Market Failure

KU-069-282

Market Failure

A Guide to the East European 'Economic Miracle'

László Andor and Martin Summers

Pluto Press
LONDON • CHICAGO, ILLINOIS

First published 1998 by Pluto Press
345 Archway Road, London N6 5AA
and 1436 West Randolph, Chicago, Illinois 60607, USA

British Library Cataloguing in Publication Data
A catalogue record for this book is available from the British Library

ISBN 0 7453 0886 4 hbk

Library of Congress Cataloging in Publication Data
Andor, Laszlo.
    Market failure: a guide to the East European "economic miracle"/
Laszlo Andor and Martin Summers.
        p.   cm.
    Includes bibliographical references (p.   ).
    ISBN 0–7453–0886–4
    1. Europe, Eastern—Economic conditions—1989– 2. Europe,
Eastern—Economic policy—1989– 3. Former Soviet republics—
Economic conditions. 4. Former Soviet republics—Economic policy.
5. Capitalism—Europe, Eastern. 6. Capitalism—Former Soviet
republics. 7. Post-communism—Europe, Eastern. 8. Post-communism—
Former Soviet republics.   I. Summers, Martin. II. Title.
HC244.A634   1998
338.947—dc21   97–36684
                                                          CIP

Designed and produced for Pluto Press by
Chase Production Services, Chadlington, OX7 3LN
Typeset by Stanford DTP, Northampton
Printed in the EC by T J International, Padstow

Contents

Acknowledgements

This book is a result of a five-year cooperation. During that time we received invaluable support and inspiration from our friends and colleagues in the United Kingdom, Hungary, Poland and other countries. The last year of this period was spent with intensified work on the volume.

The structure of the book was jointly developed by the two authors. Texts on structural adjustment, inflation, Market Maoism, agriculture and alternative policies were written by Martin Summers; those on Western policies, monetary policy, privatization, post-communist alternatives and security affairs are by László Andor.

Both authors revised the entire text several times. The coordination of the work was not easy given the frequent need to communicate between London in England, Budapest in Hungary, Lubartow in Poland and Glasgow in Scotland. We are grateful to Pluto Press for setting the deadlines for the manuscript with unbroken confidence and optimism.

1

The Long March to the Market

In April 1986 an experiment at the Number Four reactor at Chernobyl, in what was then the Ukrainian Soviet Socialist Republic, caused the most destructive nuclear accident in history:

> According to the closest studies of the disaster in the West, the experiment failed for two main reasons. First of all, the operators made a series of blunders, revealing their inexperience and inability to cope with the complexities of nuclear power. The second and ultimately much more important cause of the disaster was the design flaws in the RBMK type of reactor which was in operation at Chernobyl, and which generates 60 per cent of Soviet nuclear energy as a whole.[1]

Another experiment is now in progress. It is an economic experiment designed to test the possibility of transforming Soviet-style economies into modern, market-based societies. This experiment is being conducted simultaneously in virtually all post-communist countries. The fundamental problems that are being addressed are the design flaws inherent in such economies. Inevitably, those carrying out the experiment are inexperienced, because such an experiment has never been attempted before. Only time will tell if the inability of the experimenters to cope with the complexities of these problems will lead to disaster.

This book attempts to disentangle some of the factors which have led to these experiments and to assess the probable outcomes. It is therefore concerned with applied economics. However, it has not been written primarily for economists. Those who decided to carry out a 'turbine-tripping experiment' at Chernobyl were to have a profound impact upon the lives and well-being of millions of people. No less is true of those now promoting the 'structural adjustment experiment' in Eastern Europe. This book is written for those who do not necessarily understand either nuclear or economic jargon, but who sense that those who do may affect their lives irrevocably.

1

The term 'market failure' does have a technical definition, according to one textbook it 'describes the circumstances in which distortions prevent the Invisible Hand from allocating resources efficiently'.[2] 'The Invisible Hand' is a theological metaphor for the workings of the free market, which Adam Smith, the originator of the term, saw as the Hand of God. The distorting circumstances which prevent God's Hand from working are certainly to be found in contemporary Eastern Europe, but the title of this book also implies a wider failure – a failure of imagination by those responsible for economic policy in this region since 1989.

Structural Adjustment

Since the *'annus mirabilis'* of 1989, two processes have coalesced in the former communist countries of Eastern Europe and the Former Soviet Union. The first is the culmination of many decades of passive, and not so passive, resistance to a totalitarian economic and political system known by the name 'communism', which had emerged from the chaos of World War I. The second is the aggressive extension of a market-driven economic model, called 'structural adjustment', that explicitly rejects the social compromises which were the considered response of democratic societies to the chaos of World War II. The unfolding of the first of these processes is well documented. The latter process is more obscure, but it will fundamentally determine the shape of our shrinking world well into the next century. Most people think they understand what is meant by the word 'communism', much fewer would be able to give an explanation of the meaning of the term 'structural adjustment'.

The first structural adjustment programme (or SAP) became effective in Turkey only in 1980. The military government which seized power from civilian politicians in Turkey during that year committed itself wholeheartedly to the programme. In return for the adoption of specified policy measures a loan of $200 million was granted by the World Bank. This was the very first structural adjustment loan (or SAL). In the next few years many other countries set off along the road to adjustment with the blessing of the Bank. Other international financial institutions, such as the International Monetary Fund (or IMF) and the regional development banks reinforced this trend. This mutual reinforcement became known as 'cross-conditionality'. Some Eastern European countries, such as Poland, Hungary and Yugoslavia, were being integrated into this process well before 1989.

Policy-based lending was not a new phenomenon for international financial institutions, but the extent of the intervention in national policy making was unprecedented. Why were national governments of all political orientations so willing to accept such far-reaching interference in their internal policy making? Because they needed the money. They needed the money not primarily because of internal factors, but rather due to external factors over which national governments had very little control. Of course, some countries had been disastrously mismanaged, and every country can always find room for improvement in their economic performance. That is an inescapable reality. The fact that so many countries found themselves simultaneously in such great difficulties cannot be explained in this way.

The two leading international financial institutions were set up at the Bretton Woods conference of 1944 by the victorious Western powers and had been designed to deal with a world in which trading imbalances between countries were thought to be essentially temporary and caused by short-term internal problems. This situation no longer prevails (if it ever did). Of the three major pillars of the Bretton Woods system, the IMF was designed to provide short-term assistance during temporary balance-of-payments crises, to prevent the kind of cash-flow problems which had exacerbated the Great Depression. The International Bank for Reconstruction and Development (IBRD or World Bank) was to give long-term loans which supposedly would raise the productive potential of borrowers. The General Agreement on Tariffs and Trade (GATT), a substitute for the originally planned International Trade Organization (ITO), was to act as a nominally neutral referee in trade disputes in order to maximize the potential for international transactions.

The belief that the increase of international trade is a 'good thing' is deeply ingrained in conventional economic thinking. If each country specializes in producing those goods in which it is most relatively efficient (in those in which it is said to have a 'comparative advantage') and then trades those goods on the international market, then production is theoretically maximized and everyone gains. That is the theory. In practice, a series of unprecedented events in the 1970s and 1980s have rendered traditional trade theory historically obsolete.

The most important underlying factor in this obsolescence has been the explosive growth of international capital markets. In 1971 the US government declared the dollar unconvertible into gold even in theory: the value of the dollar and the quantity of dollars in circulation was now to be entirely determined by the US government's policy objectives. A massive expansion of US budget deficits as a means of financing the huge costs of the war in Vietnam led inexorably to the collapse of the fixed-exchange-rate regime agreed at Bretton Woods because the dollar no longer provided a solid anchor. In effect, because the Bretton Woods system had nominated the United States as the world's banker, the US President Richard Nixon was able to manipulate that system to the advantage of US interests. In 1973 the mainly Arab oil producing and exporting countries (OPEC) forced up the price of oil as a political lever against the main oil-consuming countries, who were perceived to have supported Israel in the 'Yom Kippur War' of that year. Ironically this was much more damaging in Europe and Japan than in the oil-rich United States which was Israel's main ally. Most of the funds generated in Arab countries by this manoeuvre were redeposited in the international banking system.

Though there have been international capital flows since the sixteenth century, there was never anything remotely comparable to the huge rise in availability of 'eurodollars' (dollars held outside the US mainly in European banks) which these events precipitated. This massive increase in supply was matched by a massive increase in demand, as countries sought to pay their recently inflated oil bills. Many countries, including those in Eastern Europe, took on large sovereign debts and, as we shall see, many debts contracted by private enterprise during this period became in the end the responsibility of governments. Even those countries with their own oil supplies took advantage of the funds on offer because at the time interest rates were extremely low. Private banks, with the encouragement of the international financial institutions, engaged in fierce competition to place loans. Detailed assessment of the viability of individual projects was impractical. More often than not, banks looked for the security provided by state approval and support. The conventional wisdom of the time was that a state could not be bankrupted, which made repayment absolutely assured provided a sovereign state was involved in guaranteeing the loan. Huge 'moneycentre' banks like Citicorp specialized in syndicating loans to governments of all political orientations with no real assessment of risk whatsoever.

Communist governments in Eastern Europe borrowed this money for two main reasons. First, they were affected by the oil price rise in direct and indirect ways and increasingly forced to pay their oil bills in hard currency. Second, mounting economic and social discontent, such as the workers' revolt of 1970 in Poland, had to be pacified if these undemocratic regimes were to survive. The undemocratic governments of the so-called 'free world' – such as those in the Philippines, Brazil, Zaire, Indonesia and Egypt – faced similar dilemmas. Every one of these governments believed that if they could just buy time by borrowing money then their internal economic problems could be resolved without unwelcome political change.

Despite the oil shock, a full-scale depression was prevented in the West by a relatively permissive attitude towards inflation, which made real interest rates low or negative. This convinced borrowers that they would easily be able to repay the loans from the proceeds of economic growth, which everyone, including the banks, assumed would continue in an unproblematic fashion as it had done with only minor interruptions since World War II. Despite bitter distributional conflicts triggered by rising inflation (such as the British miners' strike of 1974), the economic situation gradually stabilized as the decade progressed.

The second oil price shock was dealt with very differently. It came about in 1979 as a result of the Iranian revolution and the subsequent territorial aggression against the newly established Iranian regime by Saddam Hussein with the tacit support of both the Arab and the Western powers. In the West an ideological sea change was underway. First in Britain and then in the United States, a hitherto discredited economic theory was being revived: 'monetarism'. Technically, monetarism refers only to certain beliefs about the causal relationship between the growth of the money supply as a result of government borrowing and the subsequent rate of inflation. In a broader sense, those who had a visceral antagonism to the intervention of the democratic state in the private-property economy were known as 'neo-liberals'. The most prominent modern exponent of this school of economics was the US economist Milton Friedman who was based at the University of Chicago (which sometimes led to the appellation 'Chicago School').

From Keynes to Hayek

The idea that the state had a right, and a duty, to intervene in economic processes, in order to stabilize national markets and promote full employment, had been most famously associated with the British economist John Maynard Keynes during the Great Depression of the 1930s. The post-war economic and political consensus in the West was based on Keynesian ideas, and they rendered developed Western countries with growing economies and stable, inclusive societies largely immune to the blandishments of communist ideology. The Bretton Woods system was itself a product of those ideas although Keynes, who attended the Bretton Woods conference on behalf of the British government, was unhappy with the final agreement which gave the United States a destabilizing veto over the world financial system through the use of the dollar as a reserve currency. His fears were entirely justified. In 1972, the right-wing, conservative, Republican President Richard Nixon had declared 'we are all Keynesians now', although it is certain that Keynes would never have approved of Nixon's floating dollar policy. Keynes had explicitly rejected the anarchy of uncontrolled global capital movements; as far as he was concerned the purpose of the Bretton Woods system was to tame and direct such flows:

> I sympathise with ... those who would minimise, rather than those who would maximise, economic entanglements between nations. Ideas, knowledge, art, hospitality, travel – these are the things which of their nature should be international. But let goods be homespun whenever it is reasonably and conveniently possible; and above all, let finance be primarily national.[3]

Keynes feared that the redistributive management of domestic demand that he regarded as essential to economic prosperity and social stability would simply be impossible – the more short-term balance-of-payments problems caused by uncontrolled private capital flows tied the hands of national governments. However, by the early 1980s, partly as a result of Nixon's subversion of the Bretton Woods system, Keynesian ideas and policies were under sustained attack. This was despite the fact that the inflationary consequences of Nixon's policy were exactly what Keynes would have predicted. Unfortunately the dead are unable to defend themselves from those who claim to speak in their name.

Unlike Keynesians, the resurgent monetarists and neo-liberals believed that the public and private sectors of the economy were in perpetual conflict. Even in fundamentally market-based economies they felt that any increase in state activity would inevitably 'crowd out' the private sector. In conformity with this belief successive administrations in the US and Britain made largely unsuccessful but socially painful attempts to reduce state expenditures. This led to downward pressure on both private and public investment as Keynes, who saw the activity of the state and that of the market as complementary and interrelated, had predicted. Lowered tax returns and increased welfare spending destabilized government finances in both countries, defeating the declared object of the whole exercise.

The effects upon those countries which had borrowed heavily in the 1970s were dramatic. As world demand fell, export earnings declined. As interest rates rose ('to defeat inflation'), debt repayments increased. Many countries simply could not cope. This primarily externally generated crisis was seized upon by the monetarist vanguard which now occupied the commanding heights of the international financial institutions as evidence of widespread internal failure. Then, as now, the international financial institutions were dominated by their major shareholders – the most powerful Western governments, particularly the US which still controls 21 per cent of the voting stock in the IMF. The institutional consensus was that all the countries in difficulties had been badly mismanaged, largely because of what was caricatured as softheaded socialist interference with natural market mechanisms. It did not seem to matter that this was a gross oversimplification of very complex realities. As the success of communist ideas in the first part of the century had demonstrated, simple ideas are usually the most powerful and so it proved in this case. According to the leaders of world finance, it was high time for all these different countries to take a stiff dose of monetarist medicine. Structural adjustment was born; a technocratic formula pregnant with ideological meanings.

In 1988 the World Bank rather inelegantly defined structural adjustment as 'Reforms of policies and institutions – microeconomic (such as taxes), macroeconomic (such as fiscal imbalances) and institutional (public sector inefficiencies). These changes improve resource allocation, increase economic efficiency, expand growth potential and increase resilience to future shocks.'[4]

A plain English translation of the rationale for structural adjustment in Eastern Europe might be presented as follows:

Real economics is about the functioning of markets. Structural adjustment is simply another way of describing the necessary change from a centralised, communist, command economy to a normal market-based economy. If Eastern countries want to have such a normal economy they must integrate as rapidly as possible into the international market and accept the impersonal discipline it demands. Any other strategy is based upon utopian wishful thinking. After all, if these economic policies are good enough for Western countries they are good enough for the East.

The supporters of structural adjustment believe that most of the problems of the twentieth century have been caused by excessive government interference in natural market mechanisms. The most extreme examples of the failure of government-directed economic development are seen to be found in the communist world. According to the structural adjusters, government intervention in Western economies has also been excessive but, thanks to the bold decisions of key politicians, a reinvigorated private sector is now ready to perform its traditional role and usher in a great age of prosperity. Of course they accept that there are some difficulties with the implementation of these policies, but these are temporary. In any case, as time has passed, and whatever their personal proclivities, politicians world-wide have all come to be on intimate terms with Margaret Thatcher's bewitching brainchild TINA – 'There Is No Alternative'. In the British election year of 1997 TINA was still dangerously captivating to a whole new generation of middle-aged men in suits.

The essential elements of a structural adjustment package involve increased integration in the global division of labour. This requires that currencies should be fully convertible and, if necessary, their value should be allowed to depreciate in order to create a 'real' or 'hard' exchange rate. All controls on the import or export of capital or foreign exchange should be ended. Prices administered by the state should be liberalized. Government spending should be reduced. Loss-making public enterprises should be privatized (or liquidated). Exports should be increased and imports diminished, not by administrative methods, but simply by 'getting the prices right'. The private energies released by these measures should lead to economic growth and ever-rising prosperity.

Structural adjustment has sometimes been summarized as the three '-ations': liberalization, deregulation, privatization. A fourth component often added is stabilization. Strictly speaking, stabilization is a macroeconomic policy whereas the others are essentially microeconomic or so-called 'supply side' measures.

To an 'Old Believer', concern about the distributional effects of such policies are misplaced. The wealth generated will eventually trickle down even to the most disadvantaged ('a rising tide floats all boats'). The belief that the state can improve economic performance is heresy. Once the principle that the state can intervene in the economy is accepted then the distortions brought about by initial interventions will be used by powerful bureaucrats in order to justify further interventions, which will simply make things worse and worse. These 'rational choices' – rational, that is, from the point of view of bureaucratic vested interests – undermine economic efficiency and load burdens onto wealth-creating entrepreneurs. In the famous phrase of the patriarch of the Old Believers, Friedrich A. von Hayek, this is the 'Road to Serfdom'.

This latter observation is by far the most convincing contention of the structural adjustment paradigm. The abuse of state power by special interests all over the world has been systematic and destructive. This abuse has been most obvious where democratic structures do not exist or have been subverted by powerful elites. Even in ostensibly democratic societies, such elites often have a disproportionate influence over the social allocation of resources. Structural adjustment has seemed most credible where those who have opposed it are most clearly involved in special pleading.

The Politics of Indebtedness

In reality, the abuse of state power by vested interests has been as essential a feature of 'really existing structural adjustment' as of 'really existing socialism'. (This latter phrase was originally coined by the East German dissident Rudolf Bahro in order to characterize Soviet-style societies and to distinguish them both from capitalist societies and any yet-to-be-realized utopian ideal.) In really existing structural adjustment the manipulations of the state are sometimes indirect. For example, there is the provision of hard currency to the private sector in order to allow the service of privately contracted debts. This occurs despite the fact that the process of foreign exchange liberalization has allowed the build-up of private hard-currency accounts abroad from which such debts should logically be paid. Each depreciation of a currency, encouraged in order to bring about 'real' exchange rates and supposedly efficient price signals, increases the local purchasing power of the lucky few with access to such accounts.

Sometimes the manipulations are more unsubtle. For example, in 1985 international banks refused to accept the liquidation of Argentina's Banco de Italia, which would have wiped out $250 million of their assets. The Banking Advisory Committee telexed the Argentine government pointing out that unless the Argentine state accepted responsibility for the debt, current negotiations on a $4.2 billion loan would be jeopardized. The debt was nationalized.[5] A similar process occurred in Chile under the Pinochet dictatorship as Barbara Stallings relates:

> Believing that private sector indulgence was not the same as similar activity by the public sector, the government refused to stabilise the former. In addition, after the economy entered into crisis in

1982, the government found itself forced to nationalize much of the country's banking sector together with the non-performing firms that the banks had repossessed. Ultimately, at the insistence of the international banks, it was even forced to take responsibility for the foreign debt of the financial sector.[6]

In the very worst cases, genocidal kleptomaniacs such as Mobutu Sese Seko or Ferdinand Marcos have used the government machine to loot their own countries with the tacit support of Western public-sector bureaucracies like the CIA. In recent years lip service has been paid to the idea of 'good governance' in indebted countries by hypocritical Western governments. But who can doubt that in the grotesquely unequal and undemocratic societies which are most heavily indebted, austerity tends to fall on the poor and the marginalized rather than bankers, bureaucrats or generals? The international financial bureaucracies frequently insist upon such a skewed distribution of burdens, as we saw in the case of Chile.

Social inequalities in former socialist countries were not so vast as in Latin America or the Philippines, but real wages were always cut and shortages intensified during financial crises, the most notorious example of this being the deliberate policy of starvation in order to satisfy external creditors pursued in Romania. As Barbara Stallings says: 'In certain respects, Ceausescu was a neo-Stalinist Pinochet.'[7] However, in most East European countries it was only after the changes of 1989 that social polarization and the unfair distribution of sacrifices began to truly resemble that found in the Third World.

The allocation of government revenue for the purpose of servicing supposedly public debts, and private debts which have been socialized, such as that in the Argentine and Chilean examples mentioned above, has very negative economic consequences. (Of course it can be argued that in undemocratic states all supposedly public debts are conceptually private.) These expenditures inevitably drain resources from investment in infrastructure, production and human capital. Where the crisis itself has made it impossible to reduce government indebtedness, the result has been expanding budget deficits which are indeed one of the causes of inflation, just as the monetarists contend. This inflation then becomes the justification for further austerity at the expense of the most vulnerable and the long-run economic health of the country concerned. This vicious wheel turns faster and faster until the realization dawns that the vehicle is irretrievably stuck. This matters more in some countries than in others.

In August 1982, the threat by the Mexican government to default on their enormous and unpayable debt finally brought the whole international banking system shuddering to the verge of collapse. After a period of agonized horse-trading, the public sector, in the form of the IMF and the governments of creditor countries, stepped in and arranged further loans to the Mexican government (at a suitable rate of interest, of course). This exercise had to be repeated after the second major collapse of the Mexican financial system in January 1995. A similar public rescue had to be organized for the deregulated savings and loans sector within the United States at the end of the 1980s. Similar policies in Scandinavia had similar outcomes. The pattern has become depressingly familiar everywhere and has now appeared in South-east Asia. The whole of the international financial system is in reality dependent upon indirect subventions from the despised public sector, that is to say upon the ordinary taxpaying workers of the creditor countries. Far from being penalized for their reckless and inefficient allocation of resources, the banks have been rewarded by public subsidy, creating a clear case of what insurers call 'moral hazard'. So much for the 'discipline of the market'.

We now have the paradoxical situation in which public-sector bureaucrats in the international financial institutions, who are charged with supervising ostensibly private financial markets which are themselves ultimately dependent upon public subsidy, are empowered to lecture client governments about the absolute inviolability and infallibility of private markets. This is not really such a mystery. The current situation might be characterized as an example of the old adage 'Do as I say, not as I do'. However, another old adage is 'The proof of the pudding is in the eating'. There has now been over a decade of experience with the structural adjustment process and the results have been far from what was promised. A growing chorus of criticism has arisen, most notably from the non-governmental organizations (or NGOs), especially those concerned with tackling the problems of global poverty, environmental degradation and the abuse of human rights, whose grassroots knowledge of the real effects of these policies is unrivalled.

The stated goals of structural adjustment are macroeconomic stabilization, increased productive investment and a return to economic growth. Even the strongest supporters of structural adjustment are unable to point to more than a handful of cases where these goals have been even minimally achieved. Frequently, the 'short-term' stabilization measures such as drastic cuts in government expenditure on health and education, make it impossible to develop human capital and therefore long-term productive capacity.

Most countries have adopted adjustment programmes only under duress and in a desperate attempt to service their debts. Between 1982 and 1990, the debtor countries as a group paid out $1,300 billion in debt 'servicing', that is, interest payments, not paying back the money originally borrowed. As Susan George, a leading critic of these policies has pointed out, this is the equivalent of six Marshall Plans from the poor to the rich. In 1990, the indebted countries as a whole were 61 per cent more in debt than they were in 1982; Africa was 113 per cent more in debt.[8] Eastern Europe experienced the same two major waves of debt creation as in the Third World: first, in the 1970s as eurodollars washed through the international system, and then, in the late 1980s. Hungary had the highest per capita debt burden in Eastern Europe; after several years of austerity an unsuccessful attempt to return to GDP growth in a period of dollar depreciation led to a doubling of foreign debt between 1985 and 1987.

The main thrust of the criticism directed at structural adjustment is that the adjustment demanded of the poor is never visited on the rich and is in any case an adjustment to a fundamentally unjust status quo. The major problems in the world economy did not begin in 1973 – they are inherent in an international trading system dominated by the wealthy industrialized economies and the large corporations which are based in them. Seventy per cent of world trade is now controlled by five hundred corporations, which also control 80 per cent of foreign investment and 30 per cent of world gross domestic product.[9] Governments in the past have operated under the assumption that they possessed a degree of economic sovereignty. With the exception of the United States, which is still able to frame policies which will fundamentally affect every other country on earth, this sovereignty has now been proved to be illusory.

Global environmental degradation has accelerated during the last decades, despite an extensive public relations offensive by the major culprits. A significant factor in this has been the pressure to earn hard currency, not for productive investment, but rather for debt servicing. Irreplaceable natural resources, such as tropical timber, oil and minerals, are being looted in a desperate and futile scramble for solvency. The emphasis upon export-oriented agriculture demanded by structural adjustment programmes has driven more and more of the poorest people from the most viable agricultural land. Agricultural markets actually work most effectively as a motor for development where production of food is primarily for local consumption; that is the inescapable lesson of the relatively successful agricultural reforms in Japan, South Korea and both republics of China. This is a fact about the so-called 'tiger' economies of South-east Asia which monetarists are at great pains to obfuscate. In other more dependent parts of the world, rural people are progressively displaced by externally imposed systems of 'farming for foreigners' and forced to eke out an existence by degrading already marginal land, as in the Amazon or the Sahel, thus intensifying the underlying ecological crisis. The only alternative for such people is to migrate to burgeoning city slums in such unsustainable mega-cities as São Paulo, Manila or Johannesburg, which are breeding grounds of disease, violence and crime.

As most producers of raw materials have been simultaneously instructed by the international financial institutions to increase exports, the supply of raw materials to the industrialized countries has increased enormously. As a result, prices (and therefore earnings) have collapsed; a process which has comprehensively destroyed the market management structures which had been evolved after World War II in order to mitigate the uncertainties of international commodity trade. This has exacerbated a long-term secular trend of lowered prices because demand for food products is income inelastic (wealthier consumers can only eat so much) and manufacturing industry has become less resource-intensive due to technological change (for example, copper wire is being replaced by fibre optics). This does not mean that quantities supplied, and environmental damage done, are necessarily reduced (rather the opposite). It can lead to countries being forced to sell their exports for less than their costs of production because they are trapped in an obsolete and disadvantageous production structure, usually the legacy of colonial coercion.

This outcome has been a predictable result of the fatuous idea peddled by the international financial institutions that each country is independent of conditions in every other country; the so-called 'case-by-case' approach. It is surely obvious that if all producers of a commodity such as coffee or copper simultaneously increase export volumes, then the prices and earnings for those countries will fall. The institutions which gave the instructions – termed 'advice' – for this policy, are the same institutions that in other contexts wax lyrical about the supposed inevitability of globalization and the accelerated interdependence of world markets.

A leading critic of structural adjustment is the Malaysian Martin Khor of the Third World Network. At an international conference of non-governmental organizations held in Washington DC in 1992 he stated:

The main beneficiaries of structural adjustment are the international commercial banks and the major multinational companies. These institutions were in large part responsible for the debt crisis because they made unviable loans. Now they want their money back, but many of the countries owing are bankrupt. So there is an adjustment to be made. Either the banks' profits will fall, or they will get those loans back even if they cannot be repaid, by giving new options to the Third World countries. That is, new loans to pay back the old loans to prevent a banking crisis in the North.[10]

As Haggard and Kaufman coyly hint: 'Reform initiatives are more likely where and when political institutions insulate politicians and their technocratic allies from particular interest group constraints.'[11] Professor Leonor Briones of the Philippines is more forthright:

The very logic and framework of structural adjustment policies require the repression of democratic rights. This is because these policies demand drastic fiscal, monetary and economic measures which cannot help but raise very strong reactions from the public. And such reactions have to be repressed. It is not surprising that many structural adjustment programmes are successfully implemented in countries like my own, under a dictatorship. When we complain to the World Bank and the IMF, they tell us; so sorry, we don't talk to people. We only talk to governments. We only talk to your President. We only talk to the governor of your central bank. We only talk to your Minister of Finance.[12]

What has all this to do with the situation in the former communist countries? Surely they must adopt a market-driven economic policy which, whatever its failings, is at least better than a defunct, communist, command economy? This was certainly a widely held view in 1989, not least among the high priests of the international financial institutions. Their liturgy found a sympathetic ear among the new generation of political leaders in Eastern Europe, many of whom had very little knowledge or understanding of conditions in the world at large. Ordinary people, sick of a system which seemed to have no redeeming features and beguiled by the all-pervasive images of Western consumerism, were psychologically ready for dramatic changes. Paradoxically, this willingness to embark upon the most ambitious economic experiment in modern times was wrapped up in sentiments about the need to conform to supposed 'normality'. 'No more experiments' was the rallying cry of a new generation of economic reformers who found the longstanding debates about the improvement of economic performance in Soviet-style economies at best an irrelevance and at worst a coded attempt to preserve the status quo.

This moment also represented the high-water mark of neo-liberalism in the West. In fact the conventional neo-liberal explanations of the collapse of the communist system were curiously inconsistent. On the one hand, it was asserted that it was the US government-led arms race which had forced the Soviet Union into a submissive posture. In other words it was the role of the state in the West which had been decisive and not the market at all. This was the same state which at the level of ideology was condemned as inefficient and inimical to economic rationality and political freedom. It was in the Reagan years above all that the policy of using deficit financing to simultaneously prosecute the arms race and stimulate the private economy through public subsidy was most ruthlessly pursued, a policy which has sometimes been termed 'military Keynesianism'.

What might have happened if the largely fortuitous rise to prominence of Mikhail Gorbachev, who must surely be given much of the credit for the dismantling of the totalitarian system in any fair-minded historical assessment, had been destabilized by this bellicose posture? Even convinced Cold Warriors such as the conservative English journalist Peregrine Worsthorne now recognize that the world came much closer to general war during this period than was widely believed at the time. In all conscience the human cost of the Cold War confrontation in the 1980s was high enough in such places as Mozambique, Angola, Afghanistan and Central America.

On the other hand, the conventional wisdom suggested that the communist system had fallen under its own internally generated economic and social contradictions. Economic growth was sluggish, living standards were stagnant; the revolt of the frustrated Eastern consumer against the absurd policies of the egalitarian redistributive state was inevitable. In the West therefore the role of the state was presented as benign, not because of the provision of such goods as health care or education, but because of its most barbaric and militaristic activities. In the East the role of the state was entirely bad, even in its most humane and nurturing manifestations. This contradictory set of attitudes led inexorably to the wholesale condemnation of every aspect of the pre-existing system and in particular of the social guarantees provided by the state. Ironically, this analysis frequently found the most ready response from those who had previously been the most high-ranking vassals of that state and the major beneficiaries of its largesse. As the world's ideological field shifted, the ruling class of 'really existing socialism' realigned themselves with the new pole of power with varying degrees of psychological distress. Ordinary people, like ordinary people everywhere, hoped for the best. However, reality was always more complicated than either the communist or the neo-liberal ideology was able to admit. It still is, as we hope to demonstrate in the chapters which follow.

2

The Cold Peace

Common contemporary stereotypes suggest that the nations of Eastern Europe badly mismanaged their economies during the communist era. This is often seen as the only reason why they find themselves in impossible difficulties today. The conventional wisdom suggests that communist rule isolated these countries from their natural environment in which they would have developed in a stable, Western European, manner. The results of this isolation were as the Austrian economists von Mises and von Hayek had predicted: economic inefficiency combined with political tyranny. Other similar explanations emphasize that ruling parties and the Soviet Union did not allow ordinary people any significant economic initiative and imposed political requirements and constraints on the economy, which led in the end to a general collapse of these regimes. Western governments, when they saw the emerging crisis and the first stirrings of systemic change, did their best to help political democratization and to facilitate economic recovery.

All these stereotypical evaluations include important elements of truth. For example, it is obvious that communist rule did indeed isolate countries of the East from important relations with the West. But it should not be assumed that these countries would, in more favourable circumstances, have developed in exactly the same way as Austria, France or Sweden. Similarly, although it can be claimed that Western governments have done their best to help these new democracies, it has to be recognized that their best has been extremely disappointing by any measure. The most important task of this chapter is to convince the reader that developments and events in Eastern countries cannot be seen as totally independent from those in the West, even in periods when the isolation of the two blocs was at its most severe. Analysis based solely upon internal factors cannot explain the malfunction and eventual crisis of Eastern European state socialist regimes.

The role of the West in Eastern developments has to be examined even more carefully in the post-1989 period when ideas, policies, goods, tourists, aid and capital investments started to flow from

17

West to East. The active role of Western governments became apparent and was much more obvious than before. Since these governments also tended to control the flow of information concerning these relationships, it becomes very difficult to judge just how much influence they have been able to exert. Nevertheless, we must attempt to sketch a balanced picture of the credits and debits of the handling by the West of the Eastern crisis.

The Impact of the Cold War

Western regimes played a far from passive role in Eastern societies even in periods of acute confrontation. The dominant role of Western European ideas and institutions in Eastern Europe is centuries old and is related to the emergence of Western Europe as the core of world economic development in the sixteenth century. The recognition of the relative backwardness of the East has led to a tendency for Eastern political forces, recognizing the relative weakness of their countries, to seek to 'catch' up with the West. Usually this has implied the mechanical copy of Western institutions and behaviour following a straightforward, if simplistic, logic of modernization. This process did not always automatically lead to the same institutional arrangements as in the West. The most obvious example of this is the reimposition of serfdom in the sixteenth century, by 'modernizing' Eastern regimes, at a time when this institution was gradually dying out in the West. The practice of attempting to mobilize an economic surplus from the rural population in order to build up the economic potential of urban areas, with a view to enhancing military potential, is a recurrent pattern in Eastern Europe and Russia. In this sense Stalin was a direct descendent of Peter the Great. In the long run, all such attempts to force the pace of history have distorted social relations so badly that further and more abject dependence has been the ultimate result.

The fundamental idea of accelerating development through the process of Westernization continued unchallenged during the communist era. As Stalin put it in 1931, 'we must achieve within the space of ten years what has taken centuries in the West'. Indeed, the Soviet Union did make substantial steps forward in the creation of a heavy industrial sector during the first and second Five-Year Plans, which facilitated eventual victory in World War II but exacted a terrible human price unique in world history. The methods of Stalin were denounced by Nikita Khrushchev in 1956. The West however, remained the model for Eastern Europe's future. Khrushchev's declared objective remained to 'catch up and overtake' the West by 1980. This goal was not simply wishful thinking but was supposedly based upon the economic trends of the preceding three decades. In the event, these goals were not achieved (but it must be appreciated that Stalinist methods were not applied either). Nevertheless, the chronic inferiority complex of Eastern European political elites has been a constant feature of modern history.

By the 1970s, the non-arrival of the promised economic convergence began to create a crisis of political legitimacy in the East. For several decades the ruling communist parties were able to remain united, and to maintain some measure of popular acceptance, as long as ordinary people saw the gap in economic and cultural development between East and West being bridged. From the early 1970s onwards, as the gap began to grow wider, people began to resent more and more the existing institutions and ruling ideology. The overriding goal remained the same: to find a path to inclusion in the developed core of the global economy.

The people of Eastern Europe arrived at the turning point of 1989 with the expectation that the achievement of Western standards of living and consumption patterns would be a rapid and relatively straightforward process, albeit with a few painful transitional adjustments. These expectations were not based upon any serious understanding of the economic crisis, a large part of which was attributable to the political, military and ideological competition between East and West – in other words, to the Cold War.

Given the hostility between the post-war superpowers and their allies economic discrimination was a constant feature of East–West relations before 1989. This kept trade relations and other possible cooperation at a very low level. Hostility and suspicion were mutual, but it is obvious that the negative consequences were more severe for the East than for the West. This was most apparent where the import of advanced Western technologies might have been used to modernize Eastern production. The Western powers had a list of technologies, banned for export to the East supposedly because of their military potential but in many cases because the US did not want to see technical cooperation between the West and Eastern Europe for economic reasons. An equivalent list of COCOM technologies could not be found on the Eastern side. The East possessed just a very few technologies unavailable in the West, in areas such as space research.

This technological embargo became even stricter after the decisive round of the Cold War began in 1979–80. Given the smaller size of the industrial base and the lower productivity of the Warsaw Pact countries, the arms race had already imposed a much heavier economic burden on the peoples of the East. This burden was increased still further when the Reagan administration determined to outspend the Soviet Union and its allies in this competitive struggle (whatever the consequences for the US budget deficit). This contest was in any case fundamentally asymmetric. A market economy responds to public investment, even in such ultimately unproductive goods as weapons of mass destruction, by growing in size and complexity in self-reinforcing cycles of investment and growth (at least in the short run). This is the basis of military Keynesianism. A Soviet-style economy on the other hand has a limited investment fund. If it is used in the military sector it becomes unavailable in other sectors. There is no natural process of investment feedback. The strain of the arms race on the Soviet system, which relied entirely upon planning, was much greater than the strain on a Western economic system based upon the symbiosis of plan and market operating simultaneously.

Western sanctions following the Soviet military intervention in Afghanistan (1979) and the imposition of martial law in Poland (1981) hit all Eastern countries very hard. This was at a time when the deterioration in the international economic environment heavily aggravated the emerging liquidity crisis of all indebted countries, in Eastern Europe and elsewhere. Under new and tougher sanctions, and the impact of international price and interest shocks, policy makers had no choice but to sacrifice previous priorities concerning living standards and domestic consumption.

One expression of increasing Western influence in the East was the powerful role played by the international financial institutions during the 1980s. The financial exposure of certain countries in Eastern Europe led to complex dilemmas in economic and social policy, not to mention difficulties in general foreign policy orientation. It is important to recognize that economic policies in such countries as Poland, Hungary and Yugoslavia were already heavily influenced by the IMF well before the communist parties lost ground and collapsed. Indeed, the austerity measures demanded by the IMF helped to expedite that collapse.

Another ironic aspect of the crisis of the 1980s was that the ordinary people of the region increasingly appreciated the confrontational approach of the West, believing that Western leaders were fighting communism out of an attitude of benevolence towards the Eastern peoples. Badly disillusioned by the system in which they lived, people increasingly found their heroes in figures such as Ronald Reagan and Margaret Thatcher, who were actually imposing sanctions and embargoes on their countries, directly attacking the standard of living of ordinary people as a means of pressurizing their governments. Opposition groups in the East found vociferous rhetorical support from the neo-liberal 'New Right' in the West. This had a big impact upon their attitudes and policies. The opposition in the East created an image for themselves of the West and its motivations which led them to believe that a replacement of the communist leadership would be followed by substantial support and financial assistance. This was made apparent, for example, when President Bush visited Budapest in 1989. During his public speeches, the liberal opposition held banners inscribed 'Do Not Give Money to Communists' with the implication that serious money was on offer. In the event he gave just $25 million dollars in 1989 (and there were no more really significant sums made available to post-communist governments). Quite why Eastern people should have believed that large amounts of money might have been made available is a mystery. Within Western society the New Right heroes which Easterners admired were firmly associated with the idea that aid was in general a 'bad thing'. Due to their isolation from Western ideas and debates, most East Europeans did not realize this. They were blinded by their own wishful thinking.

The Role of Western advice

The underlying crisis in the Eastern economies emerged because the centrally planned system, even in a more or less modified form, had consumed its own internal resources and had become incapable of developing new capacities. Even so, the resulting crisis was significantly aggravated by the pressure exercised on the East by Western countries, with the long-term goal of winning the ideological struggle between the competing social systems. Even before 1989, however, Western advice had a far from negligible role in the mismanagement of the macro economy and misguided responses to the financial crisis adopted in Eastern countries.

A large part of the difficulties experienced in Eastern countries since 1989 can be attributed to the failure of prevailing ideas in economic and social science to supply useful analysis and recommendations for handling the crisis. There were even suggestions that the 'End of History' had arrived; this is eagerly accepted in the East, and resulted in hopelessly unrealistic economic programmes which identified crisis management with the transformation of the system towards a poorly understood idea of a 'free market economy'. External conditions were either not given sufficient attention when ambitious recovery projections were presented, or else some kind of public or private Western support was taken for granted.

The only significant debate concerning economic policy at the time was concerned with the speed of the transformation; whether there should be rapid 'shock therapy' or a more long-term, gradual transformation. Well-known economic experts from the United States, such as Professor Jeffrey Sachs, having served their time in such economically successful countries as Bolivia, arrived in Central and Eastern Europe with the panache of Francisco Pizzarro in order to supervise the surgical operation they considered necessary for economic revival. The acolytes of neo-liberal economic policies, having worked for a decade in Latin America and elsewhere with the determination of Don Quixote to destroy the non-performing parastatal windmills built by misguided popular (and not so popular) governments, now came East to privatize, deregulate and liberalize what had previously been planned, regulated and redistributed.

Eastern economic systems in the late 1980s were not just in crisis but also, as a consequence of a complex set of external and internal problems, in a state of bankruptcy. However, the extremity of the circumstances does not excuse the neo-liberal policy makers from critical judgement. It is now becoming clear that they completely misinterpreted the nature of the Eastern economic crisis. First, they completely ignored the negative outcomes of the pursuit of their recommended policies in both the First and the Third Worlds. Second, they failed to appreciate the fundamental differences between Eastern and Western economic structures and behaviour. Third, they did not take into consideration the social and political aspects of economic restructuring, which has inevitably led to widespread disenchantment with the entire transformation process.

A major illusion emerged in post-communist Eastern Europe concerning the direct application of speculative economic theories into policy practice. Some Western economists seemed to consider this region as a laboratory, where scientific hypotheses could be tested with no particular reservations. However, some of these economists, including Jeffrey Sachs himself, maintain that their therapies were never sufficiently applied due to deepening social and political turmoil. It is now common to find indigenous criticism of the model upon which such policies were based. As Andras Inotai, Director of the Institute of World Economics of the Hungarian Academy of Sciences states, 'Methods taken directly from economic theory, which have caused more harm than benefits, have spectacularly failed.'[1]

Perhaps the most striking example of this failure has been the handling of the economic crisis in what was then Yugoslavia. Wholesale austerity measures were introduced without any consideration of the consequences for the creeping disintegration of the federal state. Watching the multiple tragedy in the Balkans, and without any systematic understanding of the global debt crisis and the appalling social and political consequences of that crisis elsewhere in the world, orthodox economists could only treat Yugoslavia as some kind of puzzling special case. Yugoslavia had not been an optimal monetary union, they sagely concluded, nor had it been an optimal customs union and indeed 'from an economic point of view, Yugoslavia never was a country'.[2]

As the optimism, even euphoria, of 1989 was steadily replaced by fearful concern, so were ambitious economic figures about the benefits of marketization discounted as a multiplicity of problems began to reveal themselves. In the early phases of this process, there was an over-supply of optimistic forecasts and predictions about the possibilities of growth and integration into the Western market. After a while, a revision of these forecasts became unavoidable. Figures concerning sales and investment plans of Western companies had to be adjusted to the harsh realities of long-term structural crisis.

As uncertainty increased, the attachment of hard figures to opinions and recommendations become more and more infrequent and supposedly qualitative criteria were established instead such as the 'liberalization index' invented by the World Bank. An overriding psychological importance was given by Eastern elites to the question of joining the European Union. This helped to make more bearable the uncomfortable recognition of painful present realities. But it also failed to address the concerns of those in countries with no chance of being included in this exclusive club within the lifetime of a generation. The Czechs continue to hope; the Slovaks hardly bother.

Such hopes about speedy accession to the EU have in any case been wildly over-optimistic. In March 1993 the London *Economist* encouraged EU leaders to set a deadline of the year 2000 for the Visegrad countries (Poland, Hungary and the Czech Republic). This assumed that the negotiations and ratifications of the accession of the EFTA countries proceeded smoothly and that the realization of the Maastricht Treaty would proceed according to plan. Such expectations proved clearly unrealistic, not least because of the deep ambiguity in Western policy toward the East displayed since 1989.

The leading OECD countries, and especially those in Western Europe, soon realized that they had to play some significant role in the stabilization of Eastern Europe. If they wanted to integrate the newly democratized countries into the international market, and to forestall a return to communist rule, they had to provide both policies and resources to support these aims. Given the vast problems with which East European governments had to deal, it seemed that Western governments were the only actors capable of providing advice and finance for the foundation of a new order in the region. This situation raised fears in many Third World countries that resources such as aid and credit would be diverted from them towards Eastern Europe.

This fear proved to be at least partly correct. Eastern Europe immediately became the recipient of aid packages denied to others, although in terms of the underlying problems this aid was both inadequate, inappropriate and tokenistic. Within the period between January 1989 and June 1992, 11 per cent of global food aid (4.4 million tonnes) went to Eastern Europe (Poland, Romania, Albania, Bulgaria and the USSR).[3] In 1989–90, Poland alone received 1.4 million tonnes of food aid from the European Community (while Ethiopia received 0.3 million tonnes in the same period). Ironically, this helped to depress Polish agricultural markets. Individual Western governments also restructured their aid budgets in order to make new finance available for this strategically important region.

The total figure for commercial and official borrowing in Eastern Europe was already fairly large when this aid process began. In fact, several countries had for some time been struggling with the same type of debt crisis as in Latin America. However, in the case of Eastern Europe, Western governments and financial institutions were quick to understand that the scale of adjustment after the collapse of the planned economies of COMECON would demand much more financial support than the usual programmes for indebted countries. New standby agreements with the IMF and World Bank were signed and this triggered fresh loans from these institutions.

Debt relief was also approached more generously in Eastern Europe than elsewhere. Poland, which had struggled with debt repayments since 1981, received 50 per cent debt relief from official creditors in 1991, in return for implementing the IMF-sponsored Balcerowicz plan. This economic programme then became the model which other Eastern countries were invited to emulate. We shall return to the analysis of that model in later chapters. In Russia massive debts became a matter of political bargaining when President Boris Yeltsin needed external support during the referendum of 1993 and they remain so today.

An entirely new institution, the European Bank for Reconstruction and Development (EBRD) was set up in 1991, in order to organize a concerted flow of resources from West to East. The idea for the EBRD came from a think tank patronized by the French President François Mitterrand. Jacques Attali, a close aide of the President, became its first chief. The head offices of the Bank were established in the City of London, as part of a complex trade-off of the interests of shareholder governments. The idea, promoted by Attali, that soft loans (at less than commercial interest rates) should be made available for Eastern Europe was not generally popular in financial circles. Attali was finally removed from his job in the spring of 1993, shortly after the defeat of the Socialist Party in the French general election.

The extravagance of the Bank was the ostensible reason for Attali's demise and it was indeed the case that the EBRD spent more than half its expenditures in the first two years on its own overheads, welfare, decoration and entertainment. However, attacks on Attali and his Bank mainly represented a coded assault on a development concept, which attempted to take into account social, political and environmental factors beyond the narrow scope of pure finance. The essence of this personnel change was unequivocally revealed when the vacant job went to Jacques de Larosière, a former managing director of the IMF. Celebrating his new appointment, the economic and political press hailed him as the saviour of the indebted countries, although in fact he earned his reputation in the period following the Mexican default of 1982 by saving the loan portfolios of the transnational banks. He ensured that the indebted countries made the sacrifices necessary to preserve global liquidity while the banks were assured of minimizing their losses by IMF assistance.

Thus, Western countries have not only supplied financial assistance but, more importantly, the diagnoses and therapies for the stabilization and adjustment of Eastern Europe. These policies were based upon orthodox neo-liberal economic ideas, which at the end of the 1980s appeared to be triumphant nearly everywhere. From the very beginning of this process, the IMF and the World Bank appeared as the prime sources of policy prescriptions for a supposedly rapid, intelligent and moderately painful transition to a modern market economy.

The IMF Arrives

It is worth asking why the Bretton Woods institutions got the job of supervising the restructuring process in Eastern Europe. As we have seen, their main field of operations had been for many years in dealing with the countries of the Third World. As the isolation of the Second World was breached, the similarities between these countries and Third World countries became more obvious. Eastern Europe also had 'low standards of living, low per capita income, underdeveloped potentialities, a weak export capacity and other ills of underdevelopment'.[4] Yet there were clearly some visible differences inherited from the previous era, including a certain level of human infrastructure, a relatively skilled labour force and a reasonably broad industrial base.

The IMF was not a newcomer to Eastern Europe in 1989. It had already enjoyed a decade of close cooperation with governments in Poland, Hungary and Yugoslavia. However, as Anne Henderson points out:

> The IMF's approach to economic reform in Eastern Europe has been considerably more ambitious in the 1990s. This shift reflects the Fund's conviction that based on the unsatisfactory standby experiences of the 1980s, it must demand more in the 1990s; it also reflects the funds assessment that because of the European revolutions of 1989, it can demand more as well.[5]

These new ambitions of the IMF for a greater role in national policy formation were reflected in the demand for very severe reductions in real wages in the standby agreements with countries in the region. The actual outcomes of these programmes, however, were rarely in accordance with those forecast. For example, it probably took the IMF by surprise when, despite a horrifying contraction in their GDP, Bulgaria and Romania were unable to eliminate their current account deficits. Since the rate of inflation far exceeded the targeted levels in the programme period, nominal wages were usually able to increase a little faster than laid down in the agreements but the difference between the two ratios remained substantial. In its 'World Economic Outlook' of May 1992, the IMF could declare the 1990–91 stabilization policies in Eastern Europe 'relatively successful'.[6] However, unlike the reforms of the 1960s in Eastern Europe, which had been aimed at an increase of popular consumption, those of the 1990s were predicated upon a sharp decrease in the living standards of the general population.

After the forced industrialization of the 1950s, economic reforms in most East European countries gradually relaxed the drain of resources from agriculture and the human and physical infrastructure. Thus, a modest but real rise in living standards became possible for broad layers of the population. However, after 1989 the pressure to exploit the primary sector and the infrastructure arose once again.

This was not in order to artificially accelerate industrial development – however controversial that might seem – but rather to finance a de-industrialization process (as the exploitation of North Sea oil facilitated de-industrialization in Britain in the 1980s) to provide for capital accumulation by privileged groups and, most importantly, to service foreign debt.

In the first period of this process, the domestic political attitudes concerning these policies were surprisingly different from those evinced in most indebted countries under IMF supervision. The only possible explanation is that there was a widespread belief that nothing could be worse than the old discredited system. There was also a high expectation that current sacrifice would be rewarded by future welfare. External observers were impressed by the attitude shown by the new regime in Poland for example, where an extraordinary amount of 'courage and determination', inherited from the struggle against communism, developed into a perceived 'social compact between the governing and the governed'. This factor appeared as a core ingredient of the structural reform and stabilization programme. As Dr Boutros-Ghali put it at the time: 'Real wage declines that were fought bitterly on the barricades of Gdansk several months ago are accepted magnified today.'[7]

Eastern governments embraced such tough policies partly through ignorance and bravado and partly because Western governments did not sufficiently understand their mounting difficulties and did not initiate a more conducive external environment. For example, the new post-communist government of Hungary rejected all ideas about applying for debt relief or rescheduling, even though many experts and businesspeople, including George Soros, recommended such steps. This was because Hungarian policy makers feared that such 'laxness' would give them a bad name with potential foreign investors. Nothing was done by Western actors to reassure them to the contrary. Easing of the nominal debt burden did take place in Poland, as an inducement to implement the highly controversial and deflationary Balcerowicz plan. A similar agreement was also made in the case of Russia when President Yeltsin needed evidence of external backing in order to outmanoeuvre a Duma that wanted to force him to turn towards more pragmatic policies.

Debt relief came onto the agenda in this region belatedly and selectively. A desperate need for hard currency earnings continued as Western assistance dwindled. The survival of pre-existing trade barriers, involving both open and concealed protectionism, was remarkable. In addition to these existing restrictions, EU countries implemented new protectionist measures as their own recession deepened in 1992. According to EU calculations some 40 to 50 per cent of East European exports fell into the 'sensitive' category. This state of affairs fuelled nationalist sentiment in Eastern countries and resulted in pressure for retaliatory measures.

It is not only direct barriers which have restricted East European foreign trade. For example, the sale of heavily subsidized French wheat at the Baltic ports pushed Hungary out of one of her traditional markets. Eastern agriculture cannot compete, even in home markets, with Western producers bolstered by huge public subventions and export subsidies. The disintegration of existing trade arrangements, when trade between Eastern countries became dollarized in 1991, caused vast losses for the former COMECON countries. The rush of Western exporters towards the potentially huge Russian market exacerbated these losses for Eastern producers.

These developments highlight the complete lack of a sustainable Western policy towards the East. In 1989, there were calls from many quarters for a Marshall Plan for Eastern Europe (modelled on that for Western Europe at the end of World War II). Yet the lack of such a plan does not simply mean a failure to provide large-scale funding. More importantly, it presages a failure to discover a coherent strategy to deal with the interrelated problems thrown up by the continuing crisis.

The unchallenged hegemony of the IMF has been disastrous for East Europeans. First, because as experience elsewhere has shown, IMF policy tends in practice to secure a net outflow of resources from indebted countries, which eliminates the potentially favourable impact of other forms of assistance. Second, the 'case-by-case' approach of the IMF is a major obstacle to any concerted effort to deal with the problems of the region as an integrated whole, gratuitously provoking interregional jealousies and tensions.

By the end of 1993, the European Union had established association agreements with Hungary, Czechoslovakia, Poland, Romania and Bulgaria. By adding Slovenia and the Baltic states to this group, and after the divorce of Czechs and Slovaks, the number of associated countries grew to ten. These agreements set up a schedule to abolish trade restrictions between these countries and the EU. The more obvious trade embargoes had already been lifted by this time. However, Western governments did not hasten to dismantle the bulk of existing trade barriers and match their rhetorical support for Eastern recovery with painful domestic adjustment.

The agreements of 1992 and 1993 embodied a plan for an asymmetrical system of preferences, which gave apparent advantages to the East in terms of longer timescales for the removal of protectionist measures. On the other hand, the fundamental structure of the agreements implied various advantages for the EU countries, particularly by excluding groups of products in which the new democracies could hope to be successful such as steel and agricultural goods. In the circumstances, it is hardly surprising that the new democracies have often been unable to fill the new quotas provided by the agreements in areas in which they lack comparative advantage.

Furthermore, it was made clear that these agreements did not automatically imply full future membership of the European Union in a foreseeable future. Entry to the EU remained a mirage on a receding horizon. There was no deep understanding of the costs and benefits of enlargement either in the West or the East. Nevertheless, governments were able to justify current sacrifices by suggesting that they were necessary requirements of European integration. At the same time, underpublicized visits by representatives of Western vested interests made crystal clear their own special requirements and demands.

There are many complex and longstanding problems which have led to the present miserable condition of Eastern Europe. The rapid collapse of the Soviet bloc took Western policy makers by surprise, but there has been ample time since then for a coherent response to be articulated. It has not been forthcoming. The idea of a ´Marshall Plan for Eastern Europe' was rejected by Western leaders. President Bill Clinton, for example, ruled out this form of coordinated assistance on the fiftieth anniversary of the announcement of the original European Reconstruction Program.

The West has tended to treat the post-communist world as a new frontier opened up for the exploitation of raw materials and cheap labour and as a playground for economic theorists. However, this highly problematic transformation is very far from reaching the point of stability and consolidation. Therefore it is quite justified to speak about this period as a 'Cold Peace'. The open conflict between two homogeneous blocs is over, but a multilateral settlement, which truly lays a foundation for peaceful economic and social development is as far away as ever. The revolution of 1989 has had such a disappointing, and potentially dangerous, outcome that some coherent explanation is urgently required.

3

The Great Bourgeois Cultural Revolution

A revolution is not a dinner party, or writing an essay, or painting a picture, or doing embroidery; it cannot be so refined, so leisurely and gentle, so temperate, kind, courteous, restrained and magnanimous.

(Mao Tse-tung, 'Report on an investigation of the peasant movement in Hunan', March 1927, *Selected Works*, vol. 1, p. 28)

Ideology was always at the heart of the centrally planned system. Even in countries with substantial elements of decentralization, such as the former Yugoslavia, the directive role of the party in all social institutions, unified by an officially sanctioned political theology, ensured that economic planning was essentially subordinated to political considerations. The party was the essential glue which held the economic system together. It was through the disciplines and mechanisms of the party that conflicting interests were reconciled and the inconsistencies of any economic plan were papered over. The exact ideology which provided what passed for political legitimation differed from country to country but the structural functions of the party as an organizational form were substantially the same. It soon became apparent after 1989, when political events undermined the leading role of the party in each of the Eastern dominoes in turn, that the existing economic system was unworkable without the mediation which the party had provided.

Ideology in Command

In the system of so-called command economies, ideology was functional. It served as a test of loyalty which gave coherence to what would otherwise have been chaotic social practices. The underlying reality was of endemic fragmentation. The real socialist economy was no more a product of planning than the real market economies are the product of free competition. However, the social importance of ideology, and the pivotal position of intellectuals as the supposed guardians of this ideology has had a far-reaching impact on events since 1989. In an extraordinary process of intellectual contamination, the New Right in both the East and the West absorbed completely the virus of the supposed centrality of ideology in the formation of economic policy. The mindset of many of the alternative elites which came to power in 1989 was perfectly attuned to this attitude. Many of this new elite were of course the younger and professionally frustrated members of the old elite. For example, the Polish finance minister Leszek Balcerowicz was twelve years a member of the Polish United Workers Party and the radical Russian monetarist Yegor Gaidar the son of a leading Red Army General. Such people had no problem absorbing the idea that ideology was central to the conduct of economic policy.

In the case of the Western advisors who descended on the region this obsession with ideology was more curious. During the 1960s and 1970s – the era of the most intense ideological competition between the communist and the capitalist systems and the high summer of Keynesianism – the ideological posture of the West was extremely sophisticated. The market was presented as a reformed institution. Strenuous efforts were made to differentiate between socialist and social democratic ideals and the totalitarian ideology of communism. Trade unions, provided they had 'moderate' leadership, were seen in the West as essential bulwarks against communist subversion (hence the huge subventions from the CIA for the international work of the US trade union movement). As the covert Information Research Department of the British Foreign Office noted in 1949 in reference to the left-wing British Labour Party newspaper *Tribune*: 'It combines the resolute exposure of communism and its methods with the consistent championship of those objectives which left-wing sympathizers normally support ... Many articles in it can be effectively turned to this department's purposes.'[1]

Just as communist propaganda played upon inconsistencies in the Western ideal of freedom, for example, in relation to administered colonial territories, so Western responses concerned themselves, at least in part, with the conditions of life for the working class under Soviet socialism. One important practical outcome of this tendency was the huge moral and financial support extended to the Polish trade union movement *Solidarność* from across the political spectrum in the West. For many years, the West itself was seldom described as living under a capitalist system – the word was considered to have negative connotations and so the more neutral term 'market' or even 'mixed economy' was used instead. It was a signal of the resurgent power of a more crude ideological interpretation of reality that the New Right increasingly and unashamedly termed themselves as 'capitalists' during the 1980s. This ideological tendency was even further emboldened by the political changes in Eastern Europe which they had neither predicted nor expected.

As a result, ideology played an enormous role in the formulation of post-1989 economic policy. Above all, there was an enormous assault upon any conception of a 'third way' in economic policy, which was particularly noticeable on the part of born-again ex-communists such as Balcerowicz and intellectually sophisticated Western liberals such as Jeffrey Sachs, who might have been expected to have some sympathy for such ideas. In order to understand this attitude, we must revisit some of the debates concerning economic reform which took place before the political collapse of the Soviet system.

It has been frequently asserted that the centrally planned system became increasingly unable to respond to demands for higher living standards and that the technological level of the economy was stagnating. It is therefore more than a little ironic that the recent period has seen enormous collapses in both living standards and investment – from a level considered as a source of explosive discontent in 1989. This is not to suggest that in some way the old system was sustainable. As time passed its failings became increasingly apparent. This has often been seen as a result of the unsuitability of a planned system for the more flexible and intensive production required in developed economies.

As a result of these perceptions, and in order to forestall social unrest, market oriented reforms took place in several countries in Eastern Europe as early as the 1960s. The best-known case of such reforms began in Hungary in January 1968 leading to what eventually became known as 'goulash communism'. In the Soviet Union and Czechoslovakia, such reforms remained largely on the level of theoretical discussion. Yugoslavia engaged in successive waves of decentralizing reform. Although much of this was welcomed in the West at the time, there is now an all but universal consensus that these attempts were doomed to failure since the market and economic planning are assumed, with hindsight, to be incompatible.

The political organization of society by leading parties is certainly incompatible with market relations, a fact which became blindingly obvious as the second wave of economic reforms was attempted in the indebted socialist countries in the late 1980s. However, it must be recognized that all the countries of the region had gone through a shorter or longer period of reform before it was anything like obvious that the reform process would lead to a full-blooded capitalist restoration.

The last communist governments of Poland, Hungary and Yugoslavia, under Messner, Nemeth and Markovic, accepted the sale of some state companies and positively welcomed foreign investments. Anti-market forces in the ruling communist parties were brought to a compromise for the curious reason that wholesale privatization was widely regarded as economically irrational and therefore presented no threat to the dominance of public ownership. At the time, a general superiority of private ownership was not assumed. In fact, many of the most faithful communists accepted pluralism in ownership because their experts suggested that it would be the least efficient and outright bankrupt state companies that would be denationalized. The solution of problems of ownership and management were seen in a great variety of patterns and instruments.

There is little point in engaging in 'what if' speculations concerning these various attempts at reform. As Alexis de Tocqueville long ago pointed out it is precisely when authoritarian systems attempt to reform themselves that they become vulnerable to revolution. The non-engagement of the population in these elite projects ensured their ultimate failure. The legacy of these reforms for economic thought was ambiguous. At the very least they detached the idea of socialism from a strongly centralized or even militaristic model which was a potentially progressive step. On the other hand, discussions about reform were framed in terms of an assessment of different economic 'mechanisms', with the implication that it is a matter of choice, perhaps of value choice, which mechanism works in a country, regardless of general economic and cultural conditions. In practice, this gave rise to a new type of voluntarism which was no longer about quantities of steel production as in the 1950s but about institutions and their relations to particular economic outcomes.

As the economic specialists argued over the 'mechanisms', the ideologists had to find plausible phraseology in order to justify the evolving party lines (which varied from country to country). The usual terminology (still applied in China today) was the term 'socialist market economy'. The term 'market socialist' was studiously avoided since it was associated with the Polish economic heretic Oskar Lange who had always predicted the failure of the planned system and had developed his own curious hybrid proposals (long ignored by both capitalists and socialists).

One legacy of this hair-splitting was the widely held belief that only a market economy 'without qualifications' made any sense at all. That such an attitude bypassed most significant economic debates in the West was an irony lost on the fiercely parochial reformers who came to power after the political earthquake of 1989. Hereafter, governments were not expected to carefully measure the impact of their policy steps. The 'transition' (as it was widely called) was conceived as a changing of dirty clothes for clean ones, albeit with a short period of nakedness, and the need for a bath. The ideal model to be taken after the bath was 'the West', regardless of the significant differences between the existing US, Japanese and Latin American capitalist regimes, or even the substantial differences within Europe.

Such Western experts as Jeffrey Sachs have asserted that the basic building blocks of a capitalist economy are the same everywhere and that choices are for dessert only. This has the convenient corollary that no detailed understanding of existing conditions is necessary in order to suggest policy prescriptions. What to do if the initial policies do not lead to a choice of dessert, but rather back to the original problem of how to make 'an aquarium out of fish soup' was very rarely discussed. Sachs now seems to have retreated into blaming lack of Western finance for the failure of his recipes. The fiscal problems of these countries clearly are very acute and possibly terminal, but the role of textbook theories and radical ideology in the crisis cannot be so easily exorcised.

The theoretical basis for most of the reform programmes suggested with such supreme self-confidence by experts such as Sachs was singularly weak. In reality it was a vast over-extension of policies originally cobbled together by the Bretton Woods twins to deal with the first wave of the debt crisis in the Third World in the early 1980s. Policies of structural adjustment designed to eliminate supposed price distortions were elevated to the level of a programme for complex systemic change from central planning to a 'free market'; these policies had been debatable even in their original context. So-called 'price distortions' were vastly more numerous in Eastern Europe than in Central Africa or Latin America (and the belief that price liberalization would magically remove them was almost certainly erroneous). The human costs of such policies elsewhere in the world were scarcely mentioned.

In fact, much of the driving force behind this set of policy recommendations was primarily political. There was a widespread fear among Western policy makers that unless economic reform was made 'irreversible' then the communist system could be reconstructed from the roots – a curious contrast with the equally widespread belief after 1989 that the old order was terminally unsustainable. Thus, many of the economic policies which were suggested and implemented had fundamentally non-economic political and cultural goals. So pervasive and all-encompassing was this phenomenon that we might characterize it as putting 'politics in command': a phrase used by Mao to describe the policy adopted in China during the Great Proletarian Cultural Revolution which he initiated with a wave of carefully orchestrated youthful enthusiasm in 1966. In other respects, the economic policies in Eastern Europe corresponded to those adopted during the earlier stages of Maoist rule in China in the 1940s when a whole new class of property owners was created in order to provide a political base for the revolutionary regime. Mao achieved his goal of revolutionary consolidation by dispossessing a substantial minority of the Chinese population. The Market Maoists of the Great *Bourgeois* Cultural Revolution would achieve theirs by dispossessing the overwhelming majority of the populations of Eastern Europe and the Former Soviet Union.

Leading Market Maoists

Whilst it was grudgingly accepted that institutional changes, including privatization, would inevitably take longer than macroeconomic stabilization (which was in any case maddeningly elusive), there was a determination that as much should be done to disorganize the existing institutional arrangements as quickly as possible – the so-called 'shock therapy'. In a sense, this was logical, because a more pragmatic approach would inevitably have raised difficult questions about the ultimate purpose of the reform and would have bogged down the reformers in detailed questions about policy outcomes. For all sorts of reasons it was much simpler to adopt an all-encompassing policy of 'storming the heavens'. Abstruse academic debates about the 'sequencing' of reforms were effectively ended. The young reformers fresh from their sojourns in such representative Western locations as Harvard University were no longer interested in such semi-socialist nonsense. They wanted action on all fronts simultaneously and they were encouraged in these attitudes by a swashbuckling cadre of peripatetic academic stars from the West such as Sachs himself and his 'sidekick' David Lipton.

A key personality in this drama was the Polish finance minister, Leszek Balcerowicz, who was second to none in his contempt for gradualism and half-measures. His pivotal role in IMF policy in Poland and personal endorsement by Jeffrey Sachs gave him an enormous visibility in the rest of the region where the 'Polish way' was given a very hard sell by the travelling salesmen of the revolutionary roadshow. By the time the real effects of such policies were becoming apparent in Poland, Jeffrey Sachs had moved on and was advising Yegor Gaidar's economic team in Moscow. The success of shock therapy in Poland became an undisputed axiom among the new elite of reform technocrats throughout the region. The opinions of ordinary Poles concerning these policies were not so well advertised.

In a book entitled *Post Communist Economic Revolutions; How Big a Bang?*, the influential Swedish neo liberal Anders Aslund argued in typical fashion that the existing system was so bad that the only possible policy was the utmost radicalism: 'If there is a gradual path, it appears to be very difficult to find. In the meantime, the collapse of the old system brings havoc.'[2]

It scarcely seemed to occur to any of these experts that the outcome of the extremist policies they were advocating might be exactly what they themselves were postulating: havoc. Of course, there are degrees of havoc; it is probably better to be hopelessly unemployed in Poland than dead in Bosnia. But this posture seems extraordinary coming from quarters which in other circumstances would be emphasizing the importance of 'stability' and 'continuity' in such places as South Africa, Indonesia and Chile. In the same work, Aslund dismissed attempts by the state to control the monopoly power of post-communist industrial firms, which one might have thought to be an obvious step, on the grounds that:

> Only when prices are liberalized and begin to rise excessively, does the harm of the effects of monopoly become evident to everyone. Similarly, when people see cheaper and better domestic or foreign products enter the market from new sources, there will be a public outcry against state monopolies.[3]

This is a very curious argument. One is reminded of the apocryphal statement attributed to Lenin by Keynes that the best way to destroy the capitalist system is through the promotion of inflation. What Aslund is suggesting is nothing less than a destruction of popular living standards in order to mobilize a mass movement against the 'socialist roaders'. This is nothing less than Market Maoism! In no sense can such a policy be described as an 'economic reform'. Unfortunately for the Bourgeois Cultural Revolutionaries, once popular discontent was mobilized it began to flow in unauthorized channels, as it had done in the original Cultural Revolution in China, even questioning the legitimacy of those who had initiated the policy in the first place. The arrogance of those who sought to re-educate the population through such manipulations is breathtaking. In what remained of the Soviet Union, the victory of the Market Maoist line was somewhat delayed, only coming to the fore after the failed coup of August 1991. As the direction of events became clear, the young economist Yegor Gaidar resigned from the Communist Party and threw in his lot with that other former communist Boris Yeltsin. Upon the advice of Gaidar (who was acting on the advice of Sachs), Yeltsin adopted a radical policy modelled on the Polish shock therapy initiated by Balcerowicz. Yeltsin promised that 'everyone will find life harder for approximately six months, then prices will fall and goods will begin to fill the market'.[4] If, with hindsight, this was an extraordinarily complacent prediction, then the economically illiterate Yeltsin was in good company. All the best Western economic brains were unanimous in their support for the policies adopted and sanguine about the outcomes expected.

In any case, just as in Poland, the main goals of this policy were political. When asked to justify making price decontrol the centrepiece of his strategy, Gaidar suggested that it was the one economic lever the government still controlled and therefore the only thing which the government could renounce! This revealed a fundamental truth, that the so-called 'planned economy' was a myth. The Soviet economic system was based upon a truly fantastic capacity for economic actors to improvise despite the plan and to engage in complex and opaque bargaining procedures. With the removal of the leading role of the party which had mediated these processes, the Soviet system disintegrated into warring fiefdoms. After the attempted coup of 1991, the Communist Party was comprehensively legally suppressed. With its disappearance any hope of a coordinated economic strategy was destroyed. Meanwhile the *nomenklatura* regrouped and reinvented itself.

And so the old world was swept away. All those tedious debates concerning the exact mechanisms of reform were resolved. It was all so simple it was astonishing that no one had seen the light before. There was no need for incremental reform. The past should simply be destroyed in a revolutionary gale. The victory of this revolutionary line in Russia had an eerie parallel with the debates of the 1920s. There is indeed an important lesson to learn from the experiences of seven decades ago. Maintaining peace within society – which was a possibility when the civil war ended – would have required a project of gradual economic progress as suggested by Bukharin. The alternative blueprint was elaborated by Preobrazhensky, who argued for rapid industrialization and an accelerated transition to socialism.

In the event the uncertainty of the internal support for the new system precipitated a policy of even more extreme radicalism by Stalin in which both the gradualist Bukharin and the former radicals such as Preobrazhensky were liquidated.

Just as in the 1920s, there was a fatal ambiguity at the heart of the new line of the 1990s. Ordinary people had been promised higher living standards. The realists within the new elite (in fact drawn overwhelmingly from the old elite) knew very well that they only had a short time to consolidate their recently acquired power, hence the overwhelming importance of the most rapid possible privatization. As the then mayor of Moscow, Gavril Popov, wrote in an article in 1990 in the *New York Review of Books* entitled 'Dangers of Democracy':

> ... it seems to me we must make an intense effort to find new and different political mechanisms to bring about the transformations that must take place if we are to move into a new society. It is absolutely obvious to me that the purely democratic model now being pursued is leading to contradictions that can only grow more severe in future. The participants in the political struggle in our countries today lack the element that is most needed for them to shape a workable society: new forms of property.[5]

Mao could hardly have put the case more succinctly.

In the 1990s the promoters of cultural revolution justified their radicalism with the borrowed theory of rational choices. The essence of this approach when applied to government action was an *a priori* belief in what was termed 'government failure'. Any attempt by government (any government) to formulate detailed economic objectives was doomed to failure. This was because all planning is irrational. Planning is irrational because planners cannot know enough to make rational decisions. The simple fact that all economic agents have to make attempts at planning despite this supposed 'truth' can simply be ignored in this abstract model, which effectively leaves strategic planning to the economically powerful without any transparency, accountability or popular control.

Paradoxically, the other main pillar of rational choice theory was that government interventions would always create rent-seeking opportunities which would allow special interests to develop and 'distort' economic decisions. (Rent seeking means attempting to obtain income from the control of positional goods such as land or administrative power rather than through productive activity). If a bureaucracy is created in order to supervise such things as the allocation of foreign currency or export licences, then the bureaucracy itself becomes an economic actor and attempts to extend the scope of regulation (in the worst cases in order to obtain bribes). Therefore supervisory bureaucracies should be eliminated through the minimization of supervision (also known as 'cutting red tape' and 'making a bonfire of regulations'). In reality, a policy of non-supervision in a post-communist context simply gave free rein to the incipient feudalization of the economy. This has been true of privatization in a long-established liberal market state such as Britain. It was even more so in the chaotic conditions pertaining in the post-communist world. All attempts to build popular institutions underpinned by stable rules was abandoned for the duration whilst the commanding heights of the economy were carved up between newly liberated competing bureaucratic interests.

This process was itself riven with conflict as different factions of the *nomenklatura* engaged in the economic equivalent of the Wars of the Roses. These elite contests underpin much of the political history of post-Soviet Russia. In the end, what has proved decisive, in Russia as elsewhere, has been the massive political and financial support of the Western powers for their chosen champions. There was a significant ideological goal being pursued in Western capitals. It soon became apparent that in hard-cash terms there was far less of interest to multinational capital in this region than the political hype suggested, particularly in the former Soviet Union (although Germany now exports more to its immediate Eastern neighbours than to the US). However, the ideological goal of destroying the socialist idea was pursued relentlessly by the US with British support. In this respect any change which could be presented as any kind of reformed and humanized socialist system was the most significant potential threat. That reformist attitude might easily have spilled over into parts of the world where US investment was heavily exposed: Latin America, South Africa, South-East Asia (or even Western Europe itself). When one considers the terrible consequences of the structural adjustment polices imposed with such doctrinaire inflexibility on such economically unimportant countries as Rwanda, Somalia, Nicaragua, Haiti and Mozambique, one is tempted to use the only word which seems to fit such single-minded determination to impose a standardized world view: 'totalitarianism'.

As elsewhere in the world, there were significant power blocs within the governing elite which were net losers in this process of realignment. Their struggle to retain their relative privileges has ultimately determined the final reach of the radical wave in each of the post-communist countries. In Russia the struggle between President Yeltsin and the Russian Duma was an epiphenomenon of

this contest. Yeltsin's decisive move against his political opponents
was orchestrated closely with Western foreign policy manoeuvres.
On 30 September 1993 the expiry agreement of the 90-day agreement
on Russia's $27 billion debt to the commercial banks ran out; the
Russian finance minister and Market Maoist Boris Fyodorov, was
scheduled to report to the G7 finance ministers in Washington on
25 September. The annual meeting of the World Bank and the IMF
was to take place in Washington on 28 September and the decision
on an IMF standby loan was to be taken on 1 October. On 13
September Yegor Gaidar was restored to the government after a
period of political retreat by Yeltsin and the G7 embassies were
informed of Yeltsin's decision to suspend the Duma, a decision
which was fully supported. On 21 September Yeltsin acted. His
successful coup ushered in a period of even more drastic monetarist
policies which unlocked further Western aid. The fact that this 'aid'
was in the form of loans, all of which would have to be repaid at
market rates of interest, much of which was tied to the purchase of
Western exports and all of which was conditional on the surrender
of economic policy to foreign interests, was not dwelt upon in the
media, either in the West or Russia itself. However, a growing mood
of slavophile resentment was reflected in the relative success of
Vladimir Zhirinovsky's neo-fascist Liberal Democratic Party in the
subsequent parliamentary elections.

A *modus vivendi* between the competing factions of the elite has
now been found in most post-communist countries. Viktor
Chernomyrdin at one time criticized as the very incarnation of a
recidivist 'red director' is now widely regarded as a 'safe pair of
hands' largely because the energy industry empire he used to
administer as a bureaucrat he now owns outright. The opening of
the Russian energy sector to Western multinational capital in 1997
has further mended fences between the old and the new
Nomenklatura. There is a general acceptance of the irreversibility of
the redistribution of public assets by all major elite groups. Now
'privatized' centres of economic power bargain with each other and
with the residual state bureaucracy for market shares and explicit and
implicit subsidies. The non-payment of tax constitutes a significant
source of such subsidies in this feudal economic game. The problems
for the economic elite in each country are now becoming political
in a wider sense. Slowly and haltingly, ordinary people are beginning
to exert a restraining force on bureaucratic greed.

At its most apologetic, the defence of the Market Maoists is the
assertion that corrupt, venal and self-serving though the carve-up of
social assets has been, at least the 'private property' basis of a market
economy has been created. What alternative was there to the decisive

move to a private property economy and the destruction of the existing economic structures? Those who still criticize the new dispensation are characterized in two ways. Either they are unreconstructed Stalinists (who provide a useful bogey with which to frighten children and the more unsophisticated Western politicians) or they are some species of 'market socialist' who failed to understand that tinkering with the planned economy was doomed to failure. Such tinkering was indeed doomed to failure, but not for the reason the Market Maoists assume. Alternative policies would have required a vigilant and politically mobilized population and a coherent presentation of such alternative polices. Except in Poland, such a population did not exist in any post-communist country and even there demoralization and confusion had early set in. Even so, the relatively modest scope of the 'privatization' policy in Poland to date is a tribute to the potential veto power exercised by society even in the most unfavourable conditions. If such popular forces had been deliberately consulted and included rather than summarily bypassed, a very different policy outcome might have been seen. Needless to say, the ruling forces both locally and internationally had a very strong interest in suppressing such tendencies.

The current situation has curious parallels with that pertaining during the 'years of stagnation' before perestroika. An official ideology limps on, though fewer and fewer people believe in it in its pure form. This doesn't matter too much because the real wealth and power in society is now concentrated in the hands of a relatively stable elite group who will retain that power through the manipulation of economic and political processes whatever happens on the surface. Balcerowicz himself suggested that the Polish economy had become 'Italianized', that is, immune from political shocks despite the continuing uncertainties. There is something to be said for this view. The divisions opening up within Polish society are rather like those of Italy – the Italy of the 1920s. A tentative capitalist dispensation has been created within favoured enclaves even though much of the final demand in the economy and the survival of much of the population is still dependent on government expenditure, tariffs and industrial subsidies. Huge disparities are emerging between the 'developing' and 'underdeveloping' regions of Poland in which, like the southern Italy of the 1920s, the peasant farmer can only look forward to a life

> ... without machines ...without credit with which to await the harvest, without cooperative institutions which might acquire the harvest itself (if he lives to see the harvest without first having

hanged himself from the sturdiest tree in the woodlands) and save himself from the clutches of the usurers.[6]

A social gulf is opening up between '*il paese ufficiale*' of economic growth and privatization opportunities and '*il paese reale*' of mass unemployment, low wages, rural poverty and regional marginalization. This social polarization feeds a mood of popular disillusion and a desperate search for work beyond the Polish border but it also provides ... discipline.

Slow Awakening

Just as China awoke from the long night of the Proletarian Cultural Revolution to the cold light of an economy in which all the fundamentals had been ignored for years, so Eastern Europe is now coming to terms with the fact that ideology is no substitute for the rational consideration of concrete policy options. As Milton Friedman put it in a televised panel debate on CNN in 1990: 'Politically, these countries are not in the red any more, but economically they are.' In the lucky countries such as Poland, the Market Maoist policy has worked for a significant fraction of the population. From now on they will be locked into an escalating political struggle with the losers comparable with that seen in countries such as Italy in the past, but on a larger scale and for higher stakes. The state will be completely unable to deliver the level of social welfare promised by politicians in order to win elections. Disillusion with democracy itself will become increasingly prevalent. This situation is not dissimilar to that found in Eastern Europe during the inter-war years where 'with the exception of Czechoslovakia, every one of the fragile democracies established in Eastern Europe after World War One had collapsed by 1939'.[7]

In the unluckier countries, the policies have worked only for a tiny minority of the population even though they have only been partially applied. Of course, they have only been partially applied because such policies could only possibly be attempted in the most favourable of circumstances; in this sense, using shock therapy in Poland as a 'model' would have been impossible even had it been a genuine success. In the unluckiest countries, social disintegration is far advanced. There will now be a period of extended crisis management similar to that under Brezhnev in which the explanatory tools of the commentators will be less and less able to describe what is happening because it will be determined by open or covert political struggles which conventional economic analysis is at a loss to explain.

The Western academic fellow-travellers of the Great Bourgeois Cultural Revolution will retire to their academic fastnesses and attempt to explain to themselves why their prescriptions were not carried out in the correct manner. There are none who are sadder and wiser than Jeffrey Sachs, who despite the market orthodoxy of his remedies was also keen to preach the necessity of fiscal stabilization through debt relief and large injections of multilateral money. As he correctly foresaw, lasting economic and political stabilization without such support was impossible. Like many professional economists blind to political realities, he had convinced himself that ordinary people in the West had an interest in a successful economy in the East in general and in Russia in particular and that his bold economic theories would be backed up with other people's hard cash. He simply failed to take into account the vested interests and bureaucratic inertia within Western governments and financial institutions. As Sachs himself put it:

> In 1992, the West promised $24 billion of assistance and delivered only a few billion. In 1993, the West promised $28 billion and on my calculations they delivered only $4 billion ... I thought that each sign of instability in Russia would prompt the recognition that we ought to be doing more, but it hasn't happened that way.[8]

Japan has so far played a very minor role in East European affairs, being noticeably reluctant to commit funds to the transition process. This is partly to do with the continuing dispute over the Kuril Islands and also partly to do with a continuing insularity in all international endeavours. However it is also because Japanese economists had no faith in the policies being pursued, specifically those associated with Sachs and his acolytes. They thought, quite reasonably from their own point of view, that there was no point in throwing good money after bad. Eastern Europe was seen in general as a German concern.

In the United States and Western Europe the picture of Russia as a rival and an enemy long pre-dates 1917. A successful Russian economy would be an economic threat and a strategic headache. The same is true of Eastern European economic competition as a whole in relation to Western Europe. In the US on the other hand, policy makers see this potential Eastern competition as an opportunity. Meanwhile the Japanese greater co-prosperity sphere is being quietly established in the Russian Far East and Siberia. The lack of coordination between the Western powers in their policies towards this region is therefore rooted in fundamental differences of geopolitical interest. As Peter Gowan suggests:

> The lack of profitable outlets for productive investment feeds the global speculative bubble. It also threatens fierce industrial wars between the main Western states as the semi-monopolies of each state try to grab market shares from their rivals. To prevent such conflicts, the Western states seek through globalization to grab extra market shares for their companies in the East and South.[9]

One might be excused for mistaking the 1990s for the 1890s. Market Maoism provides a necessary unifying ideology for these otherwise conflictual processes.

We discuss the detailed economic prescriptions of the Market Maoists in Chapters 4 and 5. Their main achievement to date has been to stifle genuine economic debate in the countries under discussion. Astonishingly, this consensus extends to continued obeisance to the idol of privatization despite the mounting evidence for its grotesque inefficiency as a policy instrument all over the world, especially in its birthplace: Britain. As the British have discovered, the formal withdrawal of the state simply renders more opaque the relationship between the government and the economy. It certainly does not solve the fiscal problems presented by such things as the provision of necessary public services or the revenue demands of private interests such as the agribusiness lobby. In the end, as the Chinese people discovered when emperor Mao went to meet Marx, there is no substitute for detailed analysis of concrete problems rooted in the operation of the real economy which feeds, clothes and houses people – or fails to do so.

4

Price Wars

One of the most enduring stereotypical images of the Soviet system prevalent in the West was that of the queue. Like most stereotypes, this had a considerable basis in reality. It was an essential mechanism of distribution in a system in which prices were largely administered and goods were in insufficient supply at those administered prices. In market economies, prices are ideally clear signals which indicate when supply and effective demand (demand backed by ability to pay) are in imbalance. When prices rise, this indicates that demand is unsatisfied, profit margins rise and attract new entrants into the market (or encourage existing producers to supply more) thus bringing the market back into equilibrium. This process, so simple and yet so wonderful, has cast a spell of enchantment which still retains enormous appeal. As Adam Smith first suggested, it is as if an Invisible Hand were directing economic affairs in such a way that as every individual pursues their own self-interest the greater good of society as a whole is served. In eastern Europe after 1989, this primordial economic myth replaced the Marxist myth of a society in which individual interests are miraculously reconciled to social goals because the contradictions and antagonisms of the capitalist mode of production have been overcome.

At the end of the twentieth century, humankind may still need myths for all kinds of deep-seated psychological reasons but the way in which mythological thinking has infected conceptualization of the economy is a barrier to rational understanding. With the rise of complex computer-generated econometric modelling, some economists seem to believe that economics can be an exact science comparable to chemistry or physics. The belief that economics is an arcane and highly technical subject, only understandable by experts, is widespread, not least in post-communist Eastern Europe where many finance ministers, such as Lajos Bokros (finance minister in Hungary in 1985–86) are 'non-political', that is, 'non-elected' technocrats, and where technocratic governors of central banks such as Hanna Gronkiewicz Waltz in Poland run for President. Vaclav Klaus, the rhetorical Market Maoist prime minister of the Czech Republic has covered his highly astute political programme with a thick varnish of econometric voodoo. Nevertheless, economists have never really been able to render their predictions as infallible as they sometimes like to claim. As a result, they tend to retreat into myth of one variety or another, or more dangerously they mistake the mathematical certainties of their models for the real world. The disjunction between myth and reality is nowhere more pronounced than in the centrepiece of the market model: price formation.

Liberalization and Inflation

Understanding the initial conditions in post-communist economies and elaborating policies which took those conditions into account was simply off the agenda for political reasons as the Great Bourgeois Cultural Revolution got under way. Before 1989, attempts to reform the economic system were doomed to failure, partly because the population refused to cooperate and partly because any genuine reform would have undermined the political position of the leading parties. After 1989, all talk of reforming the existing system became taboo because only a supposedly entirely new system of economic relations could offer a way forward. In addition to the ideological and financial pressures, there were also the preconceptions of the Western experts parachuted into the region who had little or no idea about how the existing economic system operated and even less interest in finding out. The first thing they wanted to see were familiar landmarks. Hence the centrality of price liberalization to the usual reform strategy they proposed.

It must be emphasized that the relationship between prices and competition is far more complicated than Adam Smith's homely metaphor might suggest. Prices in market economies are not set by God's Providence as Smith indicated. The disjunction between what is found in economic textbooks and the real world is enormous. Conventional economic thinking deals with this uncomfortable gulf by suggesting that the Invisible Hand model is the norm and that deviations from this norm are 'distortions' which are a 'bad thing' to be 'progressively eliminated'. (Thus did Vaclav Klaus justify the continuing subsidies which underpinned his political base: 'Lord let me be without sin – but not yet.')

In economies dominated by rapid changes in technology (that is, all economies in the late twentieth century), price formation is not static but rather dynamic. Large organizations, the multinational companies, dominate the production and distribution of most goods.

Their pricing strategies are geared to the conquest and maintenance of market share. This may imply selling goods at below their costs of production for a time in order to destroy potential competition (a 'price war'). It may then involve selling goods at much higher prices than their costs of production to recoup the losses incurred. It may involve huge advertising expenditures on differentiating essentially identical products. The main purpose of this is to create a barrier to entry for new firms who will have to match this expenditure if they want to enter the market. In Adam Smith's terms, this is an 'anti-competitive strategy' although it is the essence of modern marketing technique. In the real world there is really no such thing as a 'distorted' price which can be differentiated from an 'undistorted' one. Prices are indeed set by competitive pressures; but it is a competition in which the strong have an overwhelming advantage. If they can simultaneously convince the weak that this process is entirely free and fair then so much the better. Economic competition is analogous to ecological conflict between organisms. Various mechanisms exist in market economies for vitiating the undesirable effects of this conflict, such as anti-monopoly laws. These however, tend to be prisoners of the Invisible Hand mythology in that, relatively mild and ineffective as such regulation tends to be, it is based upon the idea that free competition is a norm and all other situations 'deviant'.

As the Austrian-American economist Joseph Schumpeter pointed out many years ago, this process of monopolization through technological dominance is in fact the norm in modern market economies. He saw this as a positive feature characterized by 'creative destruction' as large corporations use patent law to entrench market advantage obtained through technical innovation. He saw such technical innovation as the real driving force of the capitalist market economy. Successful industrial policies in such countries as Japan, South Korea and Taiwan have been based upon deliberately 'distorting' price signals in order to accelerate these processes, for example, by mobilizing cheap credit for technically innovative companies and by rationing scarce foreign exchange to ensure that imports are of essential capital goods, not luxury items for elite consumption. Of course, such policies have not always been successful, the great danger being that the direction of 'distortion' may be to protect special interests rather than promote the common good, however that might be defined. In any case, successful policies in one country may have negative consequences for other countries. Competition is conflict.

Rational choice theory, which provides much of the intellectual justification for the policies adopted in Eastern Europe since 1989, is predicated upon the inherently implausible idea that all interventions in markets are artificial distortions serving special interests and that all uncontrolled private economic activity generates undistorted price signals. In the real world, there is a very complex struggle constantly taking place in which all agents adopt asymmetric strategies in order to advance their perceived interests. The state provides a central focus for these struggles in most modern societies, especially in the advanced market economies in which final government consumption still represents anything from 40 to 60 per cent of spending in the economy. Even today, and despite the market rhetoric, all modern capitalist states underwrite popular consumption as a spur to innovation and productivity, not to mention an essential prop to political stability. In any case, as Karl Polanyi pointed out long ago, 'The road to the free market was opened and kept open by an enormous increase in continuous, centrally organised and controlled interventionism.'[1]

Yet, when market reforms began to be fully implemented in eastern Europe, in conditions which were specific and quite unlike those in Western countries, the most simple-minded version of the competitive model was the one which was adopted. This was partly for ideological reasons as we have seen. There was a fear that if there was any serious discussion of alternative options, then the communist parties as parties might retain significant social influence, which was unacceptable to the Western powers, unlike the preservation of power by a 'depoliticized' (that is, anti-socialist) *nomenklatura*. About this latter outcome there was a 'relaxed' and 'pragmatic' attitude. Worse still, in those countries with a tradition of popular organization and social struggle such as Poland, serious discussions of alternative options might have led in all sorts of disagreeable directions, although it has to be recognized that even in Poland there was a widespread public naïvety about the implications of rapid marketization. Yet another reason for the ubiquity of the Invisible Hand model was simply the arrogance and ignorance of Western-trained economists and their young and inexperienced Eastern disciples. By the time economic policy was being formulated for the post-communist societies, a universal panacea for economic problems had gained centre stage in the prescriptions of the Bretton Woods institutions which dominated the international agenda. This was the dogma of 'liberalization'.

Despite the ubiquity of this concept, it is astonishingly vague. In fact, it could only be defined by what it was not: 'regulation'. The removal of market regulation of all kinds, whether it was those for food safety, minimum wages, trade regulations, state monopolies on policing and imprisonment or the supply of energy, was lumped together under the heading 'liberalization'. In the context of this discussion, the most important liberalization recommended for Eastern economies was that of prices.

The dogma asserted that all interventions in markets by state agencies or organized groups of workers, were 'distorting' and led to 'inefficiency' (the interventions of other organized groups were largely ignored). The obvious conclusion to be drawn was that economic progress demanded the indiscriminate dismantling of these distortions, whatever the initial rationale for them might have been, in order to allow for an ever more perfect allocation of resources. The workings of real markets were always presumed to be competitive, provided such distortions were removed. But this assumption, like many others of the Market Maoists, assumed that which ought to be proved. The spectacularly uncompetitive workings of the newly liberated Eastern markets, which hardly even approximated to conditions of imperfect competition, has been the most dramatic, but by no means the only, real-world refutation of the basic intellectual framework underpinning this dogma.

Even in 1996, the yearly World Development Report of the World Bank, entitled *From Plan to Market*, heavily relied for its analysis upon a 'liberalization index' which was defined as:

Estimates of three dimensions of liberalization: (1) internal trade, prices and markets, (2) external transactions and currency convertibility, and (3) measures to facilitate new entry. The weights on these components being 0.3, 0.3, and 0.4 respectively. Estimates being made on the basis of comparative information and rounds of consultation with specialists working on individual countries.[2]

In other words they made it up.

The report then sought to demonstrate that the more 'liberalized' an economy, the more successful (or rather the less unsuccessful) the country concerned had been. Quite simply, this is pseudo-science, which conceals far more than it illuminates. It completely sidesteps the fundamental empirical questions about the real structure of really existing markets. Failure to understand the importance of these vital questions was a crucial factor in the misunderstanding of the root causes of inflation in post-communist economies.

The conventional analysis of post-communist economies in 1989 suggested that there was considerable repressed inflation. Prices for most goods were 'too low' – hence the institution of the queue. Simultaneously, it was believed that there was a massive 'savings overhang' because the population had salted away a substantial portion of their incomes, finding nothing available worth buying in the shops (and in order to pay for consumer goods in the future, consumer credit being unobtainable). This analysis implied that rapid upward adjustment in prices was required. This would increase profit margins on goods in short supply and encourage new entry into shortage markets and increased production by existing firms, thus bringing demand and supply into equilibrium through the operation of the Invisible Hand.

There was a fear that as the savings of the population flooded the newly liberated markets, this might create 'demand pull' inflation. This was used as an argument in favour of rapid privatization of such goods as housing in order to soak up this supposed excess demand (and to create at least the illusion of private ownership). In the initial stages of the 'reform', a degree of inflation was therefore regarded as inevitable and largely beneficial. It was seen as a once-and-for-all adjustment in order to allow the reform to proceed. The monetarist consensus which dominated the policy agenda was firmly of the conviction that inflation in general was a purely monetary phenomenon. Provided a strict financial discipline was enforced by government then the expected inflationary pressures would stabilize once prices had reached a 'market clearing' level. Slightly more sophisticated analysts, such as Jeffrey Sachs, also recognized that the debt-repayment problems that many governments faced would drain domestic resources unless substantial financial support were forthcoming from the West. However, the more sanguine experts believed that after a rapid adjustment, growth would resume and the low wages and relatively high skills of the population would automatically provide the basis for a classical economic miracle, once the 'market' had been 'freed up'.

In other contexts the idea that a degree of inflation might be a good thing was fiercely resisted. During the Keynesian era, governments in the West had often tolerated moderate inflation, arguing that there was a trade-off between controlling inflation and the loss of output and employment and that the functioning of the real economy was more important than the absolute value of money. Monetarists such as Milton Friedman were regarded as cranks and obsessive by the mainstream economics profession during this period. One should be careful however to distinguish between what Keynes himself had said and what governments actually did during this period. The role of the US government in manipulating the international financial system using Keynesian methods would undoubtedly have been opposed by Keynes. He would have predicted the inflationary consequences and his fear of just such a manipulation was the reason that he argued for the international reserve currency to be created *ex nihilo* at Bretton Woods rather than using the existing dollar.

During this post-war Keynesian era, monetarist academics such as Friedman developed the theory of rational expectations which posited that any rate of inflation eventually became embedded in the expectations of economic actors in such a way that they made allowances for it in their market bargaining. Thus the inflation rate was institutionalized and any attempt by governments to 'artificially' stimulate the economy was defeated, each further dose of government credit creation simply raising the rate of inflation. There was a degree of truth in this, not least because of the psychological nature of the argument, which was in a way a backhand tribute to Keynes who had always emphasized the importance of human psychology to the real workings of markets. However, in its most extreme form, this theory was simply another version of the Invisible Hand model; democratic governments can do nothing to influence the working of the economy because the market is infallible and will second-guess them.

Thus the main theoretical difference between Keynesians and monetarists was a different mechanism for the explanation of inflation. The monetarists asserted that there was a single cause of inflation – excess money supply – and that there was a single cause of excess money supply – excess government spending. Keynesians tended to emphasize the multiple causes of inflation and particularly stressed the downward inflexibility of money wages. This inflexibility was seen as a potential source of 'cost push' inflationary spirals because, in the imperfect markets found in the real world, wage increases can be passed on to the consumer as price increases (which then feed into higher wage demands). In the classical monetarist explanation of inflation, this is impossible because no individual firm can increase its prices without losing business to its competitors – wage increases in this model simply reduce profits and therefore should have a deflationary effect as investment is thereby reduced. For Keynesians, the monetarist explanation of inflation – excess government spending – is considered to be one special case. The Keynesian theory, or rather theories, of inflation were therefore more potentially applicable in the highly imperfect markets of eastern Europe.

However, neither of the mainstream Western economic theories was really adequate to explain the impact of price liberalization in post-communist economies. This was largely because both were highly abstract models developed to explain the operations of ideal market economies with all kinds of features which were simply absent in post-communist conditions and which exhibited all kinds of peculiarities not allowed for in any Western theory. For example, advanced market economies have an economic structure in which the size distribution of individual firms is approximately 'log normal' (that is, there are a large number of small firms, a smaller number of medium-sized firms and a small number of large firms). Soviet-style economies had an almost inverted size distribution of firms with hardly any of small or medium size. As we have noted, even in Western market economies the large firms have a disproportionate influence on the formation of prices not really allowed for in monetarist theology. In post-communist economies, the industrial giants had all kinds of economic leverage which operated in ways scarcely dreamed of by Western economists.

Some locally trained economists, such as Sergei Glaziev, the head of the economic commission of the Russian Duma, did have a much better grasp of these problems, but since the whole goal of the structural adjustment process was to create 'normal' market economies, not to reform the existing economy, their warnings could be safely ignored. To those who objected to the radicalism of the policies adopted it was frequently pointed out that 'a chasm cannot be crossed in two leaps'. But as the Indian economist Padma Desai has commented: 'It cannot be crossed in one leap either unless Steven Spielberg is around to ensure that one gets to the other side. Otherwise one drops a bridge.'[3]

In every case the level of inflation precipitated by the 'big bang' of price liberalization, whether it took place earlier, as in Poland, or later as in Russia, was far greater than had been anticipated. Generally speaking, the healthier the fundamentals of an economy the faster it can be driven without causing inflationary pressure. So for many years the West German economy was greatly admired because it grew quickly but without undue inflationary pressure – the economic equivalent of a BMW. It soon became apparent that the Eastern economies were the economic equivalent of a Trabant. Though the inflation unleashed by general price liberalization was huge, the economies of the East collapsed – a perverse outcome which Western experts which were at a loss to explain. In general they attributed this disastrous result to the legacy of an entirely failed communist economic system, conveniently ignoring the role of their own egregious misdiagnosis.

Redistributive Effects

Price liberalization was supposed to be about altering relative prices and if the economy had responded in the way which had been predicted, then the supposedly more 'rational' price structure created by the liberalization would have allowed a much more efficient utilization of the factors of production and a surge of new output. In fact, output collapsed because the economy was simply unable to respond to the new price signals in the way the theory required; the price signals themselves were not 'rational' simply because the state had washed its hands of supervising them. Production of most goods was in the hands of the highly monopolized firms which were the legacy of the old system, and they were simply able to pass on cost increases as price increases to less monopolized sectors and ultimately to consumers. Attempts to control this phenomenon by tightening of government credit allocations led these firms to run up debts with each other which were ultimately the responsibility of the state, although entirely beyond state control. As inflation took hold the expectations of economic actors allowed for it, as Friedman's theory suggested would be the case, and institutionalized those high levels of inflation despite huge drops in real wages. The economically strong, freed from central control, were able to pass on the costs of the inflation to the economically weak. The supposed 'savings overhang' disappeared like snow in spring; living standards collapsed.

An inflation of this type always has pronounced redistributional effects. Those economic actors which have inelastic demand for their products are placed in a much stronger position than those without such advantages. Those actors supplying absolutely essential goods, such as fuel oil, with entirely captive markets are in the strongest position of all. In market economies such an inflation also provides the government with an 'inflation tax' because, as the issuer of legal tender, government agencies handle each tranche of money whilst it has its highest possible value, each subsequent handler losing some of this value as the money circulates. Large state enterprises quite rationally concluded that they could capture some of this inflation tax for themselves by their own manipulation of inter-enterprise credit, which the government would be forced to accept rather than allow the bankruptcy of the most important players in the national economy. In other words, by writing each other IOUs, these large enterprises were able to create money outside of government control. The only way of preventing them doing this would have been to force the bankruptcy of the enterprises concerned when these debts were not honoured. Even if this had been possible in a few cases, promoting the bankruptcy of the whole economy was impossible and unthinkable. The government was therefore powerless to prevent inflationary credit creation in such conditions. The economic actors in the post-communist economy did not behave like those in a market economy. This should not have been a surprise – after all these were not market economies and that was exactly the problem reform was supposed to address. Instead, the lateral-thinking Market Maoist reformers 'solved' this problem by ignoring it; they were under the illusion that if they treated the post-communist economy as if it were a textbook Western market economy, eventually everyone would come to believe that it was one. The 1996 World Development Report concluded that in Russia 'the inflation tax took a quarter of household income' and that 'large enterprises and conglomerates were the main winners'.[4]

Even in modern market economies, it is far from clear that the government has ultimate control over the money supply or that inflation is entirely a monetary phenomenon. During the 1980s, in such countries as Britain, Japan and the United States, paper (or rather electronic) increases in property and share prices continued injecting more and more credit into the economy despite attempts by governments to control the official money supply. This then fed into higher wage demands and even higher prices in a classic Keynesian inflationary spiral. In fact, it was the embarrassment of the British government at its inability to control the money supply which led to the quiet abandonment of the money-supply fetish during the mid-1980s. The inflationary Lawson boom, which could have been created by any free-spending old-style Keynesian such as Mitterrand the younger or Sir Anthony Barber, was touted as an 'economic miracle'. This miracle was supposedly the result of the sado-monetarist deflationary policy of Geoffrey Howe, which had allegedly forced British industry to be 'lean and mean'. In fact, both the deflation and the inflation had been the most incompetent and dishonest periods of macroeconomic governance in modern British history.

The severity of the inflationary explosion in Eastern Europe differed from country to country depending upon domestic circumstances. Those countries which had the most opportunity to respond to price increases through production changes and restructuring were best placed to ride out the storm, especially those such as the Czech Republic whose geographic position and low level of inherited debt allowed them to adapt rapidly to West European export opportunities. Those which began the process with significant macroeconomic imbalances, such as Poland, which had been in a crisis throughout the 1980s, had a rougher ride than might otherwise have been the case (inflation in Poland in 1990 was 586 per cent). In other cases the degree of monopolization of the economy tended to be the deciding factor which meant that inflation was usually worse in the Former Soviet Union than in Central and Eastern Europe. In Russia, the price decontrol ordered by Yegor Gaidar in January 1992 led to an overnight increase of prices by 250 per cent. The hope that this would be a once-and-for-all adjustment would be misplaced even in a developed market economy because even there the degree of practical monopolization is far higher than the Invisible Hand theory suggests, and in any case monetarist rational expectations theory implies that any level of inflation becomes institutionalized in the psychology of economic actors and is not therefore necessarily self-correcting. It is not unique to Eastern Europe that those who are most rhetorically 'anti-inflationary' actually stimulate inflationary pressure by their own misguided actions and then demand public affection for slaying the dragon they have themselves created. In 1992, inflation finally peaked in Russia at 1,353 per cent per annum.

The negative social effects of hyper-inflation are well known from other parts of the world. Perhaps the most important examples are to be found in Latin America. Brazil is a prime example of the phenomenon. Over many years inflation has been used as an instrument to entrench the huge disparities of wealth in that society. Inflation primarily hurts the poor who do not have access to dollars. The government deficits which are the main driving force of Brazilian inflation are hard to correct because the elite has successfully entrenched tax avoidance as a permanent feature of economic life, a phenomenon well advanced in Eastern Europe and the Former Soviet Union. At the same time, servicing debts run up by successive military governments, which first came to power with US blessing in 1964 in order to frustrate the political goals of the reformist João Goulart, continues to bleed the public treasury. Much government spending in any case is concentrated upon the needs of the elite in the form of subsidies for such unproductive activities as land speculation.

The current regime, led by the formerly left-wing economist Henrique Cardoso, came to power committed to the eradication of inflation by tough fiscal measures with the votes of millions of poor Brazilians who know from bitter experience how damaging such inflation is to their vital interests. Cardoso won the election of October 1994 against the Workers Party candidate Lula da Silva who campaigned upon a programme of institutional reform, arguing that the inflation was a symptom of much more serious underlying problems. Lula, a former trade union leader from São Paulo, once considered the Lech Walesa of Latin America, pointed out that privatization was no solution to the fundamental problems of the economy. He argued that the state, having already been captured by private interests, needed to become more publicly transparent and accountable. He lost the election because many of the poor shrewdly calculated that the social conflict engendered by elite resistance to Lula's more radical proposals might intensify the exclusion of the most marginalized (the elite themselves supported Cardoso for more obvious reasons). This election has many parallels with the Russian presidential election and for a while Cardoso has been able to curb inflation by overvaluing the currency and curbing the subsequent trade deficit through administrative controls. But the country remains vulnerable to the kind of precipitate economic collapse recently experienced by Mexico. In Latin America, these huge levels of inflation (Brazilian inflation in 1993 was 2,489 per cent) have been experienced whilst the economy has continued to grow (by 2.9 per cent in the same year). In the countries we are considering, huge levels of inflation have been experienced simultaneously with huge losses of output; a phenomenon unique in economic history.

Current textbook orthodoxy suggests that there is no long-term trade-off between inflation and output, because inflation becomes institutionalized and discounted by rational expectations and therefore cannot provide a stimulus to increased supply in the medium term. However, most mainstream economists accept that in the short run a degree of inflation is usual during periods of growth in market economies. After all, rising prices should lead to rising supply via the Invisible Hand. The converse is also true: policies designed to curb inflation, by curbing demand through rises in interest rates and taxes or cutting government expenditure, will depress output. The way in which governments attempt to curb demand in market economies very much depends upon political considerations. For example, in Britain, Margaret Thatcher's first finance minister Sir Geoffrey Howe raised sales taxes in order to reduce government borrowing and therefore reduce inflation (since the sole cause of inflation was supposedly excess money supply caused by government borrowing and spending). This had the perverse effect of raising measured inflation in the short run quite dramatically whilst it simultaneously redistributed income from poor to rich households (because sales taxes fall disproportionately on those with low incomes). As a result of this, interest rates had to be raised higher than would otherwise have been the case in order to curb the inflationary pressure the government had itself intensified.

Using interest rates as the main method for curbing demand has the side effect of redistributing income from those who borrow money to those who lend, the owners of capital assets. Conversely, increasing taxes on property income or luxury imports would have deflated the economy more effectively without excessive loss of output – but different, and more powerful, groups would have been affected. The Conservative Member of Parliament Robert Harvey noted in a perceptive book published in 1995 entitled *The Return of The Strong: The Drift to Global Disorder* that the use of interest rate increases as a weapon against inflation during the crisis of the late 1980s had very significant redistributional implications:

> High interest rates, coupled with a continuing sharp expansion of credit were an unusual feature of that crisis, but one of great assistance to banks strapped for cash. High interest rates, wheeled in invariably as the orthodox solution to inflation themselves in the short run help inflation, not just because they increase production costs for businesses and customers, but because they increase returns to the banks on a vast number of ordinary deposit accounts, on which no interest is paid.[5]

The political factors influencing the distribution of pain during inflationary episodes have been very much in evidence during the 'stagflationary shock' in Eastern Europe. In Poland, for example, the Balcerowicz programme did not simply rely on monetary measures to restrain inflation as absolute economic orthodoxy would imply. State-owned enterprises were also subjected to a wages tax known as the '*popiwek*' from which private enterprises were exempt (despite the fact that according to the theology of Old Believers wages cannot be a cause of inflation). This penalized any attempt by public sector firms to increase output by increasing labour inputs. The workings of the tax ensured that each state-owned enterprise had a centrally allocated wages fund. Any wage payments in excess of this imposed ceiling triggered penal tax payments much greater then the initial wage creep. This effectively prevented state enterprises from increasing production to take advantage of market opportunities and gave competing private enterprises significant indirect assistance. Milton Friedman was critical of this tax since it implied a departure from the catechism that inflation is 'always and everywhere a monetary phenomenon'. In fact, the policy, which was much disliked by ordinary workers, performed the ideological function of suppressing the public and subsidizing the private sector, reducing real wages and undermining trade union organization.

Big winners during the hyper-inflationary period in Russia were the mushrooming private banks who were able to exploit the interest-rate spreads which such conditions generate. In the 1980s there had been only four banks in Russia, all closely regulated. By 1995 there were an estimated two thousand. Many of these banks operated without licences or with licences obtained through bribery. A UN conference on money-laundering in Cairo in 1995 was told that 'many, if not most of these banks are reportedly fronts for criminal organizations'.[6]

Western Models, Eastern Realities

The causes of inflation in post-communist economies are complex, more complex than in Western market economies. Monetarist explanations of inflation are simplistic even in a Western context – in the Eastern context they are fantastical. For Old Believers this doesn't matter – if reality does not conform to the model then so much the worse for reality. All problems encountered can always be blamed upon the damage inflicted by communism, thus underpinning a posture of ever more drastic radicalism. Government budget deficits have often been increased by the deflationary measures adopted to control them, requiring ever more drastic cuts in government spending in a downward spiral – the economic equivalent of the medieval medical practice of bleeding with leeches. The economy may recover from this spiral despite the deflationary medicine, especially if there are practical limits to the reduction of government spending (it might be argued that this is what has occurred in Poland). On the other hand, the economy may never recover as government revenue evaporates the more government expenditure is cut (it might be argued that this is what is still occurring in Russia and the Ukraine).

Western market economies, underpinned by welfare systems which, contrary to monetarist ideology, are actually central to their efficient operation, are protected against catastrophic production collapses by so-called 'fiscal boost'. The statutory requirement to pay unemployment and other benefits prevents overcontraction of demand and places a cushion under the economic system. Conversely, excess and inflationary demand is automatically siphoned off in extra tax payments – so-called 'fiscal drag'. The large state sectors of eastern Europe could have been remodelled to mimic these effects (copying arrangements in Western welfare states was never going to be possible despite the disingenuous recommendations of the IMF).

However, this kind of policy would have required imagination and careful implementation. There were no political forces, either internally or externally, to base such policies on. In reality, the crippled public sector, or that substantial part of the 'private sector' dependent upon open or implicit subsidy does in fact provide some kind of safety net for the population. As the World Bank admitted even in 1996 'in many transition economies energy and service sector prices are still far below world levels' – subsidized heat and rent boosts real disposable income and many people remain financially dependent upon non-profitable state enterprises.[7] This is despite, rather than because of Market Maoist dogma, implying that continued pressure on living standards will be relentless and permanent as this anomaly is progressively rectified.

In post-communist economies, inflation is essentially a product of 'cost push' pressures on the supply side, which implies that supply-side measures are the only long-term solution. The 'demand pull' pressures are a short-term response to the fundamental structural problems of these economies as governments are forced to increase the money supply or face social and economic collapse. If fiscal and monetary policy had been any tighter the loss of output would have been impossible to contain; inflation is the lesser evil in the circumstances. Of course, the circumstances themselves are absurd and ought to have been avoided. The failure to recognize the supply-side causes of inflation led to the adoption of monetary and fiscal instruments of control copied from developed market economies which simply did not work because economic actors did not respond in the way that was anticipated and the government in many cases did not have an effective monopoly on credit creation. Anti-popular administrative measures to control inflation, such as the *popiwek*, were deemed to be admissible, but any attempt to control the pricing decisions of other economic actors was 'socialism' (and therefore not to be contemplated).

As a result inflation was far worse than it otherwise might have been, with drastic redistributional effects. In order to control this artificially accelerated inflation ever more draconian deflation was required leading to the progressive destruction of the existing economic structure. A denuded and crippled economic base, riddled with bottlenecks and lacking the most basic infrastructural underpinning is a matrix from which new inflation will be generated even where positive economic growth finally reappears. Worse, the price structure created by such a process is possibly less rational and certainly no better from an economic point of view than the original situation. Price liberalization as seen in Eastern Europe has been rather like blowing up the entire house with semtex in order to rearrange the furniture. Belated attempts by such second-wave Market Maoist reformers as Boris Yeltsin's protégé Boris Nemtsov to 'break up monopolies' is simply an exercise in locking the stable door after the horse has bolted.

In any case, a degree of industrial concentration might be inevitable and quite possibly desirable, because the surplus profits of oligopolistic firms can, within a suitable structure of incentives, provide the resources for investment and innovation, as suggested by Schumpeter. How much monopoly (or rather what degree of industrial concentration) might be desirable is the vital empirical question. Working out a coherent competition policy based upon a viable industrial strategy should have been the first step in any genuine economic reform – not a belated afterthought years after the process of reform has begun. The supply-side deficiencies of these economies were the fundamental problem which should have been addressed in the first place. The policies which have actually been adopted have exacerbated those very deficiencies which policy should have been directed to remedying as a first step; it is to these deleterious effects of Market Maoist policy on the functioning of the real economy to which we now turn our attention.

5

The Harder They Come ...

The main debate in economic reform should be about the means
of transition, not the ends.

Jeffrey Sachs[1]

The ostensible rationale for the policy of across-the-board price
liberalization was the belief that many goods supplied in post-
communist economies were being sold at artificially low prices
which, according to the Invisible Hand model, implied that 'market
led' increases in those prices would, after an initial shock, lead to
increased supply. It is debatable if this scenario was really believed
by those who advocated the policy – but it was certainly what many
ordinary people were prepared to believe at the time. In fact, the
disorganizing effect of the price shock, coupled with the highly
imperfect market structure inherited from the previous system led
to the most sustained collapse of production of modern times. Prices
had to rise because 'supply' was inadequate, yet credits to state
enterprises to enable them to expand production were 'irrational'
because they would simply be producing goods which were
'not wanted'.

Budget Constraints

Various 'external' factors were suggested as the explanation for the
gulf between rhetoric and reality, such as the effect of the Gulf War.
One obvious source of blame was the collapse of trade between
Eastern countries themselves. This was treated as though it were an
act of God – although it was to a very large extent the result of Western
financial and political pressure and the naïvety of those who
negotiated with the West on behalf of the countries concerned. The
explanation upon which the experts found a consensus was that the
old economic system was far more inadequate than they had initially
supposed and in any case had already been in crisis before 1989, thus
unexpectedly painful as the medicine had turned out to be, there

was No Alternative. Whilst it may be true that the economies of Eastern countries had been in crisis, the policies adopted worsened that crisis and the whole thrust of the apologetic 'explanation' offered to excuse these errors implied that those concerned did not understand the nature of the problems with which they were dealing. By simultaneously raising prices and preventing enterprises from producing to take advantage of those price rises, the state sector was fatally wounded. The managers of the enterprises concerned fought back by using their knowledge of the real workings of the 'planned' economy to subvert the immediate goals of the Market Maoists and to capture some of the gains of the inflation tax on the population for themselves. This was only a temporary expedient. By the mid-1990s, even in Russia, the old managers and the new entrepreneurial class which had been in a position to benefit directly from the inflation, had formed an unholy alliance firmly based around the ideology of privatization.

The justification for cutting credit lines to enterprises was provided by analyses of the failings of the planned economy dating back to the 1960s. The most prominent theorist of these failings was the Hungarian-born Harvard economist Janos Kornai, who postulated that the main reason for the inefficiency of socialist firms was the existence of 'soft budget constraints'. In other words, there were no penalties for failure. Resources were allocated by a process of bargaining between enterprises and the central authorities. Managers were successful depending upon their negotiating skills with external agents, including other enterprises; they had no incentive to improve internal procedures or labour productivity. Since one of the main goals of socialist enterprises was to sustain employment, reducing costs by reducing labour was not a high priority since it might cause more problems for managers than it would solve.

Much of this analysis was valid and useful, not least because it attempted to theorize the reality of the socialist economy rather than the imposition of abstract blueprints. Kornai suggested a variety of policies to reform the existing system and create a more rational structure of incentives for all concerned. In fact, in 1989 Kornai produced a best-selling pamphlet which advocated a gradual transition to a market economy thoroughly supervised by the state. He emphasized that the transition is not merely of a technical character, because it has a social aspect in terms of the creation of new forms of ownership which implies a long-term learning process for all concerned. Whilst advocating the promotion of a private sector and providing credit resources to underpin it, the government ought to maintain strict regulation, including wage and price control in the public sector. In the event, gradualists such as Kornai were swept aside and far more radical (if less coherent) policies were adopted. He himself was forced to modify his views in a more radical direction. What else could he do?

Paradoxically, many of the problems he theorized have returned in a new guise under the present dispensation. In Hungary, from 1986 onwards, new commercial banks were established from different branches of the former 'monobank'. The new banks were supposed to achieve lending on the basis of market principles. However, the first loans of these new banks were to the same notoriously inefficient state enterprises as previously. When the transition proper began there was a spectacular growth of the financial sector with high margins, high profits and high salaries for bank personnel. The banks were given responsibility for the structural policy of the country despite the fact that their staff had very little experience of the workings of the real economy. Eventually, they also became the arbiters of cultural policy since books could not be published or recordings and concerts of classical and popular music could not take place without their generous support.

The tight monetary policy insisted upon by the IMF led to considerable inter-enterprise debts and fatally undermined the position of the banks. As in many other Eastern countries, the banking system is struggling to cope with these accumulated debts which have already led to banking collapses in countries such as Lithuania and Bulgaria. In Hungary the banks with the highest number of bad debts were given more budget support from the state (a clear case of a soft budget constraint). What is worse is that decisions about which banks and companies would survive were made upon inherently political criteria depending upon links with governing parties and powerful individuals. So 'money does not function as money' even in the banking sector, and if not there, where else?

If we remember the way in which the international financial institutions have slavishly served the interests of leading Western banks exposed by the debt crisis, this capture of the state by private interests does not seem so surprising. Many of the phenomena ascribed by Kornai to socialist systems are universal. Privatization all over the world has more often than not been a process of rendering these linkages more opaque – it certainly has not ended them. The fundamental political problem of how to make the state both independent of private interests and answerable to social demands is not resolved by privatization. It simply creates another line of trenches between business bureaucrats and the populations they are supposed to be serving.

With the restructuring of government budgets, the reform of the public sector began automatically in transition countries. In theory, as subsidies and credits are withdrawn, a Western-style welfare system is to be created in order to provide a social safety net. As we have already pointed out, the welfare system performs essential functions of macroeconomic stabilization in developed market economies. In practice, complete withdrawal of subsidy has not been achieved anywhere in the East (any more than it has been achieved in Western market economies). Because there has been no strategic vision underpinning such subsidies they have been allocated upon untransparent political criteria (one of which has been justified fear of popular reaction to precipitate increases in housing and heating costs and direct cuts in old age pensions).

Depending partly upon the initial level of support for a degree of austerity, different countries hit the bottom of the depression in different years. Poland, for example, experienced its largest output collapse as early as 1990 with a return to measured growth in 1992. In 1995, it was the proud boast of the reformers that the Polish economy had regained on paper the overall size it had in the 'crisis' year of 1989. The Czech Republic and Hungary suffered the largest annual drop in 1991 and reached the sunlit uplands of zero growth in 1993 and 1994 respectively. Russian economic growth turned negative in 1990, and experienced the sharpest decline only in 1992, the year after the dissolution of the Soviet Union. In 1997, it is still unclear when Russia will return to the path of economic growth and in what circumstances. During this period, the economy has halved in size. Market Maoists remain eternally optimistic about the Russian economy, however. Russia has been 'just about to turn the corner' ever since 1993. The revelation that the budget deficit for 1997 will remain enormous (because of unpaid taxes) and that further cuts in expenditure will have to be made, despite a huge backlog of unpaid wages and pensions, hints at the possibility that the Russian economy will never recover from shock therapy.

Due to the precipitate collapse of the Soviet market, as well as the loss of the East German market with the reunification of Germany, the countries of Central and Eastern Europe were obliged to reorient their trade towards the West. Initial successes in capturing a larger share of these markets was eventually turned into trade deficits from 1992 onwards, dashing the hopes of optimistic reformers and bitterly disappointing many ordinary people. This was very largely due to the asymmetric trade agreements negotiated with the European

Union, although West Europeans tried to present the agreements in a favourable light by stressing the reduction of tariffs rather than the more fundamental non-tariff barriers.

The emergence of trade deficits in East Central Europe also showed that through COMECON the Soviet Union had provided substantial implicit subsidies to the other member states. Following the collapse of the trade bloc, however, Russia realized this potential trade surplus on world markets, but this time it was the new private entrepreneurial class which cashed in and expatriated its profits to West European banks immediately.

In 1994, the petty reality of Western protectionism was brought home by a dispute over a key consumer product once manufactured by the father of former British Prime Minister John Major – garden gnomes. Polish producers near the German border began flooding the German gnome market with cut-price gnomes. German gnome manufacturers claimed that the Polish gnomes were bring produced to a German design and after a trade war was threatened, the Poles were forced to withdraw the offending statuary.

The bulk of agricultural exports from Poland and Hungary were of grain, livestock and dairy products – all of these goods are highly protected by the Common Agricultural Policy. Chemical exports continued to be subject to anti-dumping measures aimed at state trading countries dating back to before 1989. Textiles and clothing were subject to a form of managed trade through the Multi Fibre Arrangement. Steel was subject to similar anti-dumping measures and Polish car exports were controlled by quotas. The rules of origin clauses in the agreements mean that exports to the EU from Eastern countries have to have 60 per cent local content, which undermines economic linkages between Eastern economies and ties them into individual dependence on the EU. Jeffrey Sachs and others had urged an export-oriented policy on Eastern countries promising them financial assistance and market access that was simply not on offer. Even the most pro-Western politicians in Eastern Europe have now been given an object lesson in Western trading practices – a lesson they could have learned much less expensively by listening to advice from the despised developing countries.

There is no dispute that there has been a huge fall in production, employment and living standards. This is best illustrated by the remarks of the Market Maoist Anders Aslund made in 1992:

> ... the cost has been lowest in Czechoslovakia and Hungary, where the GNP has officially fallen by about 16–18 per cent in the three years 1990–92. Poland follows with a decline of slightly more

than 20 per cent, while the drop will be about 30 per cent in Romania and some 40 per cent in Bulgaria. In small countries that are subject to severe external shocks through cuts in imports, such as Albania in 1991 and the three Baltic states in 1992, the GNP has actually been halved. A similar drop might be expected for most of the former Soviet Union. These declines make the Great Depression look like a relatively minor incident.[2]

The Market Maoists remained sanguine despite these catastrophic figures and despite the fact that the predicted outcome of rapid liberalization had been increases in aggregate supply after a minor hiatus courtesy of the Invisible Hand. It was widely suggested that much of the output of state enterprises had represented negative value added at world market prices and that the loss of this output was therefore a positive phenomenon. Output figures had been exaggerated under the old system because of desire to be seen to be fulfilling the plan and because GNP was now understated due to tax evasion by private businesses. In any case, welfare had not decreased by as much as the figures suggested because negative phenomena such as queues had been eliminated at a stroke. The largely imported goods now available were of much higher quality than previously, increasing consumer satisfaction. At its most extreme, this attitude led to the assertion that the slump was entirely due to the irrationality of the previous economic system. Clearly, the nature of the statistics are open to question.

However, if output by the state sector was overstated that still remained the case after five years of reform. The state sector and the quasi-state sector (ostensibly privatized companies dependent on implicit subsidies) still made up a very significant part of recorded output, suggesting that GNP was still overstated and implying that the falls had actually been greater than the raw figures suggested. Non-payment of taxes in any case implied significant implicit subsidy of the private sector. The availability of many goods was purely notional for those whose living standards had fallen (the majority). The availability of foreign imports, many of them produced under subsidized conditions in their countries of origin, was in reality a worrying symptom of uncontrolled de-industrialization in the East. Also the slump was across the board and all sectors of Eastern countries cannot have been subtracting value. This strongly suggests that short-run macroeconomic policies were the major proximate cause of the slump.

The initial surge in exports from the East, which was later reversed in most cases, implies that there were comparative advantages to be exploited before the depression took hold. In such abnormal conditions, it was difficult for economic actors to draw any useful long-term conclusions from the price signals being generated.

Going to Extremes

The slump plunged most of the governments in the region into a severe fiscal crisis. Since Western-style tax systems barely existed and most state funds derived from turnover taxes on state enterprises, government revenue melted away. Simultaneously, expenditures on unemployment benefits and other transfer payments to mitigate the social impact of the crisis enforced extra expenditure without doing anything to increase economic potential. Debt servicing took a large slice of whatever revenue was collected in many countries. The 'control of inflation', an inflation partly generated and accelerated by 'liberalization' itself, enforced more and more draconian spending cuts, which in turn deepened the deflationary spiral. As noted above, the new private sector virtually paid no taxes in many countries – a very significant indirect subsidy which goes a long way to explaining its heavily advertised 'viability'. None of this deterred the Market Maoists. Just like their Chinese counterparts they asserted that there was an explanation for these shortcomings: the legacy of Big Power Soviet imperialism. In fact, serious budget deficits only began to be a regular feature of conditions in this region after 1989, except in the most indebted economies: Poland, Hungary and Yugoslavia.

Throughout the slump, the IMF maintained the monetarist orthodoxy that there was no trade-off between growth and fiscal stabilization. In reality, a less dogmatically deflationary policy would have facilitated a more favourable fiscal environment. If fiscal support had been more forthcoming from the international financial institutions in the form of debt relief or concessional finance, then both budget deficits and output losses might have been controlled. After all, this is exactly the role played by Marshall Plan aid in Western Europe after 1945. In the 1990s, the Polish-born economist Stanislaw Gomulka argued, in agreement with the IMF, that any concessional finance made available to Eastern governments would constitute a kind of soft budget constraint allowing them to avoid painful but necessary restructuring. Jeffrey Sachs, whilst no less Market Maoist in relation to sweeping changes in ownership, has frequently stressed the importance of concessional finance to underpin the desired social revolution. In contrast to Gomulka he sees the refusal of such assistance as a 'tax on adjustment' which deters reform. To this extent his views were more pragmatic than those of the Old Believers.

The first head of the newly created European Bank for Reconstruction and Development (EBRD), Jacques Attali, was also a noted supporter of the idea of concessional finance. Attali was closely associated with the socialist French President François Mitterrand and this alone made him suspect in the eyes of conservative financial circles in Washington. They feared that concessional finance would be used to allow a significant state sector to survive in Eastern Europe and even the creation of new state-owned infrastructure – for which there was an obvious need. That is why the EBRD was instructed to make the bulk of its lending to the private sector by the dominant shareholder, the US government. This made it very difficult to dispense funds quickly, because very few private enterprises wanted to risk borrowing full-cost loans (which was another US stipulation) in the middle of a depression. After the French Socialist Party lost the National Assembly elections of 1993 the position of Attali became politically untenable. This, rather than the alleged profligacy of the bank on internal decoration was the real reason for his disgrace and exile. He was replaced by the impeccable neo-liberal Jacques de Larosière, former head of the IMF. The politics of Larosière's appointment became even more apparent after the surprise victory of the French Socialists at the 1997 May general elections. Soon after this event, Larosière resigned, giving his wife's car accident two years earlier as the explanation for his decision.

The major fear of the radical faction was that there was an obvious alternative. A modest infusion of concessional finance as support for national budgets would have allowed a much less painful reform to rapidly build a mixed economy which could have underpinned the varied democratic choices of individual countries. As espoused by Jeffrey Sachs, such an alternative could still have been made heavily conditional on rapid privatization and liberalization, although it must be recognized that the negative consequences of the microeconomic policies to which Sachs, like all right-thinking Market Maoists, was committed, might still have led to output losses and fiscal imbalances which would have nullified the potentially beneficial impact of a more generous approach to the question of finance. It is clear that the Japanese government, as economic pragmatists, regarded the provision of such finance as pointless in the circumstances. In any case, the real radicals understood, correctly from their own point of view, that all talk of the primacy of social and political stability was a slippery slope to common sense. Hence the truly hysterical reaction to any hint of a 'third way', even if all that was implied by this were practices which were well nigh universal in developed market economies. This newly liberated zone, like Chinese society after 1949, was to be treated like 'a sheet of white paper upon which the most beautiful characters can be written'.

That under certain circumstances this ideology could be unceremoniously jettisoned was demonstrated by the Mexican crisis of 1994. It was Mexico that had precipitated what came to be known as the 'debt crisis' by defaulting on its payments to the private banks in 1982. In order to protect the international system a consortium was formed, consisting of the international financial institutions, the G7 and the major private banks, to provide finance for the servicing of Mexico's astronomical debts. Throughout the 1980s the government of Mexico, whose legitimacy was derived from elections widely condemned as fraudulent, adopted their own version of the Market Maoist line under the instructions of their creditors. Mexico became the model for neo-liberal policy in Latin America but at the price of drastic austerity which, as elsewhere in the world, was visited mainly on the poorest sections of their already impoverished population. Foreign private capital, in amounts which dwarf those available to Eastern Europe, poured in. Some went to snap up the privatization bargains available in the fire sale of Mexico's public assets. Much was 'hot money' simply parked in Mexican government paper for a swift no-risk profit (because the finances of the state were underwritten by the international consortium which had stepped in in 1982). Much of this lending was denominated in pesos and interest rates were kept high in order to encourage inward investment and to bear down on inflation. Predictably this led to worse and worse trade deficits (because it increased the price of Mexican exports in dollars and therefore reduced demand). Foreign exchange reserves used to pay for imports were almost exhausted by the time Ernesto Zedillo was relatively freely elected in 1994, using methods closer to those of Boris Yeltsin than Leonid Brezhnev.

Zedillo was forced to devalue the peso, causing a financial panic as investors headed for the door as rapidly as they had entered. In 1994 Mexico owed nearly $136 billion. In other words, the Mexican collapse threatened the integrity of the entire international private banking system. Within a short space of time and despite much grumbling, the creditors' consortium was mobilized and $52 billion was made available to plug the hole in state finances. In effect, Western taxpayers were subsidizing the shareholders of the private banks via the Mexican government; a repeat of 1982. As the financier George Soros pointed out, those who opposed this public sector bail-out on the grounds that it contradicted free market ideology were like passengers in an airliner plummeting to the ground arguing against switching on the engine. The alternative was a global crash. The stabilization policy adopted by Cardoso in Brazil is creating a trade deficit which looks suspiciously like that in Mexico (in 1994 Brazil owed $151 billion). This situation should be understood by all in Eastern Europe and the former Soviet Union as a terrible warning. They too are being asked to walk on a fiscal tightrope similar to the Mexicans and Brazilians, the difference being that in Eastern Europe there is no safety net.

As Jeffrey Sachs was quick to point out in an article in the *Financial Times* entitled 'Mexican Precedent for the Ukraine':

> The discrepancy between Mexico's treatment and that received in recent years by Algeria, Yugoslavia and Russia could not be more stark ... Algeria was pressed in 1991 to transfer around 5 per cent of national income to its creditors at a crucial stage in the liberalization process. Yugoslavia's request for its debt to be rescheduled during a last ditch stabilization programme in 1990 was turned down. And Russia received a pittance from the IMF in the crucial years of reform between 1992 and 1994.[3]

He might have added a considerable number of other countries to his list, most poignantly Rwanda and Somalia. In the latter country, as the Canadian economist Michel Chossudovsky points out:

> ... in 1989 debt servicing obligations represented 194.6 per cent of export earnings. An IMF loan was cancelled because of Somalia's outstanding arrears ... Somalia was tangled in the straight jacket of debt servicing and structural adjustment ... Somalia's experience shows how a country can be devastated by macroeconomic policy... in the era of globalization, the IMF-World Bank structural adjustment programme bears a direct relationship to the process of famine formation because it systematically undermines all categories of economic activity, whether urban or rural, which do not directly serve the interests of the global market system.[4]

Unfortunately, in both these countries, unlike Mexico, the short-term interests of the private banks were not directly threatened. Crippling though the debt burden of these countries was in domestic terms, it simply did not represent enough to bankrupt Wall Street if it were not paid. Only the long-term interests of humanity as a whole were at risk.

There were only two other countries besides Mexico which have received significant debt relief in recent times. The government of Egypt was allowed an outright cancellation of 50 per cent of its debts in 1991 and a similar package was arranged for Poland in the same year. Unlike the Mexican case this was not just rescheduling. All three cases demonstrate that, contrary to market ideology, when it comes to international finance, politics is firmly in command. The Mexican government was helped out of the direct self-interest of the banks and because a meltdown in Mexico threatened the vital interests of the US. The authoritarian Egyptian government needed an inducement to participate in the domestically unpopular Gulf War. The newly installed *Solidarność* government in Poland was assisted partly as a reward for the anti-Soviet industrial unrest of the 1980s and partly because without such help the flagship of Market Maoist economics in Eastern Europe would have suffered not just the most severe depression since the 1930s, as actually occurred, but an economic collapse which would have discredited the whole ideology as a fraud from the very beginning.

In Poland the recovery in the economy, such as it is, has been driven by a revival of domestic demand, not the export-led growth which is the holy grail of the IMF. Domestic demand in Poland has increased largely because of the practical and political limits to the policy of economic destruction initiated by Leszek Balcerowicz. The inertial resistance to further deflation exerted by farmers, workers and the state-owned enterprises has created a 'floor' to the economy which in the West is provided by the welfare system. Such a floor is not just socially desirable, it is also economically indispensable, which is why attempts to dismantle the welfare state in the West are so misguided and irrational. The 'excessive' pensions payments which have been targeted by the IMF and World Bank as the number one fiscal problem facing the Visegrad countries have provided an essential boost to domestic demand. The cost is only 'unaffordable' because of the egregious errors in economic policy which have occurred since 1989.

Politically, the generation which has lived through World War II and forty years of totalitarian rule is in no mood to see its meagre living standards sacrificed on the altar of Market Maoist ideology. In the Polish election campaign of 1995, President Lech Walesa, the candidate of the right, vetoed the IMF-inspired pension reform proposals of the post-communist coalition and saw an immediate leap in his opinion poll ratings. This was a political turning-point of considerable significance, although one would search in vain for any hint of this in the analysis of most mainstream Western commentators. In Poland the post-communists have now become the defenders of a modified Market Maoist orthodoxy. In the event, Walesa's populism was rejected by the electorate largely because of his association with the even more extremist policies of the previous government which his belated U-turn was unable to smother.

In the West as in the East, the provision of public pensions has come under increasing attack from the Young Turks of the market revolution. This is an attempt to roll back not just the social gains of the Keynesian era but those of the whole post-World War I settlement in Western countries like Britain. On one point the radicals are right, a properly funded flexible provision of public pensions is incompatible with a 'modernized' private system. Such a 'modernized' private system is itself incompatible with security in old age for the majority of the population in Western countries, and for virtually everybody except a tiny elite in Eastern countries. The British experience in this area, as in so many others, is instructive. The state earnings-related pension scheme (Serps) created after much negotiation between government, employers and trade unions in the 1960s has been effectively dismantled; despite a spirited rearguard action by Barbara Castle, the ex-minister who had originally established the scheme, there now seems to be no hope of restoring it. The results have been catastrophic for the most vulnerable. As the journalist Will Hutton points out in his best-selling critique of Thatcherite economic policy *The State We're In*:

> Two million people have been persuaded to opt out of the state pension and into private pensions when their earnings were too low to allow them to achieve a comparable income in retirement for the kind of payments they had already been making to the state scheme ... They have been sold a pup.[5]

Despite the overwhelming evidence that a private pension system is incapable of providing elementary security for most of the population in Eastern countries, attempts to 'reform' the existing systems are predicated on the ideological nonsense that the private sector can somehow substitute for collective systems which embody a degree of redistributive solidarity. The compulsory private pension system imposed by the Pinochet regime in Chile is often held up as a model to be emulated in Eastern Europe. However, it is hard to see what the difference is between a 'compulsory' private and a 'compulsory' state system except at the level of ideology. In any case the age structure of Chilean society is very different from that in Eastern Europe, with many more net contributors. The pension reform in Chile was only possible at the point of a bayonet held by armed forces who ensured that their own state pensions remained intact. This issue has far-reaching implications because if the attempt to privatize pension provision fails (and it is looking increasingly to be a political impossibility) then the whole model of capitalism which is being imposed in Eastern Europe will have to be rethought. As Balcerowicz among others has noted, private pension funds are at the heart of the Market Maoist economic model.

The ideological blitzkrieg of the Market Maoists continues undaunted in the face of these realities. In countries with one-third of the population below the poverty line, excessive welfare spending is now blamed for the embarrassing stagnation created by the macroeconomic policies advocated by the Market Maoists themselves. In a Budapest lecture in November 1995 which was sponsored by the Central European University (CEU) founded by George Soros, Jeffrey Sachs called the attention of the audience to the fact that the proportion of the population over the age of 60 was only about 5 per cent in South-east Asia, while it is about 20 per cent in East Central Europe. He suggested that an improvement on this front would be a major precondition of achieving 'sustainable convergent economic growth' of about 6–7 per cent per annum. He did not specify the policy implications although it is true that other departments of the CEU have become leading advocates of euthanasia.

In Poland, the much-trumpeted economic upturn eventually occurred because policy makers have quietly accepted that continued inflation and hidden subsidy is the price that must be paid to prevent the collapse of the economy (although the losses of the radical period will ensure that real social peace remains more elusive). As the finance minister Kolodko of the Democratic Left Alliance put it in 1992 when still an academic:

> It seems that curbing the inflation rate to about 2 percent monthly (i.e. 27 percent yearly), while keeping up the trend to form market clearing prices, is sufficient at this phase of inflation fighting. Because otherwise e.g. if a goal of the order of 1 percent is laid down, the policy must be much more restrictive, thus sustaining recessionary trends in the real economy sphere and threatening it with further destruction.[6]

Kolodko was quoted in an IMF staff paper of December 1995 which admitted that inflation was a structural problem in the Polish economy which could not be dealt with by monetary methods because:

... the threat of job losses gives large established firms political power against the imposition of such constraints. In addition the sizeable debts such firms have already accumulated makes default a powerful threat against banks. In this context, a policy of high real interest rates and exchange rate appreciation would place the brunt of adjustment on Poland's emerging private sector.[7]

So despite all the intense social pain of the shock therapy initiated by the Market Maoists the fundamental problems are unresolved. Official unemployment in Poland in 1996 was around 14 per cent and inflation is stubbornly resilient. Despite Panglossian propaganda, this is another Trabant economy crawling along with an overheated engine. Polish policy makers are showing increasing reluctance to bang the heads of the population against hard budget constraints, largely because social tolerance for this pointless violence has evaporated. The 'recovery' of the economy therefore, far from being a vindication of Market Maoism and an example to the rest of the class, is the result of a return to messy pragmatism. However, truly coherent and strategic policy formation remains elusive.

The quality of the 'growth' in the Polish economy is also in doubt. As Anthony Robinson has pointed out in the *Financial Times*:

Many western companies are shifting labour intensive product lines to take advantage of much lower production costs just over their eastern border. The problem is that the resulting exports often consist of made up clothes or engineering sub assemblies made from previously imported cloth or components. This means that higher exports are dependent on previous imports, and labour is the only real net value added.[8]

In 1996, Poland had a trade deficit of over $6,154 million; around $4 billion of Polish 'exports' consisted of German cross-border bargain shopping. Poland has been in this situation before – in many respects it is a reversion to normal peripheral dependency. In the seventeenth century, Polish 'prosperity' was founded upon similarly illusory successes. As the historian Norman Davies remarks, the Polish grain trade, which dominated the economy during this period:

... did not develop many skills, techniques or forms of organization that did not exist already ... it fostered the massive import of foreign currency which was promptly spent on foreign luxuries ... In short, at the price of several decades of superficial prosperity, it preserved and strengthened the worst aspects of the medieval economy whilst preventing the growth of that variety and flexibility which enabled stronger economies to ride adversity. The state in particular, gained very little advantage from the Grain Trade. The producers had contrived to frame the laws of property and taxation to suit themselves ... In favourable years, the state benefited little from increased prosperity, and accumulated no funds to offset hard times, when the rate of taxation was necessarily low ... The really big money sped abroad in the profits of Dutch entrepreneurs, or stayed in Danzig in the coffers of the financiers, manufacturers and merchants ... people in Poland who complained of their usurious lending rates ... or of their shameless bribery of prominent politicians, found that in practice little could be done.[9]

The Czech Maverick

This dualized development pattern is continuously reproduced by the workings of a radically unbalanced world market. Islands of prosperity exist in a sea of misery. One such island is supposedly the Czech Republic where Premier Vaclav Klaus is regarded as the 'rustless screw' of Market Maoism and the Czech Republic is often suggested as an exemplary demonstration of the success of Market Maoist line. In China itself from 1964 onwards Mao had insisted that all production units should 'Learn from Dazhai', an exemplary People's Commune in Shanxi province led by ultra-Maoist acolyte Chen Yonggui. This was despite the fact that an investigative work team had concluded that the claims advanced for Dazhai were spurious, based on inflated production figures, under-reporting of available land and exaggerated figures for grain sales. They concluded that 'there are woodworms in the staff of the red banner of Dazhai'.[10] The report was suppressed. The utilization of supposedly exemplary centres of excellence as models for others to follow is also a well-established institutional practice of Market Maoism. It diverts attention from the dismal overall results of Market Maoist economic policy even where the results in the production unit concerned have not been totally distorted. Each continent now has its Market Maoist Dazhai: in Latin America – Chile, in Africa – Ghana, in Asia – South Korea and in Eastern Europe – the Czech Republic. Like Dazhai, the 'success' of this particular production unit demands closer and more sceptical investigation.

The Czech Republic has a geographic position which gives it distinct advantages in exporting to the EU. It inherited minimal debts from its paranoid and conformist communist leadership which not only made the fiscal position of the state more secure but also allowed a degree of independence from the dictates of the international financial institutions. The most unviable heavy industry of the former Czechoslovakia was concentrated in the Slovak Republic and thus removed from the analysis at a stroke by the Velvet Divorce.

The much-vaunted 'voucher privatization', in which shares were sold to the population en masse at prices which bore no relation to market value, was the showpiece policy of the Czech Republic's answer to Cheng Yonggui – Vaclav Klaus. It was supposed to imitate the 'popular capitalism' which many in Eastern Europe believe to exist in Britain as a result of the policies of Margaret Thatcher. Czech 'privatization' is in fact a species of corporatism. The bulk of the 'individual' shares are now in the hands of large investment privatization funds. These are basically owned by the commercial banks which are controlled indirectly by the state. Thus although much of Czech industry is now classified as 'private', the banks and the National Property Fund have been loath to initiate the kind of widespread bankruptcies seen in Hungary, Poland or in Britain during the initial stages of the Great Bourgeois Cultural Revolution in 1981–83. In other words, unlike Hungary, in the Czech Republic the state has attempted to pursue a coherent (if covert) industrial policy rather than allowing a *laissez faire* free-for-all. As a result unemployment remains very much lower in the Czech Republic than elsewhere in the region, even though the economy in 1995 was only about 85 per cent of the size it was in 1989 and productivity per employed worker is considerably lower than in Poland or Hungary.

In terms of the Market Maoist definition of efficiency, Czech manufacturing industry is overstaffed. Ironically, the Czech voucher scheme, once lionized by free-market propaganda as a shining example of popular capitalism, is now seen as a major obstacle to the shake-out of Czech industry seen as indispensable to continued 'reform'. The postponed Czech economic crisis broke with full force in 1997. It now appears that the popularity of Vaclav Klaus has been in inverse proportion to the real implementation, as opposed to the rhetorical advertisement, of Market Maoist policies. The political cynicism of Market Maoists who are now denouncing Klaus' 'anti-market' voucher privatization is truly breathtaking.

Let us give credit where it is due. The policies promoted by the Good Soldier Klaus have been relatively more successful than those adopted in the other Visegrad states. But they have succeeded partly by building upon the thrifty legacy of the Good Soldier Husak after 1968, who eschewed the Sugar Coated Bullets of Imperialism eaten in such disastrous quantities in Hungary. Since 1989, there has been a judicious and intelligent flouting of the central tenets of consistent Market Maoism. This has been coupled with a vociferous profession of theoretical radicalism (a tried and trusted Chinese peasant strategy over several millennia). In Britain, 'privatization' was a policy of implicit subsidy to the service-sector middle class. As in South Korea and Taiwan, it is Czech manufacturing industry which has been the main beneficiary of hidden subsidy. In fact, the relevance of the Czech experience for policy formation elsewhere is diametrically opposite to that which is frequently suggested.

One of the most appealing aspects of Czech policy has been the avoidance (so far) of mass unemployment. In other 'leading reformers' such as Poland and Hungary, unemployment has reached crisis proportions. In 'non-leading' reformers, unemployment and collapsing living standards are fuelling attempted population movements reminiscent of the last days of the Roman empire. This response to economic despair is consistent with free market theory. If there is an oversupply of labour in a given region then the price of labour will fall until a market-clearing equilibrium is established. The higher the unemployment the more wages will fall, thus spontaneously encouraging inward investment and outward migration. In the long run, there will be full employment provided that there is no misguided interventionism by government. In reality, no market functions in this way, let alone labour markets which are constrained by all kinds of economic rigidities and cultural peculiarities (not least immigration controls). The time was when attempts by Eastern Europeans to defect to the West or emigrate to Israel was seen as evidence of the intolerable nature of communist society. Those few who managed to evade the People's Police and cross the borders to enter the 'free world' were treated as heroes. Now it is Western governments who pay the border patrol to catch them.

Within Eastern countries it is very difficult for the labour market to work in the way the textbook suggests. Wages have fallen, but so has effective demand. What new jobs have been created are not, on the whole, going to the unemployed. Rigidities in the housing market, worsened by giveaway 'privatization' of the housing stock to existing tenants, makes it almost impossible for workers to move to high-growth areas. The high degree of regional specialization inherited from the old system means that skills are often mismatched to whatever local job opportunities do exist. Employers are in reality more likely to pay a premium to existing workers who understand their jobs through experience than to employ cheaper, but less productive new workers from the pool of the unemployed. As time goes on, the unemployed become unemployable, a net drain on social resources through benefit payments, lost tax, health expenditures and crime. The price of a 'short-term' adjustment in employment levels becomes long-term social cancer.

Maintaining levels of employment is not only politically desirable, it also makes economic sense. Unless there is a clear alternative source of employment, it is far better to allow workers to continue producing, and learning, than to throw them onto the scrap-heap. As in the Czech Republic, budget constraints should be hard enough to encourage a degree of restructuring and soft enough to prevent widespread bankruptcies. This may not be a classically capitalist policy, but so what? The alternative of writing off a large portion of the population is no alternative. The reason why widespread redundancy appears to be economically desirable is because the costs of unemployment are borne by society as a whole and the unemployed and their families in particular. The profits resulting from redundancies and downsizing are privately appropriated. In the Czech Republic a firm which makes workers redundant has to pay a part of their unemployment benefit. Policy makers in the former Soviet republics should take note. The dangers of a Market Maoist approach to labour market policy in these societies is probably even greater than in East Central Europe. The 'second shock' of widespread bankruptcy will not assist the restructuring of the economy in a rational way. Like it or not, the successor states have inherited the Soviet economic legacy. That legacy should be intelligently redeployed, not squandered in obedience to ideological diktat. As the great survivor Deng Xiaoping famously put it: 'Who cares if the cat is black or white as long as it catches mice?'

The rate of registered unemployment has varied quite considerably depending upon local conditions. However, there is clearly a strong correlation between 'strong' and 'consistent' policies and high rates of open unemployment. Where the creation of open unemployment has been resisted as in Russia and the Ukraine, the main brunt of adjustment has been borne by real wages. In other words, many officially employed workers in Russia or the Ukraine are paid at less than unemployment benefit level in Poland or Hungary and are frequently not paid at all. Average real wages in the Ukraine at the end of 1995 represented just over $50 per month. Generally, the Market Maoist attitude to the collapse of living standards in the former Soviet Union is to suggest that this is a result of lack of radicalism. Open unemployment in Russia in October 1995 was calculated at 13.7 per cent (including those 'temporarily' laid off).[11] A particular problem has been the non-payment of wages by the state in order to fulfil budget deficit conditions laid down by the IMF. This has provoked successive waves of industrial unrest, particularly in the mining industry. The continued employment of large numbers of workers in CIS countries is a result of structural and political rigidities which the IMF would like to see removed. In other words, it is because policy makers in these countries have not done what the IMF wants them to do that living standards for the majority have not collapsed even further than they already have.

Ironically, a country which used to be much praised for its loyalty to the Market Maoist programme was Albania (also the only original Maoist dictatorship in Europe). In 1994, Albania had a per capita GNP of $360. Unemployment in Albania represents well over 50 per cent of the active population. Dissatisfaction with the hardline and corrupt economic policies of the government of the Albanian Democratic Party, led by Sali Berisha, resulted in a strong challenge from the Socialist Party (the former communists) in the elections of 1996. Berisha won the election but many observers concluded that the result was fraudulent (and indeed it was reversed in the election of 1997 after a short but brutal Civil War). Economic growth in Albania in 1994 was officially 7.4 per cent, which sounds impressive until it is recognized that the return to pre-revolutionary living standards would take decades even at this rate. For the unemployed of Albania the future is bleak. They are very unlikely to see any material benefits from the introduction of a market economy in their lifetimes. The collapse of crooked pyramid investment schemes in 1997 which wiped out the savings of the population at a stroke has ended all talk of Albania as a model pupil of the IMF. The generalization of this model to the former Soviet Union is, not unnaturally, being resisted by those with the most to lose from it.

Implicit in the Market Maoist model is the belief that foreign direct investment (FDI) will provide the motor for investment in the post-communist world. As already noted, the levels of FDI in the region have been far less than has been projected, the lion's share of this going to the ten million people of Hungary (who had received nearly 50 per cent of FDI for the whole region by 1996). Despite this relatively large capital inflow, Hungary has suffered with consistent declines in GNP until 1995 with living standards under constant downward pressure (with the exception of the pre-election spending spree by the centre-right government in 1993–94).

Financial liberalization in Hungary has created a Disneyworld in which the supposedly 'independent' banks have inherited the bad debts of the state-owned enterprises. Bankrupting such enterprises would be self-defeating and so a system of lending has emerged in which the larger and more inefficient the enterprise the more likelihood of borrowing extra money. The main losers have been small and medium enterprises who find it almost impossible to secure new loans. The main source of revenue for the banks has been from government bonds and repurchase agreements with the central bank. Unsurprisingly, as soon as a tough bankruptcy law was enforced in 1992, the need for extraordinary measures arose. The government was forced to throw a lifebelt with one hand to enterprises it was attempting to drown with the other.

A programme of 'credit consolidation' was announced which then became a programme of 'bank consolidation' and eventually a programme of 'debtor consolidation' (that is to say, direct reorganization of enterprises by the government). When the banks were 'consolidated' they had to divide their own portfolios into good, bad and dubious (or should that be 'ugly'?) categories. There were no clear criteria for this process and so banks could virtually ask the government for any sum they wanted. Soon the few banks which behaved honestly were regarded as fools since they were missing out on free gifts from the state. No one really knows when a true reckoning may come. Bad loans are ticking away like a timebomb at the heart of this chaotic system.

Despite this shambles, 'privatization' is now the order of the day. The Budapest Bank was bought by General Electric Capital (GE had previously bought the Hungarian electronics firm Tungsram in order to destroy potential competition). The amount they paid was just a little more than the secret subsidy the bank had received just before privatization in order to meet the required capital adequacy ratio. When privatized, the Hungarian Credit Bank (MHB) was discovered to be worth less than Barings after Nick Leeson. Leaks about the dubious finances of Postabank, an Austro-Hungarian joint enterprise, triggered a run on that bank in early 1997. Foreign commercial banks (ING, Crédit Lyonnais, etc.) are also operating in Hungary. They mainly focus on financing foreign companies, usually related to their home countries. Local firms have no chance of obtaining loans from them. This is just another evidence to prove that Hungary is well on the way to becoming a dualized economy – this polarization has been a direct result of its openness to Western finance capital.

In contrast, Romania under the Iliescu regime attempted a more autarkic policy. Growth returned to the economy in 1991 and in 1995 was projected to be more than 4 per cent. This probably reflects the relatively unindebted situation inherited from Ceausescu. This is not to suggest that Romanian policies can or should be emulated elsewhere or that they are responsible for the relatively good performance statistics of the country. What it does make clear is that a policy of indiscriminate openness to foreign capital as seen in Hungary has many drawbacks. As the Mexicans have also discovered, money that can come in can also go out.

In any case, it is becoming increasingly clear that growth figures hide as much as they reveal. There is clearly less and less relationship between raw growth figures and material well-being. The increased use of gross domestic product as the measure of economic progress by the IMF and the World Bank is in itself significant. The main difference between GDP and gross national product is that the latter takes account of net property income from abroad. In other words, foreign firms have their profits counted in country in GDP figures whereas they are counted in the country of ownership in GNP figures. With the increasing globalization encouraged by the international financial institutions this is a very curious statistical change which serves to obscure very important resource flows from poor to rich countries.

Living standards are notoriously difficult to measure but the UN Human Development Report of July 1996 estimated that per capita income in the post-communist countries as a whole had fallen by about one-third, the bulk of this taking place during the 1990s. If we think of the social angst in developed Western countries when increases in growth fall below trend then we can begin to comprehend the scale of the social disaster unfolding in this region. In 1996, GNP per capita in Albania, Poland and Romania was at the level originally reached in the 1970s, for Estonia and Lithuania in the 1960s and for Armenia and Georgia in the 1950s.[12]

Perhaps the most revealing social statistic is the huge rise in death rates throughout Eastern Europe and the Commonwealth of Independent States (CIS). According to a UNICEF report published in 1994, between 1989 and 1993 the death rate rose by 9 per cent in Romania, by 12 per cent in Bulgaria and by a staggering 32 per cent in Russia (the equivalent of an extra half-million fatalities a year).[13] Middle-aged men seemed to have the highest increase in death rates, which must have something to do with falls in wages and increases in unemployment and general insecurity. Another UNICEF report published in 1997 highlighted the desperate plight of children in the former socialist countries. The report stated that in countries like Moldova, Georgia or Armenia, the public child protection system has virtually collapsed. The number of infants aged less than three placed in care homes has grown by 75 per cent in Estonia and by about 40 per cent in Latvia, Romania and Russia. Teenage male murder rates rose more than five-fold in Lithuania between 1989 and 1995. Polish social workers believe that half the prostitutes working on the German border are under 18. The report's co-author Gaspar Fajth stated that 'in many ways children are worse off and this is a scandal'.[14]

The gap between the winners and the losers in the Great Bourgeois Cultural Revolution has widened to a chasm. But there are winners. Wealth and opportunity has burgeoned out of all recognition for some favoured sections of the population. One of the main mechanisms through which this has occurred was invented in Britain in the 1980s, and has, with the fervent backing of the international financial institutions, become a universal feature of modern economic life: privatization.

6

Nouveau *Nomenklatura*

> The purpose of privatization is not to make state operations competitive but to make them private.
>
> Dr Madsen Pirie,
> President of the Adam Smith Institute.[1]

Privatization has achieved a centrality in global economic policy making which is truly astonishing. Before 1984 the word was scarcely used – such policies, where they occurred, usually being described as 'denationalization'. In the 1970s it was more normal even for right-wing governments in developed market economies to nationalize loss-making corporations, such as the car manufacturer Chrysler in the United States or Rolls Royce in Britain, in order to restructure the business with taxpayers' resources. It is a significant indicator of the ascendency of Market Maoism that from the mid-1980s a new set of slogans were promulgated which underpinned a whole new and aggressive ideology. Henceforth the promotion of the mixed economy, which had hitherto been the backbone of Western resistance to communist propaganda, was to be damned as a 'socialist deviation'.

Following the British Example

Britain under the Thatcher regime has been universally recognized as the epicentre of this world historical earthquake. Strangely enough, the Thatcher government was little concerned with the issue of privatization in its first term. The obsession of the time was with the 'control of the money supply'. This monocausal theory of inflation led to policy errors which had subjected the British economy to the most severe deflation since the 1930s, making Britain a net importer of manufactured goods for the first time since the Industrial Revolution. But by 1983 it was becoming increasingly clear that the 'money supply' was virtually impossible to define, let alone within the power of government to control in the manner which had been suggested. In 1983, the Thatcher government was re-elected under Britain's curious and anachronistic electoral system, derived like many other characteristic British institutions from the medieval past, with 43 per cent of the popular vote. This was the popular mandate for the privatization revolution which did not even appear in the Conservative election manifesto. It is surely significant that no other Western European country has such a perverse electoral system and that not one of the new democracies of Eastern Europe chose to adopt a British-style system after 1989.

Financial deregulation, which had been vigorously lobbied for by the City of London, a major pillar of the regime, had created a situation in which new forms of electronic money and ingenious sources of credit creation were continually being invented. Feeble attempts were made by Margaret Thatcher's personal economic advisor Sir Alan Walters to insist that the 'real' money supply only consisted of cash banknotes issued by the government because all transactions ultimately had to be settled in cash. Most professional economists thought that this was a desperate argument. Nevertheless, Margaret Thatcher appointed Alan Walters as her personal advisor to tell her what she wanted to hear. Walters in this role resembled nothing so much as the parrot Lin Biao, appointed by Mao to edit the *Little Red Book* of his wise sayings. In spite of continued theological wrangling by the Old Believers about the exact definition of Sterling M3 (did it or did it not include interest bearing current accounts?) the money supply had become a political embarrassment, not least because it continued to grow independently of government policy whatever method was used to calculate it. The time had come to launch a new rectification campaign. The slogan was to be 'privatization'. It was a fateful choice for Eastern Europe although no one could have foreseen that at the time.

It is worth examining the rationale for privatization in some detail because it has now taken on the quality of an unquestioned axiom in international political economy. As leading Market Maoist Leszek Balcerowicz put it in an article revealingly entitled 'Democracy is No Substitute for Capitalism': 'It is not true that every state owned enterprise is less efficient than a private one, just as it is not true that every woman is weaker than every man. What we have to compare is the averages.'[2]

This is crude, simplistic economics but brilliantly effective politics, provided there has been little or no experience of privatization in practice, which was universally the case in this region in 1989. John Howell, of the British consultancy firm Ernst and Young which was very active in Eastern Europe after 1989, noted that what was really surprising was

> ... the virtual absence of any Western opposition to the selling of wholesale privatization even amongst socialist politicians and economists ... how feeble the debate has been about the merits of a programme on which considerable amounts of money have been spent and on which considerable hopes were, and still are, pinned.[3]

At least part of the answer to this conundrum was answered by Howell himself when he pointed out that countries adopted privatization because 'they were told to do so by the IMF, the World Bank and by the other creditor institutions'.[4] There was also the widespread and seemingly common-sense view that whatever the intricacies of the privatization debate in the West, in Eastern Europe as Balcerowicz pointed out 'the state sector looms larger while the private sector is smaller. In consequence, the necessity and scope of what must be created in terms of driving forces are much greater.'[5] Real common sense would have been to recognize that conditions in Eastern Europe were so different from those in the West that caution should be exercised in the importation of barely understood policy prescriptions. What were the positive arguments for privatization? Essentially they boiled down to the view that private ownership created incentives for firm-level efficiency lacking in public enterprises. This is strange because all economics textbooks are unanimous in the view that efficiency is a by-product of competition, not a result of ownership. As the World Bank itself said in 1983, 'The key factor determining the efficiency of an enterprise is not whether it is publicly or privately owned, but how it is managed. In theory it is possible to create the kinds of incentives that will maximize efficiency under any type of ownership.'[6] This was in the days before the party line was radicalized. Opposition to the revolutionary line was neutralized by classical 'salami tactics'. As each new step was made, further and more extreme policies were advocated. The collapse of the Soviet system in 1989 had the effect of giving a further undeserved lease of life to policies which were becoming increasingly unsaleable within developed market economies.

A considerable body of critical analysis of the effects of privatization has now been assembled, particularly in Britain which has had such a surfeit of direct experience in this field. For example, it has been pointed out that if the government privatizes profitable firms, especially in large-scale programmes, it is usual for the assets to be underpriced either for political reasons, to make the sale a 'success', or because the buyers have effectively captured the state apparatus. In the long run, this implies that the government will have to increase taxes in order to maintain revenues. In Britain this has implied increases in indirect (sales) taxes which fall disproportionately on those with low incomes. Even with these tax increases on the poorer sections of the population, and stringent spending cuts on services largely consumed by the poor, there was a growing fiscal imbalance forcing government borrowing to record levels. However, since monetarism had been quietly forgotten, this was no longer regarded as a problem by anyone except foreign exchange dealers (this partly explains British Market Maoist opposition to the Maastricht criteria which resurrected the monetarist ghost). In Hungary and elsewhere in Eastern Europe the sale of 'money machines', such as energy utilities, in order to service payments on government borrowing is simply storing up fiscal problems for the future.

Where management initiates privatization it is usually the case that they are not seeking the increased competition that would force them to greater efficiency, but rather a higher private utilization of the monopoly power of the firm. This is not to say that it would not make sense for the state to pay managers according to performance and partial ownership might create positive incentives. But that would be a reform of public ownership and therefore explicitly excluded as a solution by true Market Maoists. As the economists Kay and Silberston put it in 1984, real consistency demands that 'privatization will only be effective in cases where existing management opposes it'.[7] The huge windfall profits to previous managers of public enterprises is an open scandal in Britain. The huge fortunes made by the new private owners, formerly *nomenklatura* managers, of Gazprom in Russia are an Eastern example of the same negative phenomenon. Viktor Chernomyrdin – the fattest cat of them all – used his position in the *nomenklatura* to become a private millionaire and then bought himself the job of prime minister.

Much privatization, in the West as in the East, has been to the benefit of speculative investors. Especially during the transition depression in markets flooded with newly offered assets, many bargains have been snapped up. The buyers intend to realize their gains from rises in the market values of those assets, not from the effective management and development of the enterprise concerned. Almost all the new shareholders created by the giveaway privatization deals in Britain have been motivated in this way. If such purchasers are allowed to use credit to finance their acquisition (a so-called 'leveraged buy-out'), they are even more likely to use income streams from the firm to repay creditors than for reinvestment. The ease with which such transactions now take place in the United States has placed many of its leading firms at a significant competitive disadvantage compared to firms, for example in Japan, where such transactions hardly ever occur.

Many firms which have been privatized in the West have very significant monopoly power (for example, energy utilities and railway networks). That is frequently why they were nationalized in the first place. It goes without saying that leading firms in Soviet-style economies enjoyed almost total monopoly domination of their respective markets, a domination which used to be offset by the state. Unloosened from such constraints, the flagrant abuse of monopoly has become widespread in Eastern economies. This has been a very popular policy amongst potential purchasers, but as Kay and Silberston note:

> ... if there is no more to the policy than selling off statutory monopolies to the highest bidder, it has no more to offer in benefits to efficiency than the similar practice of the Tudors and Stuarts of selling monopolies, and history will treat it with equal derision.[8]

Underlying the policy of privatization has been a visceral distrust and contempt towards the whole concept of the public interest. As the British Conservative MP John Moore put it, 'from the customer's point of view, the State is just as likely to abuse a monopoly power as a private owner'.[9] Pro-privatization public choice theorists, such as Downs, Niskanen, Tullock and Buchanan, are firmly of the view that 'politicians and state bureaucrats pursue their own self interest rather than the "public interest" or the will of the people'.[10] If it is the case, as these eminent social scientists suggest, that capitalism cannot be reconciled with democracy, then one might ask why it is assumed that state bureaucrats, acting in their own interests, would be less efficient than private owners, who would also presumably be acting in their own interests? We accept that there is a problem ensuring that public servants act in the public interest. That is why it is so pernicious for government bureaucrats to initiate policies of privatization which further weaken their accountability. The privatization process in practice has invariably borne out the worst expectations of public-choice theorists concerning the motivations and goals of high-ranking state employees.

This is not to suggest that privatization is always and everywhere an undesirable policy choice – such dogmatic ideological certainty is best left to the Maoists (of whatever political stripe). Where relatively competitive markets exist, firms are subject to beneficial cost disciplines whatever their ownership structure. However, in Western market economies, most competitive markets already function in the private sector and much of what has been privatized has natural monopoly power. Often, where for ideological reasons governments have insisted on 'competition', the results have been farcical. Thus the British electricity-generating industry was split into two 'competing' firms (whose obvious market strategy is collusive) supplying to local distribution companies with local monopoly. In order to avoid the exploitative squeeze of this government-created duopoly these local monopolies are increasingly using new short-life gas-powered generating capacity – the so-called 'dash for gas'. This was a major factor in the collapse of the markets of the British coal industry with the loss of thousands of jobs. Using fossil fuel to generate electricity for heating purposes only made economic sense because the whole market structure had become a dog's breakfast as a result of electricity privatization. To suggest that this outcome was the spontaneous result of 'market forces' is absurd. From the point of view of society as a whole (which must pick up the bill for dismantling the coal industry), this has been an economic and social disaster. For the managers and shareholders of the newly privatized industries, it has been a gift.

A positive feature of these developments from the point of view of the Conservative government was the effective destruction of the National Union of Mineworkers as a major social force. This underlines a very important truth. Privatization is a primarily political process. It redistributes wealth and power in favour of insider economic elites. Whatever the underlying economics, the rationalization of the Gdansk shipyard allowed a similar political revenge to be wreaked by Poland's elected post-communist government on the initiators of the trade union *Solidarność*. Where Poland's post-communists would deny such vindictive motives, the supporters of Margaret Thatcher hardly bothered to conceal them, although even many staunch middle-class Conservatives found it hard to swallow the callous mass sackings even of former strikebreakers who had been promised job security, which eventually transpired.

Competition can only usually be simulated in such monopolized markets as that for energy by government fiat. The result is a kind of modern feudalism in which the right to exploit the public is subcontracted to a number of hand-picked vassals – who reward the

regime with political and financial support. The same 'enfeudaliza-
tion' is an even more prominent feature of privatization in the East
where the minimal checks and balances of the West are dispensed
with altogether. Frequently privatizations have been concluded
which significantly diminished competition such as the notorious
acquisition of the Hungarian firm Tungsram by General Electric. The
Hungarian sugar and seed-oil industries were sold to foreign interests
in an even more concentrated form than had been allowed under
public ownership. The government justified the sale on the grounds
that there were 'too many' firms in the industry. This kind of process
creates an industrial policy by the back door but one which is
dominated by private vested interests. This elucidates another truth
– the search for monopoly power is the underlying drive of modern
corporations. The 'competition' so beloved by Market Maoists is a
myth. In their more candid moments, leading Market Maoist cadres
admit this. As Madsen Pirie of the Adam Smith Institute said, 'Some
observers have supposed that the whole point and purpose of
privatization is to subject state monopolies to competition. This
misses the point.'[11]

Ownership and Efficiency

Recommending privatization for all the sicknesses of the public
sector has been likened to a doctor prescribing the same pink pills
for all ailments. It should be obvious, as Hemming and Mansoor point
out, that 'many of the problems associated with public enterprises
arise not from the fact that they are publicly owned'.[12] As Hartley
and Parker noted in 1991, the vast literature which has mushroomed
since 1983 which is based on the assertion that private is superior
to public 'has little to say about performance differences between
organizations within the public and private sectors'.[13] In theory,
private firms which perform badly will die. In practice, they are
often resuscitated with social resources – witness the endless rescues
by the taxpayer of private banks which have taken place in the last
two decades. Losses are socialized; profits are privatized.

It is true that privatized firms are often more profitable than when
under public ownership. This does not however imply that public
firms have been mismanaged. It is more commonly the case that
public firms simply have lower regulated profits, to the benefit of
consumers. As Ramanadham notes they may also have 'conscious
injections of social policies into their operations'.[14] If one does not
expect an army or a primary school to be profitable, why should that

be required as a measure of good performance from a public transportation system or a housing project? Even if we accept the assertion of Leszek Balcerowicz that 'Profit Is the Seed of Growth',[15] it has to be recognized that profit is a complex phenomenon. As Michel Adelbert, the Chief Executive of Assurances Générales de France has pointed out in his influential study *Capitalism against Capitalism*:

> ... profit can also weaken free enterprise; it can be damaging to the economy; it can hinder development. Just as few would argue with the proposition that too much taxation will eventually lead to diminishing tax revenues, so it may be argued that too much emphasis on today's profits can jeopardize tomorrow's.[16]

As we have already pointed out, there is no necessary connection between monetarism and privatization. Monetarism has its own characteristic absurdities associated with dogmatic beliefs about the money supply and inflation. Privatization has its intellectual roots rather in the property rights theories of the Austrian school, which emphasize the importance of clear private property rights over assets as a guarantee of the efficient utilization of those assets. How paradoxical therefore that the 'stockholder-driven' capitalism most favoured by the Austrian school has created a 'capitalism without owners' where the concern of institutional investors with the actual conduct of day-to-day business is zero, and where, as Adelbert points out, 'Companies are now merely cash flow machines, subject to the whims of finance and exposed to the cruellest elements of stock market speculation.'[17]

Japan and Germany have both been largely immune to the privatization revolution. In Germany, until 1990 privatized state property amounted only to some DM 10 billion (£3.5 billion), as compared to the £28.5 billion privatized by the Thatcher government in Britain. Wholesale privatization only came onto the German political agenda after the incorporation of the GDR and it has appeared to be a process in which astronomic amounts of taxpayers' money from the West have been consumed with a very slight hope of a return in a very distant future. The recession triggered by this publicly subsidized privatization process through higher German interest rates ought to have triggered a revision of the privatization dogma. However, like a cartoon character which has not noticed that he has stepped over the edge of the cliff, the proponents of privatization refuse to accept the mounting evidence of the perverse results of their favourite policy instrument.

Eastern Europe has been treated as a vast and lucrative laboratory by the privatization industry. Although a main argument of the privateers has been that economic priorities are being asserted over political goals, the political character of the East European privatization, as well as its largely uneconomic rationale, has been more than obvious. As Jack Wiseman, in his assessment of privatization, succinctly remarks ... 'what is happening in Eastern Europe is essentially a transfer of power'.[18] It is probably only a slight exaggeration to claim that 'privatization' as an ideology is a vast confidence trick based on pyramid-selling like an Albanian 'investment opportunity'. Brendan Martin has described the sales pitch adopted by one of Britain's most fanatical free-market radicals, John Redwood, who visited Budapest to spread the gospel in 1989.

Redwood was formerly head of Margaret Thatcher's policy unit before moving to Rothschild's bank as founding head of its privatization unit. He left John Major's cabinet to challenge for the leadership of the Conservative Party in 1995. In 1989 he told a meeting of the newly established Budapest Stock Exchange:

> When privatization was tried in Great Britain, old industries were renewed and economic performance was improved. In the case of the British steel industry, a heavy loss-making industry in permanent decline was turned round to become profitable, modern, and one of the best in the world.[19]

Brendan Martin has commented:

> What Redwood said about the British steel industry is both true and false. The changes he described really did occur – but before privatization, not afterwards. This had been admitted at the time by Lord Young, the then Secretary of State – the very department Redwood was representing in Budapest. In December 1987, Lord Young announced that 'in view of the financial and commercial recovery of British Steel he was setting in hand the work necessary to privatize the Corporation as soon as possible'.[20]

Similar sleight of hand was evident in Redwood's claim in the same speech that British Airways was 'transformed from being a heavy loss maker, losing jobs and business, into one of the world's premier airlines', all of which occurred whilst British Airways was in the public sector.

An even wilder flight of fancy carried John Redwood through his description of the effects of privatization and deregulation on British bus services: 'The results were stunning: lower fares, more travellers, better quality services.'[21] By that time, even his own government's official figures showed that fares outside London had risen by an average of 12 per cent in real terms since deregulation. Integrated services and dependable timetables had disappeared. Bus use had fallen by 26 per cent in metropolitan areas and by 19 per cent elsewhere. Too much competition on busy routes had increased traffic congestion while off-peak services were cut because of the ending of cross-subsidization. Redwood was right about one thing: the results certainly were 'stunning'.

Brendan Martin concluded:

> Redwood's Budapest speech reveals the path privatization ideology has taken. The theoretical claims of the 1970s are foisted on the Third World and Eastern and Central Europe in the 1990s with the help of a distorted account of their practical results in the 1980s ... the ideological influence of Thatcherism has planted its seed in the fertile soil well prepared for it by two generations of totalitarianism in Eastern and Central Europe. One dogma is effortlessly replacing another.[22]

Privatization and Demoralization

As privatization becomes increasingly discredited as an economic policy in its birthplace and, politically speaking, Margaret Thatcher has gone to meet Adam Smith, figures such as John Redwood increasingly take up a radical posture reminiscent of Jiang Jing and the Gang of Four. British critics of privatization are constantly reminded of the huge success and popularity of this policy all over the world, not least in Eastern Europe. It is implied that privatization has been adopted entirely spontaneously by independent sovereign governments entirely on its own merits. Whilst not underestimating the simplistic appeal of privatization ideology for economically illiterate post-communist political elites, this ignores the huge moral and material pressure exerted by the radical faction in the West. Criticism of these policy choices in the West is muted because of the widespread perception that some degree of privatization in Eastern Europe was inevitable and out of an understandable unwillingness for Western critics of the policy to be seen to be defending the clearly indefensible status quo of Eastern Europe in 1989. This has had the disastrous consequence of diverting discussions about the hard choices in economic policy in both halves of Europe into a meaningless squabble about how many privatized angels can dance on the head of a pin.

In the real world, privatization in the East has done nothing to resolve the underlying economic problems of the countries in which it has been applied and in many cases has made these problems worse. In any case, privatization on the Western model has largely been unfeasible in Eastern societies and various untried mechanisms have been substituted for it in order to 'mimic' the workings of Western capital markets. In Poland for example, ten National Investment Funds have been created which will manage the 'private' shares offered by what were formerly state companies. In the Czech Republic, in which voucher privatization was supposed to create a property-owning democracy, management funds which enjoy an opaque relationship to the state apparatus have emerged to perform a similar function. Since the question of who owns Western firms has become so philosophically complex, it is hardly surprising that Eastern privatization programmes have not miraculously provided an answer in their situation. As might have been predicted in the first place, it has been the shrewdness and consistency, or lack of those qualities, in industrial strategy which has proved decisive. Privatization is at best a diversion, at worst a cargo cult.

Even more so than in Western Europe, in the East privatization has become associated in the popular mind with graft and corruption. It could hardly be otherwise when it is so obviously the holders of bureaucratic capital who have been able to translate the positional goods they enjoyed under the old system into money capital under the new. In 1995, during his unsuccessful presidential re-election bid, Lech Walesa vetoed the privatization proposals of the 'Left Wing' coalition, playing upon popular perceptions of what Walesa called the 'Red Web' of favours and kickbacks enjoyed by the *nomenklatura* as a result of the wholesale and uncritical adoption of the privatization ideology. The government obtained the necessary two-thirds majority in the Sejm to overturn the veto. Yet another straw in the wind largely ignored by mainstream Western commentators who find the Polish post-communist elite rather less threatening precisely because of their commitment to personal enrichment.

The other major social group which has benefited from rapid privatization are those who amassed criminal fortunes by controlling the supply of essential goods during the declining years of the old system – often in corrupt collusion with officials and bureaucrats. To have avoided such an outcome would have required a slow and measured application of privatization techniques, making sure that public property remained under tight supervision and control.

Contrary to massive disinformational propaganda, this would not have implied a retreat from the necessary reform of the economy upon market lines – but it would have meant the jettisoning of much Market Maoist ideology and the conscious search for a mixed economy, which would have dramatically undermined the position of the Market Maoists in the West. This was undoubtedly the goal of Gorbachev's perestroika in the first place, although it is clear with hindsight that the balance of political forces both locally and internationally made such a goal illusory. As such influential figures as Aslund and Sachs have also been keen to emphasize, a 'clean'-state bureaucracy did not exist in the East, nor did a vigilant and mobilized public opinion. However, their 'solution' to this problem was no solution at all, simply giving the corrupt state apparatus a free hand to steal common property without social control. This process has been admirably documented in the former Soviet Union by Stephen Handelman in his 1994 book *Comrade Criminal: The Theft of the Second Russian Revolution* (although like many Western commentators he has a blindness to the role of Western ideologies and institutions in legitimizing the processes he describes).

As under the Soviet system, there is now a huge gulf between what is officially promulgated and asserted and what is said by ordinary people. The main difference being that people are more prepared to say things publicly than in the past. (However, it is becoming a truism that Western opinion-poll techniques are notoriously unreliable in the Eastern context.) A kind of schizophrenia now dominates social discourse; all 'responsible' political forces are in favour of privatization, which is correctly seen as a policy so close to the heart of powerful Western creditors as to be unchallengeable. Even the more slow-moving of the Russian 'red directors' have now worked out how to turn the policy to their own advantage, thus ending the internal split within the *nomenklatura*, just as in the seventeenth century the service gentry deserted the plebian revolt of Bolotnikov once their own interests had been secured. At the same time it is becoming increasingly clear that the population at large detests privatization, seeing in it the imposition of a new feudalism. A poll conducted by the International Foundation of Electoral Systems in Russia in 1995 found that over 50 per cent of respondents wanted the 're-establishment of state control over the economy' and yet over 80 per cent agreed that 'state corruption was commonplace'.[23] In September 1994 the writer Alexander Solzhenitsyn addressed the Russian Duma:

I have the sense that the mass of the people are stunned, in shock from their degradation and from the shame of their helplessness; they have no conviction that the reforms and the policy of the current government are really being carried out in their interests.[24]

In the light of the widespread discontent in Russia, it is somewhat surprising that Boris Yeltsin managed to win re-election in 1996. Perhaps the answer to this conundrum (apart from the shameless practice of media manipulation) is as the old Soviet joke put it, 'In Russia we have a one-party system because the country cannot afford two parties.'

Privatization has destroyed the rationale of the new political system before it could even be properly established. Real power is economic power and democracy has become a façade behind which that real power is exercised. In a sense this is a 'normalization'; capitalist 'democracy' in Mexico or Peru is not dissimilar in its *modus operandi*. Commentators on Russian affairs now commonly refer to the 'Big Eight' pro-regime private firms whose Boyars control the commanding heights of the post-communist economy. Significantly in a large country like Russia, they have full control of the electronic media, something which has been of invaluable help to the privateering *nomenklatura* in Slobodan Milosevic's Serbia.

The symbiosis between the vested interests of the Eastern and Western *nomenklatura* was demonstrated on 24 July 1996 when the former British Foreign Secretary Douglas Hurd visited Belgrade. He was there to represent the interests of his new employers NatWest Markets. He met his old colleague Slobodan Milosevic for a discussion of the impending privatization of the Serbian post and telephone system, a contract worth some £10 million. 'Hurd came to thank Milosevic personally for the business', a Belgrade source told the *Sunday Telegraph*. 'He did this because NatWest wants to scoop up forthcoming privatizations in the electricity and oil sectors worth millions.'[25]

The explicitly sociological goal of Western policy has been the creation of an economic elite, coyly termed a 'middle class' by Western social scientists, which will underpin the permanent transformation of the former communist countries into Western satellites. This is often justified by referring to the distinction made famous by Reagan's UN Ambassador Jeanne Kirkpatrick (who pleaded Argentina's case during the Falklands War) between so-called 'authoritarian' regimes such as that of General Galtieri or apartheid-era South Africa, which should be 'critically supported' because the possibility of 'democratic' evolution continued to exist, and so-called 'totalitarian' regimes, such as those in Hungary and Nicaragua with which no compromise was possible because they were impervious to democratic reform. This bizarre attitude reached its apogee when the Soviet Union was being denied trading concessions, which Gorbachev was desperately seeking, because of insufficient commitment to 'reform'. Meanwhile, the Chinese regime, which still officially revered the memory of 'Red Emperor' Mao, was welcomed as a trade partner. As British journalist Jonathan Steele has pointed out, the climate of Western advice was inspired by the idea that 'communists never give up power voluntarily, let alone peacefully. In fact the collapse of Communist power in Eastern Europe produced a graphic refutation of that thesis.' Where there was truth in this line was in the recognition that

... some individuals from the old Communist system would try to maintain their power and position in spite of the change in the political and economic environment. But this was a normal human process of adaptation, a matter of instinct and survival rather than ideology.[26]

Privatization provided the pole around which this recomposition of power could take place.

The apologists for the new dispensation tend to stress that the creation of a private-property economy is bound to increase social injustice and inequality. These results are even considered to be positive outcomes by the real radicals. When the Hungarian Prime Minister Jozsef Antall was questioned about the immense fraud and corruption surrounding the privatization process in Hungary he pointed out that in the present American generation there are many successful individuals who are not proud of their grandfathers; nevertheless, the United States is now a prosperous economy and society and no one is really concerned about the sinful past now that good life can be enjoyed by all. As Gore Vidal has pointed out, in the US, success can only be enjoyed if failure is visible and seen to be punished. The political problem for the Market Maoist social engineers in Eastern Europe is that the narcissistic 'culture of contentment' delineated by the economist John Kenneth Galbraith and enjoyed by the lucky two-thirds of American society can only be available to a much smaller fraction of the population in the Eastern countries. Despite their monopoly of economic and cultural resources, the institution of the secret ballot presents the new elites with a growing headache.

In an article for the quarterly review *Eszmelet*, two young Hungarian economists Andras Sugar and Laszlo Trautmann have suggested that the huge growth of the black economy performs the function of facilitating structural change. Their analysis was received with appreciation by the annual national meeting of young economists in 1997, a three-day event focusing exclusively on the restoration of the link between economy and morality.

Edward Luttwak, in a 1995 article in the *London Review of Books* suggested that the Russian Mafia were 'just competitors which use physical force, or more often just the threat of force, usefully to offset monopolistic market power'.[27] This at least has the merit of recognizing that accelerated privatization has failed to create competitive markets but the idea that there is some kind of countervailing power projected by ordinary decent criminals against the bureaucratic private monopolists is nonsense. As Handelman notes, '... in the wreckage of Soviet Communism, the *vory* and the nomenklatura have grown closer together'. He quotes the words of a police inspector Kalinichenko: 'we can no longer talk about links between the old mafia underworld and the bureaucrats ... we have to talk about mergers'.[28] In a book published in 1997 entitled *Stealing the Russian State* Louise Shelley estimates that the mafia controlled about 40 per cent of what is left of the Russian economy.

Everywhere in Eastern countries there has been a pronounced militarization of daily life as the Boyars struggle to carve up the economic cake. As the Russian economist O.S. Pcheltsinev noted in 1995, there are now some 25,000 private security firms in Russia alone employing some 800,000 people, all adding to the supposed 'value added' of the private sector. He suggested that 'if the ongoing struggle for the redistribution of property continues, this sector will employ as many people as was recently employed by the armed forces, KGB and police together'.[29] Forward to Feudalism?

As an outrageously corrupt, tax-avoiding private sector has mushroomed in Eastern countries, the Market Maoists have retreated into outright racism as they struggle to explain why their economic prescriptions have had such baleful consequences. They have attempted to draw a distinction between the 'good' privatization in Hungary or the Czech Republic and the 'bad' privatization characteristic of Russia. But they still assert with the World Bank that 'bad privatization is better than no privatization'. The idea that the privatization ideology itself may be the main reason for the widespread discrediting of the whole idea of economic reform as such does not seem to enter their analysis. The problems which have emerged were always incipient within the undemocratic system of bureaucratic class domination which the Soviet system represented. But the poison of privatization as ideology rather than as pragmatic technique has exacerbated many of its worst features. The damage done by Margaret Thatcher's failure to control the British money supply in the mid-1980s is one of the sorriest and most incredible tales of the twentieth century. She was allowed to continue her ruinous reign over the economic destiny of the British Isles largely because of the political and economic windfall provided by North Sea oil.

In his penetrating study *Fools Gold: The Story of North Sea Oil*, the Scottish nationalist academic Christopher Harvie draws attention to the way in which the rises in the oil price precipitated by the crises of 1973 and 1979 followed by the price collapse in 1985 had a crucial diplomatic importance. During this period, oil had become the major source of foreign earnings for the Soviet Union. As in Britain, after the price fall, it began to run a significant trade deficit:

> Frustrated as an exporter to the West, Russia demanded payment for its oil in dollars from COMECON and forced her satellites into greater and greater debt. Afghanistan made the Soviet Army unreliable so there was little prospect of crushing dissent once it surfaced. In all of this, Britain's role ought to have been marginal. It was not. In the years 1987–8, no Western leader enjoyed such a high profile in the West and the East, as Mrs. Margaret Thatcher, the 'reconstructor' of the British economy, the victor of the Falklands, the living embodiment of those market forces which would, if left to themselves, bring instant wealth.[30]

Gradually the world is coming to terms with the fact that the 'British model' is as redundant as the Union of Soviet Socialist Republics; as bankrupt as the Commonwealth of Independent States. The Empress has no clothes. The destructive delirium of the Market Maoist era has solved none of the pressing economic problems which beset the last decade of the twentieth century in Britain or anywhere else. The world now faces the task of making sense of the future amidst the social and political debris which has been created. Paradoxically, even the Thatcherite *Economist* was concluding as early as 1992 that in China itself 'it is possible that a big and painful programme of privatization may be unnecessary'.[31] As always in human affairs, changes seem to occur slowly until the incremental creep of the floodwater overwhelms the cultural defences of social and political systems.

There is now an increasingly urgent but as yet unfocused dissatisfaction with the world created by the Market Maoist privateers. The most glaring intellectual failure of their ideology has been its entirely inadequate account of the actual functioning of real markets. The simplistic certainties which appeared so alluring to Eastern peoples with no experience of the workings of actual market economies have been brought into collision with the brutal realities which underlie the textbook dogmas. 'Primitive accumulation' was a term first used by Marx to describe the coercive processes which took place in Britain as a prelude to the birth of industrial capitalism. Apologists for Joseph Stalin have frequently appropriated this phrase in order to defend his policies of crash industrialization during the 1930s. Many reformed apparatchiks and their Western mentors now use similar arguments to justify the current excesses of organized selfishness. As all good realists know, you can't make an omelette without breaking eggs (that's what they tell the eggs anyway). The internal contradictions of all these pseudo-scientific enlightenment narratives are most clearly revealed in the functioning of the one of the most essential markets of all – the market for food.

7

The Scissors

Food is fundamental. In any society the production, distribution and consumption of food reveals underlying economic, social and spiritual assumptions. We can understand a great deal about any society by studying its relationship with food. Crucially a study of this relationship reveals the contours of the interaction between people and place – the social ecology of the land. In his meditation upon European values, 'Politics and Conscience', Vaclav Havel writes:

> For centuries, the basic component of European agriculture had been the family farm. In Czech, the older term for it was 'grunt' – which itself is not without its etymological interest. The word, taken from the German 'grund', actually means ground or foundation and, in Czech, acquired a peculiar semantic colouring. As the colloquial synonym for 'foundation', it points out the 'groundedness' of the ground, its indubitable, traditional, and pre-speculatively given authenticity and veridicality.[1]

Old and New Crises

The moral bankruptcy of the Soviet system was most brutally exposed by its contempt for the land and the people who depended on it. In quantitative terms the greatest of the historical crimes of that system was the monstrous destruction caused by forced collectivization and state-sponsored famine. Estimates of the number of human lives lost in this harvest of sorrow have been conservatively estimated as not less than 14.5 million souls.[2] This is undoubtedly the single largest deliberately inflicted European catastrophe of the terrible twentieth century. (It is possible that in China imitation exceeded the original inspiration.)

It has often been asserted that the exploitation of the rural population at least provided the material resources for the industrial development which was the declared objective of the whole grisly exercise. Implicitly, orthodox Stalinists and their apologists were conflating these anti-peasant policies with the primitive accumulation of capital resources described by Marx in nineteenth-century Britain:

> The last process of wholesale expropriation of the agricultural population from the soil is, finally, the so-called clearing of estates i.e. the sweeping of men off them. All the English methods hitherto considered culminated in 'clearing'... where there are no more independent peasants to get rid of, the 'clearing' of cottages begins; so that the agricultural labourers do not find on the soil cultivated by them even the spot necessary for their own housing. But what clearing of estates really and properly signifies, we learn only in the promised land of modern romance the Highlands of Scotland. There the process is distinguished by its systematic character, by the magnitude of the scale on which it is carried out at one blow (in Ireland landlords have gone to the length of sweeping away several villages at once; in Scotland areas as large as German principalities are dealt with).[3]

Marx saw this as an ambiguous process. His moral revulsion was tempered by his firm belief that such processes were inevitable and necessary; a view shared by more orthodox economists. Stalin justified his agricultural policies in similar terms. Where else were the resources to be accumulated for industrial development? Even Stalin's opponents have often accepted this argument. However, the historian Robert Conquest concluded that, although there clearly was a huge plunder of resources from rural society in the Soviet Union during the 1930s:

> ... investment in farm machinery, to say nothing of the hugely increased cost of rural administration, outweighed this. Thus, though a quite significant part of the foreign currency required for modern machine purchases was provided by grain exports, the gross economic result was that the industrial sector was not, on balance, subsidized by the exploitation of the peasants.[4]

The real balance of resource exchange between the agricultural and the non-agricultural economy is a critical question in any society. It is a crucial factor in understanding the economic and social situation in contemporary Eastern Europe.

Just as the Soviet system enslaved and instrumentalized its human victims, the attitude displayed to the land itself was one of organized rapacity. According to the agronomist Fyodor Morgan, in the twenty years before 1989 the most fertile European soils of Russia and the

Ukraine lost up to 25 per cent of soil humus. This was due to 'a unique fetish for scientific and technical progress. The belief that technology, fertilizers and pesticides can produce an infinite increase in crop yields has stalled agriculture and produces an endless consumption of soil resources.'

In 1989, 'out of 1.5 billion acres of cultivated land in the Soviet Union' nearly half was 'seriously imperilled; an additional 13 per cent was marginal – rocky, hilly, or overgrown. Of the endangered lands, some 388 million acres were saline; 279 million have been eroded; and 62 million were waterlogged or swampy.'[5]

Dissatisfaction with the quantity and quality of food supply was one of the most potent factors which undermined the social legitimacy of the totalitarian system. The disgust engendered in the population by standing in never-ending queues for substandard food products was one of the most powerful forces which provoked spontaneous revolt against the social order. Successive upheavals in Poland were typically triggered by attempts to rationalize the food bargain with the population. However, the disappearance of the queue, in Poland and elsewhere, does not mean that the food bargain has become devoid of conflict – far from it.

In fact, food production and consumption for the population of the region as a whole has declined quite considerably since 1989. The figures are striking. The total amount of food available (production plus imports) in 1993 in Romania was 95.7 per cent of the figure for 1989, for Poland 86.3 per cent, for Russia 80.3 per cent, Czech Republic 77.0 per cent, Ukraine 76.1 per cent, Slovakia 64.7 per cent and, for Hungary, which used to have one of the more relatively efficient collective food production systems, an incredible 53 per cent.[6] The relatively high figure for Romania in 1993 is due to the after-effect of the policy of deliberate starving of the population by the Ceausescu regime in order to repay international debts we have already mentioned. It should be noted that these figures for food availability include all imports and large amounts of food aid, so they very much overstate actual local production and tell us next to nothing about food security for the poor. It should be also be clearly recognized that even in famished Romania there was less food available in 1993 than in 1989. Also figures for food 'availability' in 1993 do not take into account the fact that, with the end of rationing and the collapse of real wages, food in the shops does not necessarily mean food on the table. Even Ceausescu fed his people better than the New World Order. The UNICEF report from which these figures come notes:

Droughts and other climatic factors are often cited to explain poor performance in the agricultural sector. However, as there has been a consistently negative trend for some years, it would appear more likely that structural causes ... have been more decisive.[7]

The effects on the health and nutritional status of the population are increasingly clear. For the vulnerable, the old, the sick and the unemployed there are no more queues. The shops are full of food products they can no longer afford. The Food and Agriculture Organization produced a paper for its April 1996 European Regional conference in Tel Aviv which concluded that in Eastern Europe and the CIS 'growth in the overall economy ... will not automatically solve the food insecurity problem ... In general, the social consequences of the crisis are expected to follow income growth with a substantial lag.' It should be remembered that in many countries in this region there is still no sign of 'income growth'. Even where there is measured growth there has been a dramatic impact upon health, both physical and mental.

It is often suggested that lifestyle and the composition of food intake are to blame for rising rates of illness and premature death. If this were the case, it would suggest that death rates would be high and stable. They are high, but they are not stable: they have increased everywhere since 1989 (although there are now signs of stabilization in some of the more fortunate countries). In any case, in this context we are not so much concerned with food consumption as with the precipitate collapse of food production. Why has it happened?

Is a new and more dynamic system of food production in the process of being born? Are these large falls in output simply the teething troubles of a healthy new infant industry? Common sense would seem to suggest that Eastern European countries ought to enjoy a comparative advantage in this sphere, after all many of these countries were major food exporters before 1939.

One factor which has clearly contributed to output decline has been the disorganizing effect of huge changes in property relations. In most countries, collective agriculture has been legally disbanded. However, the establishment (or re-establishment) of private property relations has been beset with wrangles and disagreements. Should land be divided equally or should it be restored to former owners? Who are the former owners? How should assets such as machinery and livestock be distributed? There have been problems connected with these issues virtually everywhere. For example, in Lithuania before 1940 70 per cent of the population lived on the land – today the figure is 30 per cent. Large numbers of people who no longer live in rural areas have reclaimed family land whilst many who have worked all their lives in agriculture have received next to nothing.

In the former Soviet Union proper, where there was no real tradition of private property in land before 1917, there are specific features to the land problem. The resistance of bureaucratic structures to any kind of private initiative in the agricultural field has been identified as a particular barrier to improvements in agricultural productivity. Some Western scholars have even theorized the existence of a 'farmer threat' which the bureaucratic ruling class must struggle to contain if it wishes to retain rural power. As US specialist Don Van Atta puts it in a study published in 1993:

> Because they understood that even a few independent peasant farms or voluntary rural cooperatives threatened their power, the most outspoken defenders of the old order opposed any changes in the kolkhoz-sovkhoz monopoly over agriculture ... the first few independent farmers, working on land leased from big farms, produced far too little to threaten the economic role of the big farms. But the possibility that land might be denationalized and a land market created turned out to be one of the major causes of the formation of political blocs in the first freely elected Soviet legislature since 1917. [This was the 'freely elected legislature' crushed by Boris Yeltsin later that same year.][8]

It has often seemed to be an assumption by such Western specialists that the only problem with Soviet agriculture was lack of private-property rights summed up in the widely circulated but largely vacuous slogan 'socialism and agriculture don't mix'. This is also apparent in the often quoted fact that private plots in the Soviet Union, which represented only 1 or 2 per cent of the land produced about 'two thirds of the potatoes and eggs and about 40 per cent of meat, milk and vegetables' consumed in the 1960s.[9] The 1996 World Development Report issued by the World Bank asserted that in Eastern Europe and the Former Soviet Union 'agriculture was highly inefficient and, in contrast to East Asia, was sustained by subsidies on inputs, credits and retail prices'.[10] This is contentious. Was the comparative advantage of Polish, or Hungarian, agriculture really inferior to the agricultures of Britain or France, which are very definitely dependent on 'subsidies on inputs, credit and retail prices'? Also the role of radical redistributive land reform in the economic success of Japan, Korea and Taiwan, and the huge non-tariff barriers to agricultural imports which still exist in these countries, is frequently overlooked by the apologists of Market Maoism. In this, as in other spheres, the alleged 'lessons' of South-east Asia are frequently diametrically opposed to those which are so often asserted. Not all current structural problems facing Eastern agriculture can be reduced to questions of ownership. And current problems are acute. Between 1990 and 1993 cattle herds in the CIS contracted by 13 per cent, pig stocks fell by 23 per cent, sheep and goat herds by 17 per cent. Meat production slumped by 26 per cent, milk products and eggs by 18 and 20 per cent respectively.[11]

Intervention and Regulation

While it is quite obvious that the kolkhoz–sovkhoz system created serious disincentives and distortions, it must be remembered that agricultural markets are heavily regulated and subsidized in all industrialized countries. Just because dysfunctional Soviet agriculture was allegedly a planned system, it is fatuous ideological laziness to conclude that all planning of agricultural production must be in defiance of the natural laws of economics. All agricultural systems in modern industrial states are in some sense 'planned'. The real question which must be asked is: planning for what? The indiscriminate increase of quantitative output (successfully) planned by the Common Agricultural Policy might be seen in this sense as comparable with the indiscriminate increase of quantitative output (unsuccessfully) planned by Gosplan. The determination of the ultimate ends and purposes of agricultural systems is the question which must be addressed.

The conventional rationale for intervention in agricultural markets is in order to deal with incipient market failure. Because the supply of many agricultural goods is inelastic (for example, most crop-planting decisions cannot be changed in less than an entire biological cycle, usually at least one year and often longer), there is a persistent danger of oversupply leading to unplanned price falls or undersupply leading to artificially high prices and subsequent oversupply (the so-called 'cobweb' effect) which can destroy stable farm incomes. Because of the relatively small scale of their operations, farmers often have no financial reserves to cope with such unforeseen income reductions. The vagaries of weather and disease add further uncertainty to the decisions of agricultural producers. Therefore, in order to stabilize agricultural markets, a whole panoply of price supports, buffer stocks, preferential credits and subsidized inputs have been created by capitalist states all over the world including the

US, the EU and Japan. A very substantial slice of all transfer payments in these societies are accounted for by these systems.

A further complication enters the picture when we try to take account of rapid technological change in agricultural production. Efficient producers are supposedly those using state-of-the-art technology. Typically these technologies, from machinery to chemicals, are produced by multinational corporations on a large scale. Such large companies are usually 'price makers' and are in a strong position to pass on their costs to the farmer. Conversely, farmers, because of the small scale of their operations and their large numbers, are typically 'price takers'. Also the demand for food products is income inelastic (that is, as income rises the proportion of extra income spent on food decreases). Thus even under the most favourable conditions farmers are likely to be caught in a price scissors of increasing capital outlays and falling real prices in saturated markets. Such a price scissors had been artificially generated by Soviet economic policy during the 1920s in order to drain resources from rural areas for 'socialist construction'. This process was so pronounced that 'by October 1923, when the scissors crisis reached its peak, industrial prices were three times higher, relative to agricultural prices, than they had been before the war'.[12] Incredibly, this process has been repeated during the recent 'market reform' period; as the World Bank conceded in 1996 the agricultural sector in Eastern Europe and the CIS had 'suffered an unnecessarily severe relative price shock – input prices, especially fuels, rose four times as much as output prices'.[13]

Government intervention in market economies has usually taken place in order to tilt the economic balance back towards the farmer (at least in the short run). One result of such intervention in the West has been to underwrite the profits of agribusiness corporations. The increased mechanization and chemicalization of agriculture in the West has not therefore been the product of spontaneous market forces. To a very large extent it has been promoted by state intervention and subsidy.

The above arguments should not be read as some kind of blanket defence of such programmes as the Common Agricultural Policy. They are intended simply as a reminder that a 'free market' in agricultural products never has and never will exist. The idea that price liberalization would lead to a leap in food supply has been shown to be completely incorrect. The Market Maoist account of the operation of food markets is simply wrong. Current rhetoric about a 'global free market' in agricultural products is just that: rhetoric. The underlying goals of the powerful agribusiness corporations which are pushing this rhetorical agenda are best illuminated by the words of US Senator Rudy Boschwitz, a close ally of the Cargill Grain Corporation, during the debate on the 1985 farm bill. He argued in a letter to *Time* magazine that 'If we don't lower our farm prices to discourage other countries now, our worldwide competitive position will continue to slide and be much more difficult to regain. This should be one of the foremost goals of our agricultural policy.'[14] The US controls some 40 per cent of the world wheat market, 60 per cent of the market in corn, 70 per cent in soybeans. In contrast, OPEC controls only some 38 per cent of the world oil market. There could hardly be a starker illustration of the way in which real participants in real markets actually behave in contrast to the ideological presentation of agricultural markets, which are often suggested as the closest living relatives of textbook-perfect competitive markets, in which producers have no control over prices. In reality, the large corporations which control international agricultural markets can squeeze both producers, consumers and taxpayers. The 'level playing field' sought by these corporations goes all the way downhill from Kansas via Washington.

Even if a global free market in agricultural produce were attainable (and, rhetoric notwithstanding, we are a long way from this) would it be desirable? As the maverick financier James Goldsmith (inexplicably admired by such Market Maoist ultras as John Redwood) pointed out in his best-selling book *The Trap*:

> In the world as a whole there are still 3.1 billion people living in the countryside. If intensive methods of agriculture were imposed universally and productivity per person were to reach the levels of Australia ... about 2 billion of these people will lose their livelihood. Rural communities throughout the world would be washed away as if by a great flood. Whole populations would be uprooted and swept into urban slums.[15]

This is already occurring and the process is intensified because under the disguise of the promotion of 'free trade', powerful nations are dumping their implicitly or explicitly subsidized agricultural surpluses on world markets and devastating agricultural and cultural systems which have survived in a sustainable way for thousands of years. Those seeking a living from the land in Eastern Europe and the former Soviet Union are now on the receiving end of these destructive policies. As John Eatwell, a member of the British House of Lords Select Committee on Agriculture points out in an article in the *Guardian*: 'In the Czech republic and Slovakia agricultural output makes up

8 per cent of GDP, in Bulgaria and Hungary 15 per cent, in Romania 18 per cent, and in Poland 27 per cent ... between 10 and 20 per cent of the active population is employed on the land.' The EU 'subsidizes its agricultural exports to the Eastern countries ... thus robbing Eastern farmers of sales at home and abroad'. The EU agricultural commissioner, Rene Steichen is quoted as saying that protecting Eastern agriculture will 'create international trade tensions with Gatt members'. Lord Eatwell concludes that 'far from preparing Eastern countries for membership of the EU , as is claimed, current agricultural policy makes Eastern membership impossible'.[16]

Poland is a crucial test case for current agricultural policies in Eastern Europe, as it is for the success of the Market Maoist model in general. Poland has always had a large proportion of its people dependent on the land (today 40 per cent live in rural areas and 17 per cent are entirely dependent on farm incomes).[17] The resistance of these rural communities to the communist ideology of collectivization was a key long-term factor in the defeat of the *ancien régime*. Unlike other Eastern countries Poland has always retained a predominantly private agriculture and therefore there is no scope to blame present difficulties upon 'inadequately defined property rights'. As Carole Nagengast noted in her study of a small Polish village in the 1980s, *Reluctant Socialists, Rural Entrepreneurs*:

> ... from a deeper historical perspective, what is most remarkable about Poland is not that it has emerged from the 'socialist' camp but that it was, although ever so briefly, part of it in the first place ... the recent brief interlude under the influence of the Soviet Union is recognizable as a special case in which the history of Poland momentarily departed from a more typical trajectory.[18]

Price liberalization, which as we have seen was an integral part of the IMF-sponsored Balcerowicz plan, had a predictably disastrous effect upon the cost and price structure faced by Polish farmers. Even under the previous system a negative trend was apparent because of the unavoidable growth of imbalance in the terms of trade found in any deregulated agricultural market. If one takes 1980 prices as 100 then by 1986 the price index of goods sold by farmers was 381.5, while the price index of commodities and services purchased by farmers for investment purposes was 528.7.[19] These trends were vastly accelerated after 1989.

The production of agricultural inputs tends towards monopoly (or rather oligopoly) in developed liberal market economies and this phenomenon is even more pronounced in artificially monopolized

Soviet-style economies. Not only are inputs monopolized but also the food-processing industry tends to extreme local monopoly (or rather monopsony – a single buyer) thus forcing down farm gate prices. At the same time, falling real incomes shrink the market for foodstuffs. Rapid privatization and price liberalization does nothing to ameliorate, and frequently exacerbates these fundamental structural problems. For example, privatization of the pre-existing food-processing industry in Lithuania, in the absence of any coherent competition policy, has left farmers at the mercy of such local monopsonies.

The record of such Market Maoist policies in other parts of the world is singularly unimpressive. A recent study of neo-liberal inspired agricultural reform in Africa, *A Blighted Harvest: The World Bank and African Agriculture in the 1980s*, concluded that 'reducing exploitative forms of state regulation by a regime of non regulation' allows the dominant elite 'to legally privatize its interests without transforming its essentially parasitic form of economic operation'.[20]

In Poland the results of such policies have been dramatic. Livestock production fell by 22 per cent in Poland between 1990 and 1993. Farm incomes fell by more than 50 per cent. Farm debt is rising (at the end of 1993 private farmers owed 7.9 billion old zlotys). Overall demand for food fell by 20 per cent as a result of unemployment and falling real incomes among the urban population. In the past, Poland used to export food products to the EU (to the tune of $557 million in 1989). In 1993 Poland had a deficit on food imports with the EU of $333 million.[21] As one Polish farmer said 'The European Community means we can't sell any of our milk or fruit in Warsaw any more. It's full of imported produce. The price of milk means it's not worth keeping a cow anymore, in this whole area there are only two cows left.'[22] In 1995, 60 per cent of Polish farms were technically bankrupt.[23] How is 'modernization' to take place in such conditions? If this is the situation in entrepreneurial private-sector Poland, what economic and social outcomes can be expected elsewhere?

As we have seen, urban unemployment is emerging as a key problem in all post-communist societies. Even a successful policy of orthodox agricultural modernization can be expected to reduce drastically the numbers employed in agriculture. How are these extra workers to be absorbed into the urban workforce? Enclosures in England, the Highland Clearances in Scotland and the Great Famine in Ireland caused enormous suffering even though they coincided with an unprecedentedly dynamic economic expansion and there was a huge outlet for surplus population provided by emigration to America and Australasia. Today in post-communist Eastern Europe, the industrial economy is in very poor shape and even the most relatively successful countries, such as Poland, are suffering crippling structural unemployment.

In any case, even were there to be an economic miracle in Eastern Europe, there is no guarantee whatsoever that this would translate into an adequate supply of new employment which could absorb simultaneously those displaced from inefficient Soviet-style industry and driven from the land by mechanization (or, more likely, by collapsing farm incomes and destitution). As James Goldsmith pointed out in relation to France, his then country of residence:

> Over the past twenty years, spectacular growth in GNP has been surpassed by even more spectacular growth in unemployment. This has taken place while Europe as a whole has progressively opened its markets to international free trade. How can we accept a system which increases unemployment from 420,000 to 5.1 million during a period in which the economy has grown by 80 per cent?[24]

In reality the grim situation in the rural areas of the old communist empire is an indictment of the anti-peasant economic policies pursued by the Market Maoists since 1989 and the awesome political power of Western agribusiness. As John Eatwell puts it, current policies 'would be laughable, if the consequences in human misery and potential political instability were not so dreadful'.[25]

East European societies are now in the grip of a complex multi-level crisis. At the most superficial level this is a crisis of really existing socialism continuing to exert its baleful influence; at another, deeper, level it is a crisis of subordinate integration into the world market, which has afflicted countries in this region since the sixteenth century. At the most profound level, this is a crisis of the modernization paradigm as such.

The overwhelming desire of the political forces which came to power in 1989 was to make their societies 'normal' as quickly as possible. Forty years of 'economic experiments' had created a psychology which craved the assurance of dependence upon policies and goals determined by conventional Western values and assumptions. But those values and assumptions are themselves in a profound state of crisis. The increased interaction with East European societies is itself accelerating this process. For example, the Common Agricultural Policy, which had long outlived its original usefulness before 1989, has now become a lethal agent of continental destabilization, not because it protects Western farmers, however inadequately and bureaucratically, but rather because it systematically undermines Eastern farmers.

In Britain, the economic and political chaos caused by the BSE infection in the national cattle herd has forced issues of food safety onto the mainstream agenda and has indirectly drawn attention to the essentially anti-market logic underpinning the rational choices of the Western agribusiness lobby. In Britain, in 1995, according to the figures issued by the Ministry of Agriculture, every milk cow was subsidized at the rate of £114 per head, beef cows at £93 per head, sheep at £21 per head. Cereals received a subsidy of £269 per hectare, oilseeds £456 per hectare, peas and beans at £388 per hectare and linseed was subsidized at £520 per hectare. As a result of 'reforms' of the Common Agricultural Policy, land which had been set aside (that is, not used at all) received a subsidy of £340 per hectare. Average farm sales per hectare in Poland in 1996 were 648 new zloty (about £128); profits were non-existent in many regions.

Pressure from the British agribusiness lobby was instrumental in the undermining of attempts by the Irish EU Agricultural Commissioner Ray McSharry to reform the system of CAP subsidies. The 'McSharry Principles' were intended to reverse a situation in which 80 per cent of EU subsidy went to the largest 20 per cent of farmers, favouring intensive production and large capital outlays beneficial to the corporations which supply farm inputs. The British government insisted that their large-scale farmers (and even larger-scale corporations) should not be disadvantaged by the changes. As a result, contrary to carefully cultivated popular perceptions, far more public subsidy goes to the Barley Barons of East Anglia than to marginal farmers in upland France or rural Portugal.

Large British landowners (and their suppliers) further benefited from the competitive devaluation of the British currency which took place as a result of 'Black Wednesday' in September 1992, because their subsidies continued to be paid in undevalued green pounds. The currency markets had given their definitive judgement on the relative success of the Market Maoist economic policies pioneered in Britain during the previous decade as compared to the more pragmatic social market policies pursued in the rest of northern Europe. Without this stimulus fortuitously afforded to the British economy at the expense of her EU trading partners, the real economic results of the Great Leap Forward would have been even more apparent. The defence of the right to devalue the pound sterling has now become the rallying cry of the British Market Maoist ultras. They have also made strenuous attempts to mobilize the latent discontent with the Common Agricultural Policy to their political advantage, studiously ignoring the British role in further distorting the subsidy regime in a productivist direction.

The process whereby the citizens of Western Europe subsidize fewer and fewer people to produce more and more food products which subsequently saturate global markets, to the detriment of producers in the East and in the Third World, is both suicidal and immoral. Yet this unsustainable charade continues because of the rational choices of the bureaucratic interests concerned. Urban-based policy makers in the East, so ready to engage in sweeping projects of social engineering despite their rejection of economic 'experiments', have little sympathy for the problems of the rural poor. It is implicitly accepted that in the medium term the urban population will be fed directly or indirectly by the Cargill Grain Corporation and European Union agribusiness, after all 'progress' demands it. Typical of the attitude of these urban elites is the ominous remark of the secretary of the Polish committee for EU integration, Danuta Hubner: 'We will need to re-deploy country-dwellers'. She went on to suggest that rural areas of Poland should diversify into 'agro-tourism' (rural Poland as agricultural theme park?) and she correctly pointed out that 'we can't just sit back and wait for our farmers to get handouts from Brussels'.[26] This at least is realistic. There will be no 'handouts' from Brussels probably because the existence of the Polish peasantry will make Polish membership of the European Union impossible, which is why the current dekulakisation policy in Poland is so stupid and shortsighted. Illusions about the nature of the European Union are still widespread among the urban elite in Poland. The international economic report on Poland for 1995–96 produced by the Warsaw University of Economics warned that:

> ... especially harmful in the pre-membership period would be the equalisation of Polish and [EU] agricultural prices and excessive protection against foreign competition. This would leave Polish farmers with insufficiently strong incentives to rationalize production, while other social groups would be burdened with major transfers in agriculture's favour.[27]

This kind of reasoning represents a classic case of what has been described as 'the political power of images of an archaic and backward peasantry absorbing large amounts of public investment providing a powerful reinforcement to remove other elements of social welfare and economic planning from the rural sphere'.[28] As W. Piskorz of the Agricultural Policy Analysis Unit in Warsaw points out: 'The large Polish agricultural labour force is in fact an efficient and economically rational response on behalf of farmers to the low opportunity cost of labour – economic jargon for low wages and few alternative jobs.'[29]

Despite this reality, urban Eastern European elites are as usual engaged in the process of recycling already obsolescent Western ideas and institutions long after their sell-by date has expired, whilst all the time broadcasting from the rooftops their commitment to 'modernization' and 'progress'.

These problems are not only confined to Eastern Europe. The logic of the globalization agenda enshrined in the new General Agreement on Tariffs and Trade (GATT), the North American Free Trade Agreement (NAFTA) and the European Single Market virtually guarantees the sombre social outcomes foreseen by Goldsmith (although he underestimates how intolerable the urban environment has become for many of the poorest and therefore underestimates the resistance of the rural poor to the urbanization process). The fact that 'free trade' at the global level is logically incompatible with regional 'free trade' agreements is not the sort of contradiction which bothers Market Maoists. The capacity to believe two equal and opposite things at once is a hallmark of advanced thinking (as George Orwell said of the Stalinist definition of dialectics).

Forward to the Past

Many of the debates about agricultural modernization in pre-revolutionary Russia are now returning to haunt a hungry world. The populist economist Chayanov published the first version of his study 'The Theory of Peasant Economy' in 1914. It was based upon empirical studies of the workings of the agricultural economy in pre-revolutionary Russia. Although somewhat simplistic, his theories have remained a point of reference for the study of the economic behaviour of peasant societies all over the world ever since. In contrast to analyses which stressed differentiation and struggle within peasant society between incipient capitalist farmers (the so-called 'kulaks') and the increasingly proletarianized rural poor, Chayanov drew attention to the tendencies toward convergence in social status in peasant society over time through such institutions as partible inheritance. Frequently differences in status were perceived to be 'fair' because derived from differences of effort and need. Redistributive mechanisms of various kinds ensured a degree of social security for all. His vision of a self-reproducing peasant economy modernized by the application of appropriate technology which does not undermine beneficial social solidarity now appears to have a prophetically contemporary appeal, even if the idea that such peasant societies are entirely without internal conflict is somewhat exaggerated.

In contrast, the analysis of Lenin, who saw the polarization of peasant society as inevitable and violent, has been the justification of the genocidal projects of both Stalin and Mao. It is often forgotten that Lenin had based his analysis on that of the Tsarist modernizer Stolypin whose views would be entirely compatible with those of modern Market Maoists. As Teodor Shanin writes, in pre-revolutionary Russia the belief that:

> A new social structure based on capitalist farming would finally come to be established in the countryside ... was established as a piece of self-evident knowledge – it had become part of the prevailing ideology, not only in the normative sense but also in the cognitive sense. It was in turn taken as a given and constituted the basic assumption underlying the rural policies of all the rulers of the Russian state during the crucial quarter of a century which followed the 1905 revolution. The political perspective was that the peasantry would break down into new rural classes typical of capitalist society ... This expected development was in fact a precondition for the success of the policies pursued by successive Russian governments. The major fact of Russian rural history in the first quarter of the century is that the predicted development both of the class structure and of the political response of the peasants did not happen ... in spite of the apparent differentiation and of polarization processes the villages of the Russian peasantry went on showing remarkable political cohesiveness and unity of action.[30]

Stolypin's attempt to engineer the creation of a class of pro-regime, proto-capitalist farmers, who would enclose the land at the expense of the rural poor, was dramatically reversed during the massive popular land seizures of 1917. Those land seizures would undoubtedly have been institutionalized by the democratically elected Constituent Assembly, which was dominated by pro-peasant parties such as the Socialist Revolutionaries, had the Bolshevik regime allowed it to survive. As a class the peasantry showed considerable cohesion in resisting the rural policies of Stalin. Robert Conquest remarks that:

> ... in the local documents we have, there are many references to chairmen of village soviets, Party members, and peasants trying to help the 'kulaks'. An OGPU report makes it clear that many poor

and middle peasants were against dekulakisation, would not vote for it, hid kulak property and warned kulak friends of searches.[31]

The revolt of the peasantry against those who would write them out of the future was nowhere more dramatically seen than in the southern Mexican state of Chiapas in January 1994. The North American Free Trade Agreement, which came into force on 1 January, was predicated upon the destruction of the traditional structures of land tenure in the Mexican countryside. These structures, the so-called '*ejidos*', which guaranteed access to land for all, had been successfully defended by the indigenous people of Mexico in the revolution of 1917 and had been the basis of the legitimacy of the Mexican state among the rural poor throughout the following decades. The Zapatista uprising which began in 1994 was a significant psychological factor in the intensification of the Mexican financial panic of the same year, a panic which without massive international public sector intervention would have destroyed the international financial system upon which Eastern Europe is now so dependent. Eastern Europeans who believe that these events are irrelevant to their situation have failed to understand the integrative logic of financial globalization.

Another, less dramatic but none the less epochal, change has begun to occur. The 1995 report of the Pastoral Land Commission of the Catholic Church in Brazil noted the beginning of a tendency that would inevitably pick up steam as the end of the century approaches: a large number of people living on the edges of the cities, without any prospects for making a living, are returning to the countryside because they see it as a way of guaranteeing their existence. For many, this return to their origin completes the circle: from the land to the favela and from the favela back to the land. The 'Movement of the Landless' is a growing and vocal social force within Brazil, frequently facing violent repression, which rejects the agricultural model imposed on the country by commercial landowning interests. These interests have stressed an agriculture directed towards the international market, based on the concentration of land and dependent upon machinery, fertilizers and pesticides supplied by the multinationals instead of human labour deployed for the fulfilment of domestic food consumption. This move to the countryside is also to be seen in Eastern Europe, not because living standards are higher in rural areas any more than they are in Brazil, but because urban living standards have collapsed.

The spontaneous renewal of urban links to the country and the explosive growth of 'non-market' agricultural production in order to ensure food security, which have become a common feature of many East European societies, may not just be a transitional coping mechanism. On the one hand, under current conditions, this phenomenon represents a retreat to a pre-industrial scarcity economy which will never modernize and allow improved living standards. This development alone should lead commentators to the inescapable recognition of the failure of Market Maoism even in its own terms; Eastern societies are 'underdeveloping' before our eyes. On the other hand, this nightmare scenario might also be seen as the jumping-off point for an entirely different kind of economic 'development', based on the fulfilment of human needs, which might become characteristic of the twenty-first century. Such possibilities were predicted by the pioneer of 'New Economics', E.F. Schumacher in his seminal work *Small Is Beautiful – a study of economics as if people mattered*, the 'bible' of the Green movement, which was first published at the time of the 1973 oil crisis. Perhaps the vision of Chayanov and his intellectual heirs will in the end prove more enduring than those of his critics.

Currently, rural poverty in Eastern Europe and the Former Soviet Union is becoming a scandalous spectacle of chronic human suffering. Those living in rural areas are far more likely to be ill-fed, ill-housed and sick. Children born in rural areas are particularly at risk of stunted growth. But, as elsewhere in the world these masses of people are largely invisible to the powerful. The development economist Michael Lipton long ago pointed out the problem of 'urban bias' in the allocation of resources in the Third World. Ironically, some of the themes of Lipton's work have been appropriated by the Market Maoists who presume that such bias is only a 'socialist' phenomenon. In fact such a bias is at the heart of much of what is wrong with the whole ideology of 'development', whether 'socialist' or 'capitalist'. As Gavin Williams has written in a paper entitled 'Taking the Part of Peasants', both capitalist and socialist economists:

> ... identify progress with the replacement of peasant production by capitalist or state forms of production, characterized by the application of advanced technology and increasing division of labour ... Peasants are expected to contribute to development by providing the resources for others to develop the urban industrial economy. Alternatively, they are required to give way to capitalist producers or state farms. Either alternative requires the ruthless application of violence against peasant communities.[32]

In understanding the real workings of rural societies in all their diversity and complexity, much of the conventional apparatus of economic science is at best redundant and mostly dangerous. More than ever, policy makers need a much more sophisticated picture of rural economy and society. This is profoundly threatening to the economics profession (and other powerful vested interests) who would prefer to retain their own abstract conceptions concerning the rational functioning of markets (not to mention the desirability of supposed 'progress' and 'development'). For example, in Africa successive attempts to increase the marketed output of peasant farmers by introducing new cash crops and commercial relations have left families increasingly impoverished; the abstract theories of the capitalist commissars failed to recognize that cash earnings would be diverted to leisure expenditure by men – leaving women to feed households with diminished resources.

Ordinary people in Eastern countries are increasingly and painfully aware of the inadequacy of conventional 'solutions' to the rural crisis. But discontent can show itself in all kinds of ways, some of them with a disturbingly irrational character. In this context the phenomenon of the Polish *'Samoobrona'* or movement of 'self-defence' is instructive. The organization was officially registered in January 1992 by its leader Andrej Lepper. Its programme was entirely concerned with the defence of peasant interests. From the very beginning, *Samoobrona* set out to organize the disenfranchised and alienated rural population. In all of its literature there was special emphasis on the fear of foreclosure on farm debts.

During the summer of 1992 *Samoobrona* organized road blockades and hunger strikes to dramatize this issue, receiving national attention and leading to the movement being courted by mainstream politicians, mainly on the right wing of Polish politics, such as the Confederation of Independent Poland and President Lech Walesa. Banks, especially foreign banks, were singled out for attack by Lepper. Prominent supporters of the movement included figures from the anti-Semitic wing of the old Polish United Workers Party such as Bozena Krzywoblocka and also anti-communist Polish veterans such as General Stanislaw Skalski of the Polish Air Force. Attacks on the head of the EBRD, Jacques Attali, signalled their anti-Semitic stance in a coded form. In the run-up to the 1993 elections the movement claimed up to 300,000 registered supporters but, because they did not find stable coalition partners, they were unable to breach the 5 per cent barrier necessary to secure representation in the Sejm. In Hungary the racist Party of Hungarian Justice and Life led by Istvan Csurka articulates a similar set of grievances. In February 1997, after nationwide demonstrations against a proposed extension of social security payments and enterprise taxation to the smallholding sector, the similarly minded Independent Smallholders' Party were leading Hungarian opinion polls.

In the event the largest parties in the Polish election of 1993 were the ex-communist Democratic Left Alliance and the Polish Peasant Alliance – the PSL (*Polskie Stronnictwo Ludowe*). The leader of the PSL, Waldemar Pawlak was appointed prime minister. The PSL was a reincarnation of the old communist-front party of the peasantry the ZSL. In the semi-free elections of 1989 they had been allocated seats in the 65 per cent in the Sejm reserved for pro-regime parties. Their decision to switch their support to *Solidarność* (which made a clean sweep of remaining contested seats) was a crucial factor in the formation of the first non-communist government in Eastern Europe for forty years. The fact that they were the second largest party in the fully free election of 1993 demonstrated that they had managed to build a stable political base and mass electoral appeal. The position of the party was much more critical than the SLD on such litmus issues as privatization. The SLD, desperate for international respectability, at first attempted to form a coalition with their preferred choice – the Market Maoists of Democratic Union, who had led the outgoing coalition. The refusal of these overtures forced the SLD back into the hands of the PSL whose policies so far have been largely reactive in the face of the Market Maoist dekulakisation. Desperate attempts to salvage the credibility of the PSL as the defender of peasant Poland were made a more assertive Jarostaw, before the elections of September 1997. But the vote of the PSL collapsed to the right. The question of what should be done to overcome the rural crisis remained painfully unresolved.

The real needs of farmers continue to be ignored by policy makers desperate not to antagonize the Western agribusiness lobby and without the imagination to recognize that a major trend of the twenty-first century will probably be the repopulation of the countryside, in Eastern Europe as elsewhere, either because urban society is breaking down or because sustainable development has at last begun to take root. Policies which continue to intensify rural impoverishment are the clearest evidence of the failure of the Market Maoist Great Leap Forward which, like its original Chinese counterpart, has been an unmitigated disaster for the peasants. Countries which all have significant comparative advantage in agriculture have been reduced to the status of captive markets for subsidized Western agribusiness. The gap between the urban middle class and the rural poor, has become enormous. This however is only one dimension of the huge social divisions which are emerging in this region.

8

Polarities

Collapsing food production and reduced food consumption by the marginalized and excluded are the most obvious symptoms of more deep-seated problems. Unemployment, besides being a chronic waste of human resources, is another visible symptom of those problems and is one of the clearest conventional indicators of economic failure. But statistical measures of unemployment do not really capture the essence of the social shock precipitated by the so-called 'transition' in Eastern Europe. Unemployment statistics are in any case notoriously unreliable and frequently politically manipulated. The tendency to distortion of unemployment statistics through the practice of rounding figures down or up to suit political convenience is well nigh universal.

In general, pro-market economists and politicians tend to round down unemployment figures, unless they are attempting to throw doubt upon the economic competence of political opponents. In a debate with the Hungarian teachers' trade union, the Budapest resident of the IMF mentioned that the official unemployment rate in Spain was around 22 per cent and that the 'real' rate must therefore be at least 15 per cent, implying that many registered unemployed people were active in the grey or the black economy. These wicked and dishonest people provide Market Maoists with a wonderful double opportunity. They are simultaneously cheating society and can safely be used as a rationale for disbelieving measured unemployment statistics.

Social and Ethnic Cleavages

Market Maoist economists who constantly preach the virtues of 'downsizing' and 'efficiency' are passionate about the threat to 'jobs' posed by interventionist measures such as minimum wage legislation, which if properly implemented, might make official figures more accurate. Of course this presumes that they are indeed an over- rather than an understatement. In fact, there is considerable evidence

119

to the contrary. Market Maoist policies effectively present the most vulnerable section of society with Hobson's choice: either permanent unemployment or wage levels lower than subsistence (certainly so far as the real costs of housing are concerned).

This whole discussion becomes real and actual when we leave the fairy-tale world of unemployment statistics and concentrate upon something concrete – poverty. All objective indicators show with absolute clarity that during the early 1980s the former socialist countries, and in particular the countries of the Former Soviet Union, have experienced the fastest rise of poverty and the most precipitate collapse in living standards in modern times. The fact that people in these countries are still 'rich' compared to others in even more desperate circumstances elsewhere in the world is hardly an advertisement for neo-liberalism; rather the opposite since it is the same policy responsible for the misery in both cases. It has become abundantly obvious that, as Kramer points out, the 'sacrifices required during the transition from state controlled to a free market system fall disproportionately on blue collar workers'.[1] For a quantitive analysis of the fall in real wages see Glyn and the ILO study published in 1995 entitled *From Protection to Destitution*.[2] It is working women who have been the biggest losers of all because they are relatively immobile due to family circumstances, have lost access to benefits such as free child care and are more open to exploitation when they are mobile.

As time has passed, both blue- and white-collar workers (such as teachers and health workers) have begun to recognize that industrial action and other forms of pressing popular demands are certainly one of the main building blocks of real-life market economies. As early as 1990, miners, shipbuilders and other workers started to threaten the shock-therapy programme of Balcerowicz in Poland. The neo-liberal-minded Prime Minister Mazowiecki failed to be elected president later in that year. The winner was Lech Walesa in 'Tribune of the People' mode who defeated the even more extreme populist Stanislaw Tyminski of 'Party X' in the second round. Workers gained significant concessions over the closure of some large factories in late 1991. The subsequent proliferation of strikes caused political uncertainty but the development of alternative policies proved extremely slow.

The rationalization of the workforce in the Gdansk shipyard in 1996 provided a symbolic indicator of the rapid and bewildering changes to which Polish workers have been subjected. Their erstwhile supporters from the Market Maoist right in the West were now strangely silent about their plight. Walesa himself, having ostentatiously 'returned to work' in the shipyard after his defeat in the presidential elections of 1995 at first declared his 'solidarity' with the workers and then counselled a policy of 'realism'. The approach of the parliamentary elections of 1997 lathered the Right in Polish politics and their allies in the Catholic Church into a frenzy of rhetorical support for the shipyard despite their simultaneous support for a market economy 'without qualifications'. The collapse of the shipyard has great significance as the neo-liberal Lucja Swiatkowski Cannon admits in an article in the *Financial Times* in May 1997 entitled 'Sad Symbol of Reforms':

> ... the largest Polish enterprises ... remain unprofitable and in a precarious position. Their problems are too big to be dealt with by the companies themselves, but successive Polish governments have pursued a policy of neglect in the name of economic liberalism.

She went on to note:

> The situation of the Gdansk shipyard is typical if extreme ... the economy has stabilised in the past few years but the legacy of transition has lingered. The Gdansk shipyard remained saddled with huge debts ... the closure of the Gdansk shipyard highlights the incomplete and distorted process of structural transformation of Poland ... Gdansk, once a symbol of hope, may come to represent the failure of Poland's market reforms.[3]

As early as October 1990, there was a 'petrol riot' in Hungary triggered by hugely unpopular price increases which paralysed the country for three days. In 1991 the Hungarian government was forced to compromise over further price increases when threatened with a national strike. It also had to commit itself to an employee stock ownership programme in order to share the allegedly substantial benefits of privatization with the workers of firms for sale. In 1992, an impressive demonstration of health workers provided appropriate feedback about continuing government austerity. In 1990, the Socialist Party government of Bulgaria was brought down by strikes and work stoppages, a pattern repeated in 1996–7. In August 1991, a strike by 27,000 miners had led to significant wage increases. In Romania there was a stormy gathering of coal miners in the capital Bucharest seeking higher wages, lower prices and the resignation of the government. Subsequent waves of strikes and demonstrations in both countries have kept up the level of popular pressure whatever the complexion of their respective governments.

In early 1991, the threat of widespread labour unrest forced the federal government of Czechoslovakia to back away from its plan to quadruple the prices of electricity, petrol and heating. Rail strikes in February 1997 destabilized privatization proposals. Warning strikes and demonstrations in Slovakia in 1991 saved several factories from closure and forced the government to make trade regulations more favourable for the arms industry. 'The federal government also found itself under attack from workers on collective farms in both Slovakia and the Czech lands, who feared unemployment if plans for the privatisation of agriculture went ahead.'[4] In the former GDR, where unemployment soared to 30 per cent in the first eighteen months after the currency union, industrial action was muted until May 1993 but disillusion is now widespread. At the other end of the former socialist world, the reviving labour movements in Russia and some other CIS countries such as the Ukraine, have fairly quickly established themselves as major forces in the political struggles over the speed and direction of reforms. The failure to pay back wages, particularly in the economically vital (albeit 'unprofitable') coal industry, remains as a potentially explosive and fundamentally unresolved grievance in both countries.

The overall picture is confused and confusing in many countries. Often the forces of the 'right' are the loudest in denouncing Market Maoist policies pursued by the 'left'. The political situation is contorted in many countries into shapes unrecognizable to Western political scientists. The underlying realities are more clear; popular opinion has not come to terms with the new circumstances at all. As early as 1990 a survey suggested that 75 per cent of Polish workers did not want privatization. An opinion poll in Russia before the referendum of 1993 found that a majority of the population 'did not like' businesspeople. In early 1993, a third of the Hungarian electorate would have voted for the basically Thatcherite Alliance of Young Democrats (*Fidesz*), although more than a third of those supporters thought they would return the economy to central planning![5] In the autumn of 1992, the Eurobarometer poll found that one-third of the population of Eastern Europe wanted to emigrate to the West.

As Paul Hockenos has pointed out in his book *Free to Hate*, marketization and the rise of racism do not simply coincide, but there is a certain causal relationship between the two. There is no better example than the situation of the Roma population of Hungary. This is a minority representing about 5 per cent of the population, mainly unskilled and employed in low-paid jobs in the centrally planned economy before 1989. Despite being closed into an untouchable caste, Roma families enjoyed state benefits for housing and regular income support under the welfare system of state socialism. As Market Maoism gradually penetrated economic and political thought in Hungary, the Roma people were increasingly stigmatized as parasites, though in reality they were the ones more and more explicitly discriminated against, and were the first single social group victimized by transition.

When construction was dramatically restricted among other non-tradable economic activities, many Roma workers lost their urban jobs and became rural unemployed. When state enterprises in heavy industry were closed down or streamlined after privatization, particularly in Northern Hungary, it was again the Roma to be hurt by the first waves of redundancies. The decimation of state benefits along with the increasing costs of education, health care and communication cut off the lifebelt that could have saved some of the Roma families and broader communities as potentially integrated units of a modernizing society. However, as desperation spread throughout the country after structural adjustment resulted in economic and social breakdown, the number of anti-gypsy atrocities rapidly increased. Together with African students and sometimes even diplomats, the Roma became the main targets of the mushrooming skinhead groups in Hungary.

Martin Kovats, a British researcher of Hungarian Roma politics concluded his investigation with a dramatic but certainly realistic picture:

> The last ten years have been a disaster for the majority of Hungary's Roma population. Most of those who had work have become unemployed, and young people coming through are denied opportunities. Half-hearted government policies to improve the social and economic position of the Roma have failed to halt the rapid rise in Roma poverty. Neither have they addressed poverty-related problems such as falling standards of education, anxiety, poor health, crime, prostitution, etc. The scale of problems are mounting and they have to be addressed if Hungary is to make any long-term social, political or economic progress.[6]

Another unreported feature of the East European transition is the gender character of the new division of labour. When unemployment first started to hit formerly full employment societies, it was the female labour force that was laid off for various reasons. First, it was women who worked mostly in intra-firm service jobs where streamlining was easiest. Second, in certain societies it was more acceptable for women to leave the labour market because of a general conservative trend in ideology that emphasized women's responsibilities in the household. Later, however, when unemployment was reaching mass proportions, the gender bias started to work against men, who lost their jobs in privatized or restructured industrial companies by the thousand. Many of these men found refuge in the black economy or in alcoholism, both contributing to the dramatic drop in male life expectancy throughout the region.

The workload of women was increased by the abolition of the state child-care system which previously provided daytime care of children under the age of three in most state socialist countries. The elimination of these distortions, as they were seen by the Market Maoists, placed an increasing burden on mothers and grandmothers. Because of the deterioration of these conditions, and worsening expectations, the number of marriages and childbirths significantly dropped in Eastern Europe

A most striking consequence of marketization in Eastern Europe can be observed in the explosion of prostitution in all countries concerned. Under the pressure of the foreign debts, Hungarian economic policy tacitly tried to exploit commodified female bodies for foreign exchange earnings as early as the 1980s. Dozens of new hotels and other facilities were built to provide sufficient infrastructure for 'conference tourism'. CNN reported the March 1990 elections under the title 'Budapest from red star to red light'. As employment and living standards collapsed in the early 1990s, however, a boom in red-light sectors was observed in the entire region. Russian and Ukranian girls were hired and forced to work in Poland and Hungary, while Polish and Hungarian girls went further to the West. In the Czech Republic, drivers coming from Germany or Austria could see the cheap supply of sexual services on the roadside whichever major road they took.

In principle, it would be the task of left-wing political forces to address the negative consequences of both marketization and racism. The political left in most East European countries, however, is dominated by former communists desperate to live down their totalitarian past. Unfortunately, the easiest way for them to do this has been the ostentatious repudiation of supposedly 'socialist' economics and a wholesale commitment to the fundamentals of the Market Maoist package (albeit with a 'human face'). In this intellectual and cultural wasteland, it is the extreme right which has the best opportunity to capitalize on popular discontent. Economic policy in the region therefore swings in an unstable fashion between the poles of populism and market fundamentalism. A rational and balanced approach is nowhere in sight.

Even so, 'life itself' imposes a degree of realism on policy makers (to use a phrase redolent of times gone by). It has not so much been public pressure but rather practical difficulties which have enforced more pragmatic attitudes. This has happened long before academic critique has been able to develop a coherent perspective, let alone worked out alternative policies. The political earthquake of the last few years has successfully disintegrated the previous forms of economic coordination, but economic agents operating on the micro level have been unable to reorganize the economy spontaneously from below as the market ideology suggests. Moreover, since most of the intellectual effort of commentators on these matters has been devoted to the question of how to destroy the role of the public authorities in the organization of the economy (rather than how to rationalize and democratize it), attempts to revive state intervention have been characterized by their belated and reactive nature and have been unprepared, unskilled and ill-conceived and have therefore usually resulted in creating a convenient target for Market Maoist counter-attacks. The level at which the need for an active role for the state has been recognized is in most cases simply in handling the consequences of the attempt to restructure the economy. The most pernicious of such consequences have been the emergence of mass poverty, homelessness and other forms of social misery. Strange as it may sound to Western audiences schooled in the idea of the criminal failure of socialism in Eastern Europe, it is inescapable that the main discernible result so far of Market Maoist economic policies has been the recreation of the five evils denounced by the Beveridge Report in the Britain of the 1930s.

It might be argued that many of the preceding comments are pitched at a far too general level and do not take into account the very varied nature of the changes which have taken place and the very different outcomes which have characterized the response of different societies to those changes. But the Market Maoist ideology itself has openly stated universalist pretensions which are not confined to individual countries (or even continents) and in criticizing this ideology we do not intend to imply either that there are uniform conditions or straightforward solutions to the problems discussed. It is our contention that the process of differentiation and polarization between social classes, ethnic communities and nationalities is one of the most potentially dangerous implications of current developments.

Market Maoist ideology insists that capitalist economics is not a zero-sum game. If the economy grows then everyone can win, at least in theory. In principle this might be true, but only at a very high level of abstraction. In the real world of really existing markets there are frequent conflicts of interest between actors, both collectively and individually, which make a mockery of the enlightenment narrative of textbook market economics. Too many economic technocrats are still beguiled by the illusion that they can successfully ape the manners of nineteenth-century natural scientists. Twentieth-century natural scientists have forsaken the certainties to which these economists aspire. In small ways, the intellectual edifice of conventional economics is beginning to crack. Paul Ormerod has even declared the 'death of economics' in a recent influential study. Arturo Escobar, basing his comments on McCloskey's work on the 'rhetoric' of economists has stressed how 'literary devices systematically and inevitably pervade the science of economics.'[7] If some readers find this book openly 'rhetorical' they should perhaps reflect upon the 'rhetoric' which covertly underpins the supposedly scientific expostulations of mainstream economists (such as the extravagant notion of the Invisible Hand). The fact that economics is not simply a mathematical puzzle has a very important practical implication. In the real world, economic winners frequently win by making losers lose.

Losers are often therefore acting with impeccable economic rationality when they attempt to frustrate the gains of winners. In a world in which the privatization of profits coexists with the general socialization of losses, cant about the mutually beneficial impact of free markets must be heavily discounted. Appeals to the common interest can only function in such circumstances as appeals to 'our' interests as opposed to 'theirs' (whoever 'they' may be in the particular context). In addition, both winners and losers do not always behave rationally. Winners are notoriously incapable of seeing the long-term benefits of sharing their good fortune and the market ideology encourages them in the comforting belief that their personal prosperity is to be seen as a common benefit. Losers may attempt to frustrate winners even when it is not in their direct interest to do so out of spite, envy or malice. The Serbian shelling of Dalmatian holiday resorts, whose future income streams would now flow to Zagreb rather than Belgrade, is a possible case of this (although it could also be seen as a rational, if disgraceful, act of terrorism). The point is perhaps most succinctly made by the Russian neo-fascist Vladimir Zhirinovsky when he rhetorically asked, 'Why should we suffer? We should rather make others suffer.' Needless to say, managing such intractable aspects of human nature does not appear anywhere in the elegant mathematical equations of conventional economic analysis.

Things were not supposed to be like this. Different political tendencies had different visions of the Brave New Europe in 1989. Social Democrats advocated a social market economy, Christian Democrats a Christian version of the same ideal. The hardline Market Maoists saw the East as an opportunity to demonstrate the superiority of their own economic nostrums, the complete fulfilment of which was still frustrated by social opposition (and economic reality) in the West. None of these visions bore any relation to the real situation in eastern Europe.

The Gap between East and West

When the so-called 'transition' began, most analysts and politicians believed that the chances of integrating Eastern economies into the Western sphere of influence were fairly good. Most ordinary people do not really understand why there should be such an economic gap between Hungary and Austria, or Slovenia and Italy, or northern Italy and the *mezzogiorno*, for that matter. Even less could they see, even the experts, the immense difficulties arising from the existence of the economic gap between the German states. Fashionable opinion in the late 1980s considered the existence of the state socialist regimes a crime against history and presumed that the fall of the Soviet Empire would allow these nations to return to the natural path of historic development so rudely interrupted by the Red Army in 1945, in other words, into an ever closer integration with the West European economies.

The breakdown of the previous system was widely interpreted as a liberation and Western politicians were not stingy with promises and finely tuned offers of mutually advantageous cooperation. When the first elected prime minister of the new Hungarian Republic Jozsef Antall told the public that the country could become a member of the European Union by the year 1996 he probably based his statement upon preliminary consultation with Western politicians and advisors. Under the prevailing ideology of 'systemic change', joining the European Union represented a final solution to economic problems and membership of NATO the only possible answer to emerging security issues. Membership of the two organizations has come to symbolize belonging to the Western club. The necessity and desirability of EU integration has become well nigh unquestionable within the political class in East Central European countries. The prevailing discourse takes it for granted that replacing Eastern/Socialist economic relations with Western/Capitalist ones automatically implied 'catching up' with the West. The general belief is still that entry into Western economic and security organizations will undoubtedly take place sometime in the foreseeable future just because the political elites of eastern Europe desire this outcome and because Western governments have made more or less definite promises about it.

In the countries applying for membership, very little attention has been paid to the fact that since the early 1990s West European integration has slowed to a crawl and is in no way comparable to the steps of the 1970s or even the 1980s. The admission of just one of the Visegrad countries in the next decade would require a fundamental reform of EU institutions. It can even be argued that the current direction of EU policy is away from that reform which might be necessary. Since the Maastricht Treaty, signed in early 1992, the community has turned in a direction which implies the progressive abolition of the post-war welfare state and towards a policy determined by a Market Maoist lowest common denominator. Social considerations have been subordinated to the prosecution of economic rivalry between the great powers – the US, Japan and 'Greater Germany' (the northern, more prosperous regions of western Europe). Thus despite the lengthy Social Chapter of the treaty, rejected outright for ideological reasons by the Market Maoists of the British Conservative Party, the project of 'Social Europe' is dead in the water. Far from making Eastern integration more likely, as the British Market Maoists maintain, these developments effectively rule it out as a practical proposition. This is little understood by Eastern political elites who still have a lot to learn about the ways of the world. Integration of even one Eastern country (and the elites in each country are determined that they should be 'first' – undermining any coherent common negotiating position) would imply the wholesale renegotiation of the Common Agricultural Policy and a complete overhaul of regional policy. These two aspects of European Union policy are already the most contentious between the member states and any change at all would involve long and tiresome horse-trading, let alone the complete revision necessary to integrate only the Czech Republic for example.

Received opinion still maintains that the ten associated countries with so-called 'Europe Agreements' will be eventually admitted to the EU (effectively the Visegrad four, the Baltic states and Romania, Bulgaria and Slovenia). Hitherto the enlargements of the European

Union have been of two kinds: First, the integration of net contributors to the EU budget, that is, the northern countries with the exception of Ireland, and second, countries requiring political stabilization because of the Cold War which were net beneficiaries from the budget, that is, the former fascist dictatorships of Spain, Greece, and Portugal. Neither of these criteria apply to any of the applicant countries of Eastern Europe. The main hope of applicants is to be net recipients from the EU budget but none of them threatens any kind of social revolution as was the case with the southern European states which overthrew domestic dictatorships and then lurched leftwards. In fact, these net recipients now have a strong interest in delaying Eastern integration. It must also be recognized that being a net beneficiary from the budget is often offset by being a net loser of employment opportunities due to the operations of the single market. There is no free lunch either in or out of the European Union.

Major northern beneficiaries of the existing Common Agricultural Policy such as France and Denmark also have a strong self-interest in obstructing, or at the very least delaying, the integration of the Eastern countries. The Atlantic powers of France and Britain are made uneasy by the strengthening of German hegemony through the integration of her former '*lebensraum*'; it should not be forgotten that the real opposition to German reunification came not from Mikhail Gorbachev but from Margaret Thatcher. Newly admitted Scandinavian members of the EU might veto the incorporation of the Visegrad states, considering it a betrayal of the Baltics. All these objections might be treated as bargaining counters if the main advantages of enlargement were more widely understood, namely that it could enlarge the internal market of the EU and strengthen competitiveness of West European capital *vis-à-vis* Japan and the US. Economies with one-tenth the German wage level could exercise strong downward pressure on Western wages. However, to a large extent, potential applicants have already provided all necessary facilities to Western investors without extracting any firm promise about integration at all. In these circumstances, their real leverage over Western policy makers is precisely zero.

Some East European Market Maoists used to look to their ideological cousins in Britain to help them overcome the political difficulties outlined above. There are indeed those in Britain that see the East European countries as potential allies in destroying any idea of a 'Social Europe'. However, most of the British 'debate' on this topic functions entirely at the level of rhetoric and is utterly self-referential. The real Market Maoist ultras in Britain now speak openly of leaving the EU altogether (in which case their influence over the other member states, already negligible, would be non-existent).

The real position of the British political elite was more realistically revealed by a speech given by the Conservative Foreign Secretary Malcolm Rifkind in Zurich in September 1996. At the same time as reiterating British Conservative objections to European Monetary Union as more divisive than unifying, he also suggested that enlargement to the East would have similar consequences because the associated countries 'will long remain immature for qualifying for full membership'. Seen from the inside the European Union is much more an arena of conflict than it might appear to Eastern Europeans pressing their noses against the window and peering through the 'Silver Curtain'. The enthusiasm of Eastern peoples might be summed up by the phrase 'we would love to have their problems', even among highly educated academics. It is almost impossible to explain to East Europeans today, blinded as they are by wishful thinking, why 'their problems' might be so much worse when transposed to the East.

The process of integration in the West was further endangered by the recession of the early 1990s, which was partly caused by the attempted absorption of the sixteen million inhabitants of the former East Germany and its knock-on effects on West German tax rates and European interest rates. Western countries are currently in a profoundly introspective mood as each political system grapples with seemingly insoluble economic problems and mounting internal discontent. In addition, it is scarcely recognized in East Central Europe that the former Soviet Union is falling into ever greater economic and social turmoil – of far greater immediate importance in Western capitals than the grumbles of the Visegrad states. Promises have risen to the sky: Western ministers were talking about an incredible $43 million for Russia alone in the spring of 1993. However, real support has remained pitifully low. Furthermore, the EU has defined as an elementary condition for any cooperation with the ex-socialist countries that they coordinate their economic policies with the IMF. Eastern political elites have not been keen to point out to their electorates that this coordination relegates these countries firmly to the status of the despised Third World. Sometimes it has even been suggested that those ex-socialist countries hoping for EU membership will have to conform to the Maastricht convergence criteria on fiscal austerity, whilst new members from the European Free Trade Association (EFTA) such as Finland and Sweden were not forced to do so.

The Maastricht directives envisage the reassessment of the progress of Western integration in the second half of the 1990s. The recurrent crises of the European monetary system in 1992 and 1993 ensure that this will remain the top priority in the West. The current debate within the British Conservative Party implies the questioning of the existence of the European Union in its present form altogether (at least as far as Britain is concerned). Public opinion in the newly admitted EFTA countries is strongly divided, all of which simply adds to the existing cleavages between the more longstanding member states. It seems very unlikely that whilst digesting Austria and the northern countries and revising the monetary system the Union will have anything more than words of encouragement for the Visegrad states for a considerable time to come. And this is presuming that there are no other economic and foreign policy shocks which have not been allowed for – a very complacent assumption in our increasingly unstable world.

This lack of real commitment to integration has contributed in no small measure to the tendency towards increasing divergence from Western economic performance in the East. The key issues concerning any putative integration, agricultural policy and interregional transfers are the most difficult and politically explosive issues facing the European Union in the West. The sense of urgency which motivated the founders of the Union in the 1940s, which was largely the product of the experience of total war and the fear of a repetition of that experience, has been singularly absent from current discussions. This has been another of the poisonous by-products of the bourgeois triumphalism represented by the virulent strain of capitalist apologetic which we have characterized as Market Maoism. If history had ended, no fear of the consequences of complacent self-congratulation needed to be entertained.

Where it has suited the political project of the right, a degree of scaremongering has been indulged. This has been most apparent in 'discussions' concerning questions of migration. During the collapse of the communist system in the autumn of 1989, and later after the dissolution of the Soviet Union, speculation was running high about the likely rise of immigration from the former socialist countries to the West. At this stage, such expectations did not even imply that living standards would decline as dramatically as they have done in the East. They simply stemmed from a crude market-oriented analysis of human behaviour which predicts that people tend to flow from places of lower incomes and living standards to those with higher ones. Understandably, such speculations have arisen with renewed force when the facts about declining living standards became widely understood. In fact, the level of migration has been much lower than might have been expected, partly because human beings do not always slavishly conform to the expectations of market theory and also because immigration controls in the West have become more and more draconian in response to political pressure (largely but not entirely from the right). 'Fortress Europe' is increasingly a reality, which simply increases the desperation of those who wish to enter the stronghold before the drawbridge is finally raised.

Of course it is not only East Europeans who are being excluded by such policies. Even more directly they are aimed at the former colonial subjects of the Western nations who are frequently more identifiable and therefore the targets of a more sustained hostility, which is all the more bitter for being the product of lengthy intimacy and continuing exploitation through the workings of the international financial system. The extreme right in Eastern Europe fondly imagines that the skin colour of their adherents will protect them from such attitudes. Like the more mainstream right-wing politicians in the region, they still have a lot to learn about the real world. And the fear of uncontrolled immigration is not confined to the right. The reaction of French seamen to the use of Polish workers (at much lower rates of pay) by a British shipping company in the 'English' Channel was swift and militant. How long East European building workers without proper work permits will be tolerated in a Germany experiencing the worst unemployment crisis for a generation is extremely open to question. It is also doubtful, for example, that Polish or Hungarian workers would tolerate for long a large expatriate workforce from Russia and the Ukraine within their own borders at substantially lower rates of pay. Even the threat of migration allows living standards to be ratcheted down in the interests of capital throughout Europe. It is clear that many US-based multinationals see Eastern Europe as the Achilles' heel of the European Union just as British Conservatives sometimes see it as a means of frustrating aspirations to a Social Europe. Ordinary people everywhere will be the losers in these processes; and as we have already pointed out, losers very rarely go quietly.

Intra-regional Divisions

Beyond increasing social polarization within the transition countries and the widening of the East–West gap, divisions have become more apparent between the former socialist countries too. By the mid-1990s, a number of possible scenarios presented themselves for consideration:-

Full Integration into the European Union

Complete integration is the most optimistic outcome, with relative economic and social progress. By the mid-1990s, the European Union had already established trade agreements with the Visegrad and Baltic states, Slovenia, Romania and Bulgaria. Other organizational links included the Central European Initiative (the former Pentagonale) with the participation of Italy, Austria and the Visegrad states, as well as Slovenia and Croatia. Initial steps had been taken towards Baltic cooperation between the Scandinavian countries and the independent Baltic states.

However, it was also obvious that these agreements did not in any way guarantee membership in the European Union for any of these countries for all of the reasons outlined above. In any case, it was also often forgotten that joining the EU was not necessarily linked to economic and social improvement. The southern and western periphery of Europe has had very mixed fortunes within the EU. Out of Ireland, Spain, Portugal and Greece, the first three have managed to reduce their income differential with the rest of the EU, but Ireland and Spain have also had the most dramatic unemployment crises even as their economies have been 'booming'. Joining the EU has not led to a Great Leap Forward for Greece; apparently it has not even resulted in a small step.

The possibility of a Spanish-style development (fast-growing economy with very high unemployment) is probably the best that might be hoped for in the more fortunate Visegrad states, but even this outcome is doubtful because of the very significant differences in initial conditions between Southern and Eastern Europe at the advent of democracy and the collapse of authoritarianism. As Bill Lomax notes:

> While the economies of Southern Europe were on an economic upturn with increasing prosperity and rising living standards, growth in foreign investment, and expanding domestic economies, those of East-Central Europe were in decline and recession, if not near collapse, with falling GDP, escalating foreign debts and an outflow of funds. In Southern Europe domestic growth and sound economies provided a stable background for the political transition to democracy; in East-Central Europe economic collapse brought

to a head the crisis of the old regimes, but provided no secure basis for the establishment of new ones.[8]

Newly Industrialized Countries (NICs) of Eastern Europe

Another unstable scenario for Central and Eastern Europe is rapid industrial growth but without the immediate political and social advantages of the West. According to the 1993 survey of *The Economist*, Central and Eastern Europe was a prime candidate for this in the later 1990s. However, if the more fortunate countries get closer to the EU during this period then investment flows may move further towards the east and south. The lack of political progress envisaged in this scenario implies a kind of 'expert dictatorship'. This would be based upon popular ignorance of financial affairs and a continuing mythologization of economics (and economists). Economic knowledge would remain a privilege of the few whose expertise cannot be questioned. Tougher and tougher austerity measures would be necessary in order for policy to remain upon a 'scientific' basis. A particular obstacle to this scenario is the high dependency ratio in Eastern Europe compared to the South-east Asian Tigers, in particular the large number of pensioners.

An article entitled 'Tigers or Tortoises?', in an October 1996 issue of *The Economist* reviews two reports by such experts (including one co-authored by Jeffrey Sachs). It concludes, 'East European countries can do nothing to change their demographics. But they will not catch up with their Western neighbours if they make matters worse by copying the EU's generous social welfare schemes.'[9]

This ignores the fact that East European countries are not copying Western schemes; they are simply administering existing arrangements which the populations of the countries concerned think of as their entitlement. Also, it is extremely doubtful if East European workers would accept such things as a complete absence of paid leave (which was the situation in South Korea for many years).

As we have already noted, this kind of 'success', even were it to occur, would still exclude the majority of the population. It is probably only viable upon a non-democratic basis even if the demographic situation were not so adverse. The educational achievements, particularly in technical subjects, which are often seen as the basis for this scenario are already under threat from the very austerity considered indispensable to success. As Tony Killik of the Overseas Development Institute points out, 'To the extent that IFI programmes are associated – as they are – with reductions in public sector services and investments, they will make it harder for economies to adapt to present day realities.'[10]

On the whole, and at the risk of being accused of racism, we might characterize this whole discussion as being an example of the Irish saying 'If I were you I wouldn't start from here.' The real lessons of South-east Asia – the rationing of foreign exchange, government direction of credit and long-term industrial planning – are ignored as embarrassing irrelevancies to the grand obsession of the Market Maoists with reducing popular welfare.

Balkanization

Balkanization entails permanent economic crisis with vast social and ethnic hostilities and unstable political institutions. This nightmare scenario is more likely to occur in the South-East and the CIS but of course this could have unforeseen consequences for the whole of Europe. This scenario is most likely to occur if the EU remains incapable of exercising leadership while the countries of Eastern Europe continue to take their increasingly irrelevant advice. A situation in which nations and their political leaders cannot find ways out of a desperate plight can lead to the complete neglect of economic affairs. Nation states and social groups can turn on each other for an indefinite period. People will be fed not with concrete achievements but by improvised ideologies and political promises, particularly of a nationalist kind. Societies can shift to this unfortunate destination along with a widespread criminalization of economic activity and the collapse of legal structures. The real threat embodied by the war in former Yugoslavia is not simply that the conflict might spread to neighbouring countries (although the threat is real enough) but rather that the tendency towards economic crisis, exacerbated by ill-thought out, ideologically driven, market reforms becomes institutionalized and leads to a total social and political breakdown unleashing violence on a scale unprecedented in Europe since 1945.

No sane person can view this scenario with equanimity. We make no predictions about the probability of such a tragedy. It is apposite to remember in this context that the purpose of prophecies of doom is to elicit remedial action.

New Regional Blocs

Yet another possible scenario is a partial revival of earlier forms of inter-state cooperation with strong regulation of the economy by corporatist governments. An essential part of such a scenario would be the establishment of some kind of regional payments system as has already been suggested by many independent experts such as George Soros, Hughes and Hare or the Agenda '92 group (which operates under the auspices of the Austrian Academy of Sciences and the International Institute for Peace in Vienna). We might envisage both democratic and authoritarian versions of this scenario. The authoritarian version would be a much closer approximation to the real experiences of South-east Asia than the fantasies of the Market Maoists. Far more attractive would be the democratic alternative which would imply the politicization of the policy-making process and the development of structures for multi-party collective bargaining – multi-party not just in a political but also in a social sense. This would imply that different social groups would become much more aware of their economic and financial interests; something largely lacking from debates in the region thus far. A closer identification of financial flows and items of government expenditure with aspects of real life would enable groups and individuals to define their goals and priorities on a realistic basis.

If the possibility of such an outcome still exists, then there is a potential way forward for the peoples of Eastern Europe either with, or more probably without, the EU. If such developments are blocked in Eastern Europe by the workings of the international system then they will inevitably be blocked elsewhere as well. This gives East Europeans a historic duty as well as an opportunity. We shall have more to say about these matters in Chapter 11.

The former socialist countries never followed a single and generalized pattern of development, not even in the period of strongest Soviet influence. Following the collapse of the Berlin Wall, however, the divergence of their paths has become more and more clear. The destination of a particular country mainly depended on which of the above four trends had the strongest impact on her economic and social development.

For the purposes of analysis, students of the region have often divided the post-socialist world into three sub regions.

1) *East Central Europe*: Poland, the Czech Republic, Slovakia, Hungary and post-war Croatia and Slovenia. This is the zone with the closest cooperation with the EU and with the best hope of integration in the long run. Due to their emerging special relationship with Scandinavia, the Baltic states of Estonia, Latvia and Lithuania can also be classified in this group. Poland, the Czech Republic and Hungary have already moved towards a

degree of tentative integration with each other through the Visegrad agreement of 1991.

2) *South-east Europe*: Romania, Bulgaria, Albania, Rump Yugoslavia, Macedonia and Bosnia-Herzegovina. These countries, due to their more apparent ethnic cleavages and their weaker business prospects have been neglected by the West in terms of development cooperation. The probability is that they will have to fend for themselves as best they can in an increasingly hostile environment.

3) *European CIS*: Russia, Belarus, Moldova and the Ukraine (with the Caucasian and Central Asian republics behind them). The dire situation in these countries suggests a very tough future for the peoples concerned with the alternative of becoming indebted suppliers of cheap raw materials to the OECD or restoring economic integrity on the basis of a heavily centralized and militarized system. There is the clear possibility of a Yugoslavian-style social catastrophe.

This classification can be useful for our analysis too, although bearing in mind the tentative and provisional nature of any such exercise. We also must be aware that the factors which will determine the possible outcomes discussed above are by no means technical or natural, but primarily political. In the next chapter we shall examine perhaps the most striking political phenomenon of recent years in Eastern Europe: the democratic rehabilitation of the former communist parties.

9

Left Turn?

Perhaps the most unexpected development for Western commentators on East European affairs during the last five years has been the democratic rehabilitation of the various Eastern communist parties under new names and usually under new management. The first straw in the wind was seen in the unlikely setting of Lithuania in October 1992 when the Lithuanian Democratic Labour Party – the former Communist Party of Lithuania – won a crushing victory in the elections to the Seimas (the parliament) and consolidated it sometime later by the convincing presidential majority obtained by Algirdas Brazauskas, the leader of the party. At the time the results were regarded as a fluke despite the emphatic nature of the two electoral victories and the strongly anti-communist temper of the society. There might indeed have been local factors at work – Brazuskas had after all defied Gorbachev in order to split the Communist Party of Lithuania from the CPSU. Most careful observers recognized however the economic discontent underlying the results, particularly the disastrous collapse in the standard of living of decollectivized farmers and the urban poor.

Yet another surprise for Western Cold Warriors who were content to substitute their own political prejudices for empirical examination of social trends was the outcome of the elections to the Polish Sejm of September 1993. The Social Democracy of the Republic of Poland (SDRP), the former Communist Party, having created the Democratic Left Alliance which also included other left-wing forces such as the former oppositionist Polish Socialist Party, was the largest single grouping. A government was formed with the *Polskie Stronnictwo Ludowe* (PSL) the former communist-front peasants' party. Further gains for the left were seen in the unexpectedly strong showing of Labour Union, a social democratic faction of *Solidarność*. The right were badly split (and badly beaten). Thus two of the most anti-communist countries in Eastern Europe had returned the former communists to power through the ballot box. Conventional Western political commentators were left scrabbling for explanations.

Towards Social Democracy

In some countries the former communists had hardly ever been away, particularly in the Balkans. In Bulgaria, Romania and notoriously in Serbia, the reconstituted communist parties remained electorally dominant. The standard explanation for this was cultural pathology. Forty years of totalitarianism had warped the political culture in these countries leading to the 'wrong' people winning free elections. The electoral contests in the northern countries and particularly in Lithuania and Poland belied such simplistic nostrums. When the Hungarian Socialist Party won an outright majority of the seats in the elections held in May 1994, it was clear that a general phenomenon was occurring which could no longer be ignored or dismissed. The so-called 'Warsaw Express' rolled through one country after another, even arriving in Rome during 1996 when the former communist Democratic Party of the Left (PDS) formed an Italian government for the first time since 1945. Significantly, the French Communist Party did not even bother to change their name before the election of 1997 which brought them back into government for the first time since 1981.

In the East, the former communists presented themselves as 'socialists' or 'social democrats' in their new incarnation. The two exceptions to this were revealing. In Russia, the Communist Party of the Russian Federation defiantly retained the 'C' word in their title. After the population had tasted Market Maoist shock therapy this appellation did not seem to do them much harm at the ballot box; in fact, in the country where the Communist Party had defeated Hitler, it was in some ways an asset. Although unable to form a government due to strenuous opposition from the presidential office and the Western powers, the Russian Communists remain the single biggest political force in the country and by far the best organized, dominating the Duma. In the Czech Republic, there was another exception because the main left-wing force in Czech politics has turned out to be the Czech Social Democratic Party which was directly descended from the pre-war Social Democratic Party. Elsewhere the historic social democratic parties were unable to re-emerge with any convincing strength even in the former East Germany, where the Party of Democratic Socialism retained significant popular support (to the chagrin of the primarily West German Social Democratic Party). In general the ideological and political space that social democratic parties wanted to occupy was already taken; their political clothes successfully stolen.

Of course what these different post-communist social democratic parties represented varied enormously from country to country; some retained power essentially through the use of patronage and in the worst cases by intimidation and by echoing the rhetoric of the extreme right. The best-known example of this latter phenomenon is the Serbian Socialist Party regime of Slobodan Milosevic which has retained power through the three 'Bs': 'Blinding, Bribing and Beating'. The Bulgarian Socialist Party which lost power after extended street protests in 1997 was fatally split between genuine modernizers and corrupt *nomenklatura* capitalists (it remains to be seen whether any Bulgarian government of whatever political complexion can halt the disintegration of the Bulgarian economy which continues apace).

The Hungarian Socialist Party can hardly be considered in the same category as the Balkan post-communist parties. The reformists which led the Hungarian party during the late 1980s, whose decision to open the border to those fleeing the GDR precipitated the fall of the Berlin Wall, had high hopes of winning the first democratic elections in Hungary. Although disappointed by a result which they thought took no account of their role in ending totalitarianism, they learned to bide their time very usefully. In Poland the long struggle for the hearts and minds of the working class and the peasantry had sharpened the democratic political skills of the Social Democracy of the Republic of Poland (SDRP), so much so that their candidate Alexander Kwasnieski defeated Lech Walesa in the presidential election of November 1995.

It is hard to give a single reason for these diverse political phenomena, but the positive evaluation of some aspects of the previous system plus the painful consequences of Market Maoist policies upon the most vulnerable groups clearly had something to do with it. Workers and farmers in particular, the former 'leading classes' at least at the level of ideology, were the most disillusioned by the new dispensation. Strangely enough it did not seem to matter whether true shock therapy had been implemented as in Poland or a more gradualist policy had been adopted as in Hungary; the political outcome was the same. This was probably because the economic outcomes were the same. Whether reform was 'fast' as in Poland, or 'slow' as in Bulgaria, living standards collapsed and disillusion mounted. Most ordinary people were shocked by the consequences of moving overnight from the Second into the Third World. By 1997, it became a realistic option even in the Czech Republic for a left-of-centre government to come into office after the real consequences of Market Maoism become clear.

Both the right and the left in the West were taken by surprise by this turn of events. At first, the Western social democratic parties were very unwilling to cooperate with these ideologically contaminated and unwelcome Eastern relatives. The historic social democratic parties, dissolved during the 1940s, would have been their preferred partners. The distinction between 'communists' and 'social democrats' or 'socialists' was a product of splits within the socialist movement during World War I. Originally the term 'social democrat' had been applied to parties with a Marxist (not to say revolutionary) orientation in order to distinguish them from 'political democrats' who were the liberal defenders of property unwilling to extend democracy into the social sphere. One such revolutionary social democratic party was that of Russia which split into 'Bolshevik' (majority) and 'Menshevik' (minority) factions before World War I. The Bolsheviks ultimately became the rulers of Russia (and inherited its empire); they labelled themselves 'communists' in order to distinguish themselves from 'social democrats' like the orthodox Marxist Mensheviks who believed that in the Russian context 'socialism' had to be preceded by capitalism. In Western Europe, social democrats became associated with the idea of the gradual reform of capitalism through democratic agitation and parliamentary legislation and later with the acceptance of the basis of a market economy underpinned by a developed welfare state. This was the case especially after the 1959 Bad Godesberg congress of the influential German SPD.

The high tide of social democratic reformism in the West came after 1945. During this period, Keynesian economic ideas were more or less openly espoused by social democratic parties and indeed by their liberal and conservative opponents, which gave the whole era its peculiarly social democratic flavour. As we have already noted, these were years of tremendous economic and social progress in the West. Much of what East Europeans like to think of as the 'Western way of life' was the product of this period and these economic policies. Of course, substantial sections of the population of even the most fortunate Western countries remained trapped in poverty and the continued existence of dictatorships of privilege, both within Southern Europe and in the economically exploited regions of the Third World periphery, made a mockery of democratic and constitutionalist pretensions much as really existing socialism continued to do in its own way within its sphere of influence.

From 1973 onwards, the politically initiated globalization of capital undermined the basis of these achievements. A further turning-point was reached in 1979 when the US Federal Reserve raised interest rates during a recession for the first time since the 1930s. With hindsight this can be seen as a declaration of war upon the Keynesian settlement by finance capital. At the time, conservative social democrats such as the British Prime Minister James Callaghan and Chancellor Denis Healey rejected such an alarmist prognosis; significantly they do not do so today.

It should be remembered that the main political goal of the Market Maoists during the first phase of their counter-revolution was not the destruction of communism, which their own ideology suggested was impossible because of its allegedly 'total' control of social life, but rather the destruction of social democracy. No one was more surprised than Western anti-communists by the fall of communism. The method adopted by the Market Maoists in their war on social democracy are familiar to East Europeans as 'salami tactics'. The original phrase had been used to describe the process whereby opponents of communist rule in Eastern Europe had been sliced off group-by-group preventing the emergence of a broad current of opposition to the concentration of power in communist hands. Similarly, the Market Maoists at first made 'moderate' demands for 'rationalization' of the welfare state and for greater 'efficiency' (privatization was never even mentioned). Once such 'efficiencies' had been accomplished, then further 'restructuring' was demanded and then ever more extreme exercises in 'thinking the unthinkable'.

Social democratic governments responded to these pressures by attempting to satisfy the Market Maoists that they were 'competent' and 'trustworthy' in the belief that this was the best way to blunt the attack. The phrase that 'socialism is the language of priorities' was frequently quoted. Better to concede inessentials in order to preserve the core of the Keynesian settlement, it was argued. However, each concession merely emboldened the neo-liberal Jacobins and their allies in the financial markets. Eventually they jettisoned even the language of compromise. Once installed in government, particularly in Britain and the US, the Market Maoists were able to enforce the deregulation of financial markets which could then be relied upon to orchestrate 'objective' pressures for further change. What Denis Healey called 'those overpaid young lemmings' – the foreign exchange dealers – were the Red Braces Guard of this particular Cultural Revolution.

In a sense, social democracy was a victim of its own success. Having created a tolerably humane social order, there seemed nothing left to do but manage it efficiently. Social democracy had run out of ideological steam. Even in Sweden, the Mecca of social democracy since 1936, the 1990s saw the election of the Market Maoist-influenced 'Moderate' party who proceeded to deregulate the financial system as ideology dictated. The banks quickly overreached themselves and had to be rescued by the state, now back under the control of the Swedish Social Democratic Party, but the damage was done. Even before this destructive interlude Sweden had probably reached the limit of the possibilities of the use of income redistribution as an economic and social tool. Further redistribution of income would have undermined economic incentives. This is not to suggest that there is some kind of universal trade-off between economic efficiency and income inequality. As the histories of Sweden and Japan conclusively demonstrate, the opposite is the case.

Over many decades the centralized pay-bargaining system in Sweden gave across-the-board increases to all workers in particular industrial sectors, regardless of the economic performance of the individual privately-owned firms for which they worked. Those on the lowest pay always received the biggest proportional increases as an expression of social solidarity. The level of pay increases was usually pegged to the average level of productivity increase in those sectors of the economy exposed to international competition. Thus firms with above-average productivity increases were rewarded and those with below-average productivity were ruthlessly punished. It was always policy in Sweden to bankrupt inefficiently managed companies with low levels of investment. The hardest of budget constraints were an emphatic underpinning of the industrial system. Labour and capital resources were kept as mobile as possible. Hence the high levels of labour productivity in Sweden which were rewarded with high wages which ensured in turn high and stable levels of domestic demand and ample resources for social expenditures. The Swedish labour market was in fact extremely flexible. This underlines an important truth: 'flexibility' does not have to imply the destruction of organized labour – it can under certain circumstances strengthen it. As Joan Nelson notes: 'Links between union strength and strike activity are ... complex ... strike activity [is] negatively correlated to strong labour movements and highly centralised wage bargaining.' For such a cooperative relationship between workers and government to operate 'two perceptions are key: confidence in the government's ability to manage the economy, and the belief that [the workers] will share in future benefits'.[1]

The Swedish system required regulated financial markets. Once the seemingly innocuous demand for more 'flexibility' in financial markets was conceded then the whole basis of the model unravelled.

Even as this occurred, some far-sighted social democratic thinkers in Sweden were plotting the potential course of policy in the twenty-first century. The economist Rudolf Meidner, who had played a prominent role in the initial creation of the Swedish model had by the end of the 1970s come to the conclusion that income redistribution no longer provided enough fuel to power the development of the Swedish economy. He suggested that the time had come to begin the redistribution of assets. He argued that employment is becoming more and more scarce as technological change intensifies. Workers need to obtain income streams from the fixed-capital resources which are replacing them if their standard of living is to be protected and the economy to operate efficiently. The Meidner Plan proposed that a tax on profits and wages should be used to create 'wage earner funds' which should be used to progressively buy up the stock of Swedish industry on behalf of the workforce by pension funds to be managed by the trade unions and accountable to their members.

There are curious parallels in these proposals with the compulsory private pension-fund systems found in Singapore and imposed in Chile and greatly admired by Market Maoists. The difference of course is really in the political goals of each system. In Chile, the workforce are forced to make compulsory contributions to private institutions controlled by finance capital; in Sweden, they would have made compulsory contributions to funds which were ultimately under their own control through the trade unions (and which would have been under strong pressure to reinvest in Sweden). Meidner suggested that it might take anything from twenty to fifty years for the whole of Swedish industry to be bought by the workers. He suggested that the current owners might be reconciled to these proposals because their role as managers would continue and the state would not be involved in ownership in any way. This was optimistic to the point of blindness. In the event Swedish capital resisted the proposals tooth and nail. With the support of horrified international financiers (and the pop group Abba), the Meidner Plan was thwarted.

So today even in Sweden social democracy has been snookered by finance capital. Elsewhere financial globalization has had similar effects. In Australasia, the hegemonic Labour Parties of Australia and New Zealand attempted to conform to the maxim 'If you can't beat them, join them' by attempting their own 'humane' version of the neo-liberal counter-revolution. They hoped thereby to maintain political dominance and to soften the blow to their core constituency. Tony Blair seems to have learned nothing from the failure of these policies Down Under. The result in Australasia has been a huge widening of social inequalities in the two countries, a patchy economic performance which only looks good compared to the catastrophic outcomes elsewhere in the world, rising racial tensions (highlighted by the political antics of Pauline Hanson's anti-Asian, anti-aboriginal, One Nation party), and a crisis of political legitimacy. In New Zealand, this crisis has led to fundamental changes in the political system through the medium of proportional representation and the emergence of large political parties on the extreme left (the 'Alliance'; effectively a radicalized Labour party) and the extreme right ('New Zealand First'). This political polarization, even in longstanding liberal democracies, has been the most worrying outcome of the Market Maoist era. In Eastern Europe in particular this has ominous implications. In this context the espousal of 'social democracy' by the former communist parties of Eastern Europe, which affected to despise this political current during the heyday of its success in improving the lives of ordinary people in the West, is rich with tragic irony.

Nevertheless, as their electoral success gave them moral legitimacy, Western social democratic forces were more willing to cooperate with their Eastern counterparts despite their dubious pedigree. Such prominent figures as Austrian Chancellor Franz Vranitsky and French Prime Minister Pierre Mauroy found themselves able to offer words of support to their Eastern 'comrades' even before elections. The summit conference of the European socialist parties was held in Budapest and some of the Eastern parties were admitted to the Socialist International at its New York congress in September 1996.

Changing priorities

As time passed it was not only social democrats who found it possible to overcome their initial reluctance to engage in political cooperation with their former communist adversaries. Liberals and Christian democrats also found themselves able to 'do business' with such individuals as Prime Minister Gyula Horn of Hungary or President Alexander Kwasnieski of Poland. In a sense, the right in the West had always been able to cooperate pragmatically with former communists; after all, what were Balcerowicz, Gaidar, Yeltsin and Franjo Tudjman but former communist converts to Market Maoism? Liberals were also shocked by the Yugoslav War of Succession into seeing the dangers represented by the extreme right and this hastened the rehabilitation of the former communist social democrats in such circles in the West.

These currents were even reflected in the rarefied world of academic economic discourse. The influential Harvard economist, Hungarian Janos Kornai, having rejected his former gradualism, began the 1990s by pushing for a more Market Maoist policy in his native land. He suggested that the priorities for economic policy should be:

1) Stabilizing foreign debt through a policy of strict repayment
2) Reducing inflation through fiscal austerity, and
3) Dealing with unemployment through remedial social policy.

By 1993, Kornai had made yet another change of direction. He no longer spoke of the 'transition' but now rather of the 'transformational crisis'. He reformulated the priorities of economic policy as:

1) A return to economic growth
2) Control of the increase of inflation within tolerable limits, and
3) Toleration of the increase of foreign indebtedness.

He was quite explicit about the political motivation for his change of heart. As he put it:

> The loss of real income for substantial sections of the population and the previously unknown scale of unemployment has triggered off a broad economic discontent. If the strength of this discontent reaches a certain threshold, that could bring dangers to the new Hungarian democracy ... we have to defend ourselves from Weimarisation in the political and ideological spheres ... we also need to draw the necessary conclusions in economic policy.[2]

Sadly, his new-found emphasis on political stabilization still seemed to take very little account of the global factors underlying the economic failure in Hungary and elsewhere in the region, as if some tinkering with short-term economic policies in a more flexible direction would be enough to deal with what he himself characterized as a 'crisis'. A hint that he might have been even more forthright in private was given during a lecture by US Ambassador to Hungary Donald Blinken at the Collegium Budapest in March 1995. Blinken had praised the austerity policies pursued by the Socialist–Liberal coalition in Hungary. Kornai publicly demanded that more flexibility should be shown by Western actors towards Eastern regimes struggling with social crisis. Like most professional economists, including Jeffrey Sachs, Kornai seemed blind to political realities. Finance capital was not going to make exceptions in eastern Europe which could undo all the 'good work' accomplished in the West and the Third World in the previous decade. Although moving from the opposite direction, Kornai's conversion to a form of social democracy was as futile as that of the former communists; social democracy on a national scale was effectively dead.

In Hungary, unlike in Poland, there had been very little sign of popular discontent before the election of 1994. The population grimly endured the collapse in their living standards then went to the polls and punished those who they believed to be to blame for their plight: the right-wing government. This was a potentially positive phenomenon demonstrating the capacity of a democratic parliamentary system to deal with economic grievances in an orderly fashion. The hope was short-lived. The initial stages of the Market Maoist counter-revolution had concentrated upon fiscal and monetary austerity. This led to reductions in what is known in political economy as the 'primary' income of the population (that is, wages and salaries). This phase was largely supervised by the IMF. The second phase of the Market Maoist policy coincided with the electoral victories of the social democrats and was coordinated by the World Bank. This involved the structural disintegration of the welfare state and constituted an attack upon the 'secondary' income of the population, sometimes referred to as the 'social wage'.

So it was paradoxically the Hungarian Socialist Party which found itself presiding over the imposition of fees for higher education despite personal pleas from the Hungarian prime minister to Chancellor Kohl of Germany. It was the so-called 'socialists' who had to impose charges for dental and medical care and impose road tolls and other anti-popular measures. It was the party of the left which was obliged to sell the monopoly regional electricity and gas suppliers into foreign private hands (something only elsewhere implemented in bankrupt Argentina by the right-wing Menem government). To add insult to injury, the proceeds from the Hungarian sale could not be used for internal investment in people or infrastructure but rather was gobbled up immediately as debt repayment. Those who criticized this policy were accused of being ignorant of 'economic realities'. Thus were monopoly industries with a 'licence to print money' and long-term strategic importance to the economy sold off for a short-term 'profit', which was taken by the international banks in return for not cutting off further addictive doses of imaginary 'credit'.

The naïvety of these former communists about the nature of Western practices and intentions was truly astonishing and requires some kind of explanation. Most of the personnel which occupied the higher echelons of these social democratic parties were former apparatchiks used to working within an externally imposed framework. In the 1980s, they had looked to Gorbachev and Moscow for parental guidance; now they sought the same emotional satisfactions in Brussels and Washington. Unlike the left in the rest of the world they were largely divorced from popular struggles. Of course it must be recognized that because of the power of finance capital and the unashamed utilization of armed terrorism, the left in the West and the Third World was itself decimated by defeat, disappointment and death by the end of the 1980s. Also, because of the need to live down their supposedly revolutionary past, the Eastern social democratic parties were desperate to operate within Western norms and expectations and it is hardly surprising that they found it psychologically impossible to challenge those from whom they so desperately craved acceptance. In any case their situation was objectively weak. Economic policy is not decided in eastern Europe; it doesn't matter who wins elections. As time goes on this will have a corrosive effect upon fragile democratic values. As Peter Taylor has put it:

> Why should the majority of a state's people participate in an election if there is little or no politics of redistribution ... in non-core areas of the world economy without a viable politics of redistribution the basic mechanism for keeping voter loyalty is absent.[3]

Increasingly it is the radical right which is picking up the gauntlet thrown down by the Market Maoists. Since their political style thrives upon paranoia and social conflict, they have been able to opportunistically capitalize upon popular grievances as they have appeared without worrying too much about viable alternative policies. Attempts by the centre left to appeal to 'reason' and 'reality' have been undermined by the idiotic social and economic policies they have been forced to impose; policies with which they themselves do not really agree. In effect, they have been left invoking entry to the European Union as a *Deus ex machina* which will magically resolve all social and economic problems. They have also increasingly attempted to play the role of international statesmen in order to hide their domestic nakedness. At the end of 1996 for example, Hungarian Foreign Minister Laszlo Kovacs made a speech in which he pointedly drew attention to the fact that a recent speech by the leader of the Hungarian Christian Democratic People's Party had questioned the existing borders of the Hungarian state and had hinted at irredentist demands in Romania and Slovakia. The intended audience for Kovacs' remarks was not in Hungary, where no one was in any doubt about the position of the right, it was rather in Western chancelleries. The not-so-coded message was clear: 'The right cannot be trusted, we are your best bet for a stable Central Europe – give us some concessions we can pass on to our electorate.'

Challenges to Internationalism

In 1996, the commemoration of the fortieth anniversary of the Hungarian uprising of 1956 had a sinister impact. In previous years all political forces had been happy to associate themselves with the revolutionaries of 1956, which had, after all, included many communists including the leader of the revolt Prime Minister Imre Nagy, a lifelong communist executed by the Soviets for his part in the events of that year. In 1996, the only group which dared to call crowds out onto the streets was the nationalist party of Istvan Csurka. Other participants included Leszek Moczulski of the reactionary Confederation of Independent Poland, prominent in opposing most of the measures of 'market reform' imposed in that country , and the anti-European Union Jean Marie Le Pen, leader of the openly racist French National Front (strangely enough Le Pen's good friend Vladimir Zhirinovsky, who invited Le Pen to his wedding, did not put in an appearance).

The problem for the left in dealing with the xenophobic demagoguery of the extreme right is enormous. The left-of-centre parties aspire to be managers of an orderly transition to capitalism and therefore must be both credible and consistent. The right has no need for such caution; for them, the worse things get the more they will thrive. Psychologically dependent on the West, the moderate left is unable to bring itself to mobilize potential unrest against the status quo. Increasingly Eastern Europe resembles the Ireland of the 1920s which the poet W.B. Yeats had in mind when he wrote the lines 'Things fall apart, the centre cannot hold; Mere anarchy is loosed upon the world'.

The anguished convolutions of social democrats saddled with Market Maoist policies in deadly political combat with opponents with no such handicaps suggest that 'The best lack all conviction, while the worst Are full of passionate intensity'.

It is hard to say who is more to blame for this parlous state of affairs. Is it the witless Weimar democrats of post-communist social democracy constantly praying for the Seventh Cavalry (or at least European Union structural funds) or the complacent Western Marie Antoinettes to whom they direct their increasingly desperate entreaties? On balance it is probably the Western political elite that should be asking itself '... What rough beast, its hour come round at last, Slouches towards Bethlehem to be born?'4

The Weimar phase is rapidly drawing to a close. In 1996 in Lithuania the Democratic Labour Party was trounced in the parliamentary elections by a resurgent right. The former communists were deserted in droves by the peasants and the urban poor who were bitterly disappointed with the continued deterioration of their lot. A pattern is now emerging of a right-wing reaction to the successes of the left in Poland, Hungary and elsewhere. Lest Western conservatives rejoice too quickly, they should confront the fact that the popular appeal of the far right is largely based upon the explicit rejection of Market Maoist economic policy. They are offering the population the modern equivalent of 'Bread, Peace and Land' not 'free markets' and 'choice'. Whether the left gets drawn into the same empty auction of promises is largely irrelevant. Without fundamental changes in continental and global economic policy the entire region is on course for unprecedented political turmoil. From drunken workers from state-owned enterprises rioting in Warsaw against 'red' austerity to armed confrontation on the streets of Albania, the game and the rules by which it is to be played are changing rapidly for the worse.

The lack of self-confidence on the left is not a phenomenon confined to Eastern Europe of course. Contrary to New Right ideology, far from being in possession of an ideologically consistent 'political correctness', the left is in fact incapable of analysing let alone combating the rise of right-wing fundamentalism either in Eastern or Western Europe. Globalization has been accepted as an inevitable act of God to which 'modern' social democrats must simply adapt themselves, posing all the time as the guardians of 'order' and 'stability'. Within the core of the world economy in such places as the United States and Britain, this may even be an electorally viable strategy as Bill Clinton and Tony Blair have both demonstrated in their different ways. Outside the charmed circle of capitalist prosperity, which is where most ordinary East Europeans are situated, it simply won't wash.

It is worth reminding ourselves of the politically driven nature of globalization and its handmaiden structural adjustment. 'The market' would long ago have solved the problem of international indebtedness by the time-honoured method of a good old-fashioned financial crash; something from which the consistent followers of Friedrich von Hayek have never shrunk. Under the bastard Keynesian dispensation under which the world now functions, such an outcome has been blocked by the action of the state operating through the international financial institutions. Both the state and those institutions have been suborned by the rational choices of finance capital; as clear a case as anything in history of what is technically known as 'regulatory capture'. The IMF was supposed to police high finance on behalf of the people; it now polices the people on behalf of high finance. A crash, consistent Hayekians notwithstanding, is clearly undesirable; although it may in the end be inevitable. What is intolerable is that institutions funded by public taxation should be so shamelessly dominated by private interests.

One social democratic modernizer who went some way to recognizing the political nature of the Great Bourgeois Cultural Revolution was the former leader of the British Labour Party John Smith. Shortly before he died he gave an important, but strangely little-reported speech to the Socialist International Committee on Economic Policy, Development and the Environment in Geneva. Since his role in preparing the Labour Party for government responsibility is now widely praised, what he had to say deserves to be quoted at length. In relation to the IMF and the World Bank he stated:

> The two institutions are increasingly doing the same job – and a major and consistent criticism is that both are doing the same job badly. Cynics in developing countries like to compare the two with a torturer's double act. The Fund does the nasty stuff and the Bank offers tea and sympathy. I believe that serious consideration should be given to merging the Fund and the Bank into a single institution and at the same time bringing the new organisation into a closer and more cooperative relationship with the UN specialised development agencies – such as the UN development programme, the World Food Programme and UNICEF. A combined Fund and Bank could be administratively leaner and, I hope, more effective in mobilising both resources and economic policy advice. I appreciate that such a proposal will send a shiver through Chevy Chase, Maclean and other Washington suburbs – but after all the army of economists that work for the Bank and the Fund are all experts at coping with structural adjustment.[5]

This speech is not so important for its specific proposals, which seem to suggest plenty of opportunity for the reconfiguration of vested interests behind a smokescreen of reform, but rather for the political logic which underlay John Smith's analysis. In effect in his own understated way he was raising that very old revolutionary slogan: 'No Taxation Without Representation'. It is not the place of private capital dependent upon public subsidy to dictate economic policy to elected politicians. This speech was the first shot in what promises to be a long war. The struggle to regulate international finance capital will be every bit as hard fought as the battle to regulate national finance capital in the first part of the twentieth century but such a political struggle is the manifest destiny of social democracy and the common sense of the twenty-first century.

All over the world a strange and troubled recognition that things cannot go on as they are is beginning to emerge. But this sentiment has yet to take form as a coherent alternative strategy. In referring to the growing crisis of structural unemployment in Western Europe, Hugh Compston has noted that changes in policy will only become possible in the longer term 'as the economic paradigm slowly changes – or snaps'.[6] The crisis in Eastern Europe may well lead to the latter rather than the former outcome. We have all been here before. As Michael Barratt Brown has stated:

> ... when the capitalist world failed sixty years ago to cancel the mountain of debts and reparations burdening the economies of Germany and Austria and of several Latin American countries the result was a rise to power of fascist dictators and a holocaust from which we are only just recovering. How much more warning do we need?[7]

Social democracy is not really dead; it is merely suffering from a mid-life crisis. It is by far the most successful and lasting political movement of the twentieth century. Hitler and Stalin are gone and the IMF merely a passing shadow. The ideals of social solidarity, public action for the public good and humane political debate and agitation are the only hope for a way out of the current impasse. As John Smith said, '... if we are to provide a blueprint for a better future, we must be ready to change and to think how things could be different. And instead of asking why, ask why not.'[8]

We are in need of alternatives based on a different perspective than the neo-liberal utopia, not only for the sake of higher rates of employment and economic growth. A programme that could provide social and economic development would also be an alternative to the militarization of Eastern Europe that came on to the agenda of Western policy in the second half of the 1990s.

10

A Military Solution

'One thing is certain: Political instability is not conducive to investment.'
'It is no longer possible to pursue the eastward enlargement of NATO and remain friends with Russia.'

George Soros[1]

Controlling the darker human passions which can be unleashed by economic and social change is the role of security policy. Which brings up the question of the future of that other putative pillar of European integration: the North Atlantic Treaty Organisation. Most of the foreign policy establishment in East Central Europe consider integration in the EU and in NATO as two sides of the same coin. This twin-track policy is sometimes described as 'Euro-Atlantic Integration'. It is not self-evident why there should be such a clear consensus within the political elites about such a double integration but it certainly does exist. And it is usually an unconditional support for the idea of membership in most cases.

Economy and Security

According to the opinion polls, nations which have only recently achieved independence after long struggle would be more than happy to abandon their currencies, foreign ministries and other national institutions. Among politicians this 'EU phoria' can be seen as an expression of loyalty by would-be vassals of the Western powers. It is felt that any slackening of this infatuation might shake the sympathy and assistance of Western governments and private sources, although like all adolescent passion, this enthusiasm can sometimes be a trifle embarrassing to those at whom it is directed (even if they have been guilty of soliciting it). Among non-politicians, such attitudes can probably be attributed to a lack of information about the costs and benefits of joining such exclusive clubs.

The real relationship between economic and security policy has been critically examined by very few. Most analysts are happy to mouth platitudes about the interrelationship between them and leave it at that. Interestingly, one commentator who has taken a more penetrating view is Dr Otto von Hapsburg, now president of the Pan-European Movement, who declared in a recent article that 'our main task is to reach full membership for Hungary within the European Union'. Surprisingly for some he added that 'this is first of all a security community and just secondly an economic order'.[2] Dr Hapsburg does have a point. In the post-war period, the main instrument of security within Europe was not NATO, but, indeed, economic integration. The first steps were made by establishing the European Payments Union (EPU) in 1950, and the European Coal and Steel Community (ECSC) in 1951. Both were created following the initiative and guidance of the US, and developed into the EEC after the 1957 Treaty of Rome.

NATO was not established in order to settle inter-state disputes between the members (although these have taken place between Greece and Turkey), but rather in order to offset a military threat external to all. Nevertheless this did not occur without an intimate connection between economics and security. In order to establish NATO in 1949, the US had to promote economic reconstruction within Western Europe. It would be incorrect to assume that the framers of the Marshall Plan had the foundation of a military bloc in mind when they were elaborating the state-led financial reconstruction of Western Europe. It cannot be doubted however, that without this multifunctional aid project Western Europe would have been unable to create a viable military organization in the late 1940s.

When NATO was enlarged towards the south, incorporation into the EC was a guarantee that Spain would pay its way in military terms (Portugal and Greece had long been members of NATO even as military dictatorships). Turkey on the other hand has been the notable exception to this pattern. Although she has been provided over the years with astronomic amounts of concessional credit from the international financial institutions (including, as we have seen, the very first structural adjustment loan), she has never even been close to membership of the EU despite persistent attempts to join (and East European elites should remember that Turkey is ahead of them in this particular queue). Quibbles about human rights, particularly in Kurdistan, are often given as the reason for delay but other, and baser, motives are more likely explanations.

First, the EU cannot really afford to integrate Turkey, let alone Eastern Europe. Second, there is still a residual racist contempt in Western Europe for Muslim people. (Incidentally, are Czechs, Hungarians and Poles ready for Turkish and Kurdish competition in their domestic labour markets?) Third, the US has been unwilling to share control over this key 'strategic asset' even with her closest allies. The Turkish Army, fully integrated into NATO, has in the past overthrown elected governments potentially hostile to US interests.

The idea of NATO as a partnership of equals is clearly fictitious. There are senior and junior members (just as in the EU). The conflicts of interest between members are as important as their shared goals. In fact, with the end of the Cold War they are more important. The tension between Greece and Turkey, who are at present engaged in a massive arms race in the Aegean and who have diametrically opposite positions on the Balkan conflict, is well known. Less well known is the fact that during the Bosnian crisis, British special forces under the UN command of Michael Rose, were ordered to withhold targeting information from US forces so that the British government could frustrate US policy in the region which was more belligerent than the British believed to be prudent, in relation to Serbian interests. British-led UN forces were also involved in attempts to intercept weapons supplies to the Bosnian Armija coordinated between the US, Croatia and Iran. So much for the 'special relationship' at the heart of NATO which had already been strained in previous years by US support for Argentina, the entirely illegal invasion of the British Commonwealth country of Grenada and the continuing conflict in Ireland. When East Europeans talk of 'joining NATO', which NATO do they mean?

For all these reasons, whilst we must link questions of economy and security together, we also have to deconstruct the Euro Atlantic package. There is a real danger that the illusory security offered by NATO membership will be used as a means of avoiding the difficult questions surrounding EU membership. If security is defined in its widest sense as the basis of economic development (à la Dr Hapsburg), it should not only involve military security but economic, social and ecological security as well. If security structures confine themselves to the military sphere then at best their function can only be to preserve social injustice and insecurity within and between states. At worst they simply become reactive to endemic economic, social and political crisis.

If NATO membership is extended to the Visegrad countries this will largely be because of their residual fear of Russia. The Baltic states and the Ukraine will be left outside of the NATO umbrella. This may intensify their already conflictual relationship with Moscow. The net result may well be the precipitation of the very security crisis NATO expansion is supposed to forestall. Are East Europeans really so confident that when it comes to the crunch President Gingrich will want to send US troops to the Belorussian border? That Middle America will go to war for anything other than fundamental national interests? The unwillingness to commit US forces in any kind of combat role has been the one consistency in US policy throughout the debacle in former Yugoslavia.

NATO issued invitation to Poland, Hungary and the Czech Republic at the Madrid summit, July 1997. These three countries therefore will soon find themselves in the company of Turkey, that is, in a group of countries with membership in NATO but only with the promise to become members of the European Union some day. Feeling offended by the Madrid decision, Russia declared expansion to be 'the biggest mistake in Europe since the second world war'.[3] Even without going to such extremes, the controversial nature of NATO enlargement can be explored.

NATO expansion, as a part of the rearrangement of security structures in Central Europe, should be a step towards an era more peaceful than the pre-1989 Cold War period. Since the fall of the Berlin Wall, and in fact since the Gorbachev–Reagan summits of the late 1980s, disarmament and withdrawal of foreign troops were indeed an important feature of Eastern and Central European changes. However, the arrival of NATO in former Warsaw Pact countries would certainly mean the start of rearmament of these states, giving legitimacy to similar steps by Russia and a revitalization of security cooperation in the CIS.

It is, however, not only the East–West relationship where NATO expansion creates tension but within the security alliance too. Instead of uniting Western great powers, the debate over NATO expansion has divided them further. France until the last minute insisted on the invitation of Romania in addition to the three others, and membership for Slovenia was also supported by a number of West European governments. The French government was prepared to sacrifice their return into the military command of the alliance because Romania was left out by the US initiative.

The US position was explained by Secretary of State Madeleine Albright in a lengthy article for *The Economist*, and supported by a joint contribution by former national security advisers Zbigniew Brzezinski and Anthony Lake written for the *New York Times*. According to Brzezinski and Lake:

> NATO expansion is a creative response to three strategic challenges: to enhance the relationship between the United States and the enlarging democratic Europe; to engage the still evolving, post-

imperial Russia in a cooperative relationship with that Europe, and to reinforce the habits of democracy and the practices of peace in Central Europe.

Thus, as a third-rank issue, the problems of the would-be member countries find their place among great-power considerations. The priorities of the American Democrats can perhaps be better illuminated by another quotation from the same article. The authors explain that expansion will 'place the alliance, and the United States, at the center of a wider regional security system to which Russia is related. This is good for the future of Europe – thus good for us Americans.'4

This explanation reinforces that 'what is good for NATO is good for America', although we have already been familiar with this principle. The overall discourse about NATO, however, may create the impression that the expansion of the security alliance is primarily a symbolic political step and military considerations bear only secondary importance. The military gains for NATO are indeed hard to notice at once. David Fairhall, defence correspondent of the *Guardian* explained in detail how unfit the Czech and Hungarian armies were to fulfil military requirements in NATO:

> The best the apathetic Czech and Hungarian forces could currently manage is a couple of battalions apiece and a handful of fighter aircraft. ... Barracks and airfields are in the wrong places, laid out to defend against Nato attack or support an invasion of Western Europe. Warsaw Pact armies became bloated with middle-ranking officers but desperately short of non-commissioned officers, the experienced sergeants and corporals who form the backbone of Nato units. ... Czech pilots may get as little as 15 hours flying a year, insufficient for operational efficiency but essential to qualify for extra flying pay.5

If it was a question of military competence, NATO should have invited only Poland and Romania, and perhaps Slovenia. The leader article of the same newspaper added that 'expansion will not strengthen Nato militarily and will weaken the economies of new members'. Interestingly enough, the very same article concluded that expansion must go ahead nevertheless because a serious organization cannot afford to withdraw its promises:

> A Nato which had decided not to incorporate any eastern members would be one thing. A Nato which has decided to bring them in,

and does so, would be another. But a Nato which so decided, and then failed to do so because of a defeat in the legislature of its most important member state, would be another article altogether. A busted flush, perhaps.[6]

It is obviously bad for Western politicians to eat their words or to be voted against in their parliaments. It would however be equally inconvenient if popular opinion in the new member states would prevent ratification of the accession treaties. According to an opinion poll reported by the *Financial Times* in June 1997, NATO membership would not easily get an absolute majority if a referendum was made in the near future in Hungary.[7] The idea of joining NATO is even less popular in the Czech Republic which does not even share a border with Russia or other successor states of the Former Soviet Union, while the threat of those is said to be the main danger NATO enlargement is meant to offset.

The chances of winning a referendum for accession would be seriously undermined if Czechs, Poles and Hungarians take seriously the allegation that expansion would 'weaken the economies of new members', as has been recognized in various assessments of the enlargement process including the *Guardian* leader article cited above. (The real possibility of losing a referendum contradicts the alleged purpose of enlargement as had been explained in the *Guardian*: 'The reason Nato is expanding is that Eastern European countries pleaded, begged, argued, lectured, and hammered on the door. Could we really have just said No?'[8])

If they become members, the Czech Republic and Hungary must at least double their defence budgets: that would inevitably take resources away from civilian sectors of the economy and thus prevent a recovery of living standards long awaited by these nations after the painful restructuring period of the early 1980s. Their governments may buy fighter aircraft and other modern weapons by using foreign loans, but that would only postpone the burden of adjustment to later generations, very similar to the armament projects of some Third World governments in the 1970s and 1980s.

It might well be the case that the entire political elite, that is, all parliamentary parties of the three countries, are in favour of NATO membership, but it is still not a guarantee for winning a referendum for that cause. This was the case in Denmark where all the major parties supported the Maastricht Treaty but the people rejected it in a referendum on 2 June 1992. The situation was similar in Norway with a referendum on EU membership in 1994, when the ruling Labour Party failed to mobilize support among their own conventional constituency. Another type of potential failure can be expected on the basis of the French experience: the Maastricht Treaty was nearly defeated there because millions of people saw the referendum an opportunity to vote against a government that was unpopular for a completely different reason, unemployment. (The connection between the Maastricht Treaty and the maintenance of mass unemployment in Western Europe was discovered much later in France, affecting the outcome of the parliamentary elections in May 1997.)

Some experts concerned with the integration process have already considered these problems, and, like Dr Miklos Derer of the Hungarian Atlantic Council, started to hint that a referendum about NATO membership may not be necessary in Hungary because in most democratic states there would not be one on a similar issue. It is true that the people in Germany, for example, have never been asked whether they wanted their country to be a member in NATO or the EU (or, previously, the EC, and even earlier, the EEC). The ruling socialists of Hungary, however, did promise that a referendum would be made about this issue as soon as the terms have been negotiated with the West. The junior coalition partner, the Alliance of Free Democrats, also supports the idea of popular decision, and no major political force has so far expressed an opposite view.

To prepare the road to a referendum, the foreign policy and defence establishment of Hungary have launched a large-scale propaganda campaign. Books and articles have been written about the impossibility of neutrality in the new era. However, some elements of this campaign may easily backfire because of the inherent contadictions within this propaganda. An example of this is the frequent reference to the changing nature of NATO, meaning that it is primarily not a military alliance any longer but an organization to protect common political values. This factor was emphasized in a recent lecture by Javier Solana, Secretary General of NATO, at the Budapest University of Economic Sciences. The educational power of such statements is seriously weakened by access to information on alternative interpretations by other Western leaders. When, for instance, Prime Minister Tony Blair expressed his support for the US position at the Madrid summit, he also found it important to emphasize that 'NATO is a military alliance, not a political club.'[9]

Less learned advocates of NATO accession tell stories about how membership in NATO would accelerate the inflow of foreign direct investment. Some of them even go so far as to claim that if we become members in NATO we will have to establish professional armies and then 'only those who like that life style will be soldiers'.

'Joining the unbeatable club' is the most attractive argument for many, forgetting that Hungary has never proved unbeatable when siding with Germany in a major military conflict.

To prevent negative repercussions from Russian, Romanian, and perhaps even Serb foreign policy, Hungarian Foreign Minister Laszlo Kovacs often says Hungary needs NATO not against a particular threat but for the sake of modernization and against instability in general. The greatest problem of all, however, in the entire NATO discourse both in East and West, is perhaps the misunderstanding of the nature of instability in the former socialist countries (FSCs) of Eastern Europe.

The announcement of a US policy by the Secretary of State to enlarge NATO by inviting three countries, nearly coincided with the rejection by President Clinton of a comprehensive aid package for the former socialist countries, on the pattern of the Marshall Plan, the fiftieth anniversary of which he used to declare his principles. Whenever Western politicians rejected the idea of 'a new Marshall Plan' in recent years, they referred to foreign investment, saying that it should this time be private money that fulfils the role of reconstructing the former Eastern bloc countries, destroyed by economic warfare during the Cold War and the eventual collapse of their trading bloc COMECON (officially called Council for Mutual Economic Assistance or CMEA).

The problem with this reference to private investment is that it just too much resembles American policies after World War I, when private money also flew towards the destroyed economies of Europe, including Germany, but due to its anarchistic character it could not prevent the greatest economic and social disaster of this century. The Americans did too little and too late to remove the debt burden of Germany in the 1920s, and supported rigid monetarist policies that exacerbated the depression for years.

Private investment also started to flow to the FSCs after the fall of the Berlin Wall; however, it did not turn out to be such a great engine for the recapitalized economies of the region. Hungary, the country that received half of the foreign investment of the region by 1996, showed the slowest growth in GDP as compared to Poland, the Czech Republic, Slovakia, Slovenia and Romania – countries which preferred other forms or even a slower pace of privatization.

The failure of market principles to facilitate rapid recovery and an improvement of the living standards for a substantial majority of the population in the FSCs generated a debate about the need for, and the possibility of a new Marshall Plan time after time. This very discourse has been an evidence of the instability politicians and much of public commentators have highlighted. This instability has a variety of components in the FSCs, like personal insecurity for those affected or threatened by the loss of jobs or welfare entitlements, a criminalization of the economy from ordinary tax evasion to oil Mafiosi, the recurring danger of ethnic violence and racist aggression, and the lack of legitimacy for the new owners of the recently privatized assets.

The ultimate source of this instability is the so-called transition project proper – the attempt to re-establish capitalism by implementing a neo-liberal shock therapy (rapid liberalization, deregulation and privatization). The pressure exercised by Western governments and multilateral agencies to implement these policies have made a serious impact on all the FSCs, including those where national governments were reluctant to accept neo-liberal principles. In those countries, however, where the governments went ahead with the shock for at least a year, the consequences have been devastating.

Poland was the country where the anti-Communist *Solidarność* government elected in the summer of 1989 launched the first and purest neo-liberal programme designed by economic advisors with substantial Third World experience, including the infamous Harvard professor Jeffrey Sachs himself. Starting in January 1990, the government made millions of people redundant within a year. The collapse of workers' purchasing power made it possible to halt inflation and abolish queues for elementary goods. Nevertheless, Solidarność had to face an emerging political crisis due to the declining pubic support for their programme. They had to bring in two new prime ministers after Tadeusz Mazowiecki's fall, and even had to give way to a coalition led by the Peasant Party leader Waldemar Pawlak. They were given an outstanding reward for their pioneering role by the United States through the cancellation of half of the Polish foreign debt. Eventually, however, they were sent into opposition as early as September 1993, when in desperation the Polish electorate brought back the post-communist left.

Having seen the Polish experience, two major countries under surviving post-communist leaderships decided not to experiment with neo-liberal reform. Despite constant pressure from the IMF, Romania and Bulgaria applied moderate and cautious reforms, although the abolition of COMECON had severe impact on their incomes and general economic situation after 1991. By applying various combinations of carrot and stick, however, these two countries have been pushed towards shock therapy by the external agencies. The breakthrough occurred for both in early 1997, when their new governments sent their currencies into free fall and cut real wages by double-digit figures within a few months.

The government of the Czech Republic was talking the language of neo-liberal shock, without really doing it, while the Hungarians did the opposite, that is, doing it while talking about gradualism until 1995. Hungary, as a consequence, experienced the rise of mass unemployment and increasing social and regional polarization, while the Czechs maintained nearly full employment and did not contemplate the privatization of public services until early 1997. In Hungary, the neo-liberal programme was revitalized by the post-communist Hungarian Socialist Party (MSZP) after 1995 this made the populist right-wing Smallholders' Party (FKGP) the most popular party in certain periods as the single major opponent of the course apparently inspired by the IMF and the World Bank. The resistance of Czech Prime Minister Vaclav Klaus to practical neo-liberalism was broken by a suddenly revealed gigantic trade deficit, which destroyed the hitherto most stable and triumphant version of re-capitalization.

Hazardous financial operations led to the outbreak of a short civil war in Albania. However, the most devastating consequences of neo-liberal crisis management emerged in former Yugoslavia and in the former USSR. In Yugoslavia, it resulted in the collapse of the federal state because of unresolvable debates over monetary policy and the distribution of the debt burden between the member republics.

The economic origins of 'ethnic conflict'

Yugoslavia has been the test tube in which all of the poisonous cocktails we have been examining have become most critical. In all the millions of words which have been spoken and written about this appalling tragedy, very little attention has been given to the economic developments which preceded the conflict. We have heard far more about medieval history than structural adjustment. The development economist Michael Barratt Brown has been an honourable exception to this conspiracy of silence. In Yugoslavia, he notes:

> ... public and private debt to foreign lenders was of the order of $20 billions throughout the 1980s. In most of that decade this was the equivalent of over a quarter of the national income, and debt servicing took up some 20 per cent of all Yugoslavia's annual exports of goods and services ... diversion of production to exports

to pay off the debt was the main cause of soaring inflation and a steadily deteriorating standard of living.[10]

This is not to suggest that there were not serious structural weaknesses in the Yugoslav economic system in the first place. The much-discussed 'self-management' was a sham and a failure. As property rights theorists such as Svetozar Pejovich have been keen to point out, the Yugoslav system did not give workers real ownership over assets (quite unlike the individual ownership basis of the highly successful Mondragon cooperatives which are the major employers in the Basque country, the most industrialized region of Spain). Thus, even where bureaucratic interference in economic decisions was not all-pervasive (and of course in many respects the Yugoslav system was substantially the same as that found in other economies dominated by political and administrative command), the structure of incentives was perverse. Because any expansion of production implied increasing numbers employed (and therefore depleting the wages fund available for current employees), Yugoslav firms were not sufficiently entrepreneurial. Because bankruptcy was highly unlikely, firms became effectively price makers (the root cause of the inflationary pressures analysed in Chapter 4). Because workers did not own the assets they supposedly managed collectively, capital investment was neglected in favour of current consumption (a socialist version of Anglo-Saxon *rentier* capitalism). All these failings made the Yugoslav system dangerously prone to stagflation even without the added pressures created by international debt. As Pejovich has said:

> Inherent in the structure of property rights in the labour managed economy are some positive transaction costs and negative incentives that are specific to its institutional structure. These transaction costs and disincentives are responsible for inflation, unemployment and declining income.[11]

The failures of Market Maoism should not blind us to the failures of really existing socialism, in Yugoslavia or elsewhere. However, it should also be recognized that the irresponsible and inflationary decentralization seen in Yugoslavia was precisely the result of the policies imposed by the Market Maoist ideologues on the other post-communist countries after 1989.

In a sense, the Yugoslav economic experiment prefigured the developments of the other socialist countries by some years. The failings of the Yugoslav system should have been a warning of what might happen elsewhere once all central control was abandoned for primarily ideological reasons. Despite the handicaps which the contradictions of the Yugoslav version of self-management imposed on itself, the system had in some respects functioned relatively well during the period under consideration 'shifting from a mainly primary producing economic base to a manufacturing economy'.[12] Yugoslav exports of manufactured goods, which had represented only around 50 per cent of total exports in the 1970s, had risen to around 80 per cent by the 1980s. Yugoslavia was successfully servicing its debts and simultaneously improving the quality of its exports. Many countries would dearly love to achieve this textbook outcome. But there was a catch. Manufacturing industry was located mainly in the northern republics of Slovenia and Croatia. Increased manufactured exports from these republics did not lead to increased living standards because the income generated left the country as debt service. This was perceived by the population of these republics as a 'subsidy' to the underdeveloped south (in fact, it was a subsidy to Western bankers).

In the southern republics, on the other hand, production of absolute quantities of primary goods such as coal and copper was also increasing. But in line with world-wide trends, the prices for such products was continually forced down by technological change and saturated markets. The perception in these republics was that they produced more and more for less and less. In many ways, the Yugoslav federation was like a microcosm of the global economy with all of its imbalances and injustices. Being much more open to the global economy than some other socialist states, Yugoslavia was quickly drawn into the debt trap created by the expansion of the eurodollar market in the 1970s. The decentralized nature of the Yugoslav state and economy quickly translated these pressures into the stagflationary impasse now so familiar in other post-communist economies. The money supply was promiscuously increased as nominal incomes rose but the goods produced were exported to service the debt.

As in other post-communist economies, problems with money supply were largely the symptom rather than the cause of inflationary pressure. As we have already noted, post-communist economies have a very severe structural inflationary bias. In the Yugoslav case this was compounded by political problems. An austerity policy would have had to have fallen on consumption in the wealthier republics of the north, an outcome entirely incompatible with the sentiments of their populations. In the circumstances, preserving some measure of popular purchasing power through loose monetary policy while hoping against hope for something to turn up was probably the only politically possible line of action.

Inflation in the former Federal Republic of Yugoslavia peaked at over 1,300 per cent per annum in 1989. There was a steady reduction in living standards throughout the 1980s, unemployment became a permanent feature of life in Yugoslavia long before it began to appear in other Eastern countries (and this despite a steady flow of labour to the European Union). Barratt Brown writes:

> The deficit on foreign trade was in fact brought down from $7.2 billion to $0.6 billion between 1979 and 1988, but successive reschedulings of the debt meant that it was not reduced in total by more than a narrow margin of $1 billion and in 1987 it bounced back up to $20 billion. There seemed to be and there was no hope.[13]

It is highly significant that during the political manoeuvring which surrounded the Dayton Agreement and its aftermath, the question of the debt obligations of the individual republics were a major source of disagreement. It is often overlooked that the immediate precursor to the final breakdown of political negotiations and the first fatal bloodshed was the attempt by the federal government to institute a Market Maoist shock-therapy reform à la Jeffrey Sachs in an attempt to impose financial discipline while at the same time liberalizing both internal and external transactions. It is hardly surprising that the northern republics wanted to escape from the negative consequences of this. The fact that such a policy implied testing to destruction the constitution of the republic and the economic and cultural viability of the whole society has passed largely without comment in the West. It was so much easier to regale the bemused population of Western Europe with racist stereotypes about 'Balkan Brutality'.

The submerged economic causes of the Yugoslav Wars of Succession were also compounded by egregious Western foreign policy errors. The decisive step on the road to war was taken by the government of Slovenia which made a Unilateral Declaration of Independence in June 1991 to the chagrin of Croatian nationalists who felt let down by the 'Alpine Chetniks' in Ljubljana because they themselves were at that stage unprepared to fight the Serbs. The federal army moved to forestall the Slovenians by sealing the northern borders. Significantly it was the Slovenian national guard which chose to settle the issue in arms. Like the IRA in the 1920s, they knew that the blood of soldiers in uniform, even if they were conscripts, was the necessary price of independence. Like the IRA, they knew that they held all the cards once the fighting began, not least because of the tacit acceptance of their independence bid by the Serbian nationalists in Belgrade who were anxious to disgorge Slovenia, because they wished to dissolve the federation, purge the army of its 'Yugoslavian' elements and settle accounts with their enemies in Zagreb and Sarajevo by partitioning Croatia and Bosnia.

Western policy makers completely misunderstood these events. Obsessed as they were with their own policy of 'rollback' they perceived plucky little Slovenia standing up to the communist giant of Yugoslavia and conflated events in the Balkans with what had been happening in the Baltic states (which had pursued their campaign for the restoration of the status quo of 1940 without offering violence of any kind to the occupying power despite provocation far worse than that offered to the Slovenians). In particular, there was overwhelming pressure from the newly united Germany for what was essentially a 'pro-Catholic' policy which sought to 'punish' Belgrade by the recognition of the two republics of Slovenia and Croatia. The British Foreign Office, though subsequently (and rightly) damned for an excessively pro-Serb orientation, was surely right in its belief that such recognition, which effectively partitioned a long-existing multi-ethnic state upon confessional lines, was an extremely foolhardy course of action, not least because far from punishing Greater Serb nationalism, it was actually advancing its policy.

In contrast, the continued non-recognition of the already declared independence of Kosovo, despite the exemplary restraint of its oppressed population, is explicable only as a policy of circumspection signally absent from the treatment of Slovenia and Croatia. Perhaps it represents a residual respect for the political arrangements of Marshall Tito, who had designated Kosovo as part of the Republic of Serbia (and Croatia, Slovenia and Bosnia as integral parts of Federal Yugoslavia), or quite simply as yet another expression of anti-Muslim prejudice by Western political elites.

Such errors were encouraged by the febrile atmosphere of the time which was replete with ostentatious humbug about a supposed 'New World Order' created by the far-sighted stratagems of that latter-day Bismarck Chancellor Helmut Kohl and the victorious arms of feted generals such as 'Stormin' Norman' Schwarzkopf, who did not blush to compare his merits with those of his hero Hannibal. (Unfortunately, his opponent, the erstwhile Western ally Saddam Hussein, has demonstrated a Fabian resilience.) It is one of the most tragic consequences of the rake's progress of British Market Maoism that their fanatical belief in the merits of deregulated labour markets led John Major to the conclusion that in order to escape the tyranny of the Social Chapter of the Maastricht Treaty, Britain would be willing to indulge the realpolitik of Chancellor Kohl against the better judgement of their own foreign policy experts, including the EU special envoy Lord Carrington. Both Slovenia and Croatia were given international recognition, supposedly within their existing 'natural' borders. John Major's diplomatic triumph at Maastricht, which succeeded in preventing the partition of the British Conservative Party, did not have the same happy result in Bosnia. The full horror of this modern Munich was to be seen some months later in the Muslim ghettos of western Bosnia when Chancellor Kohl's co-religionists, with the full support of the now-independent government in Zagreb, enthusiastically demonstrated their contempt for the international boundaries he so unwisely saw fit to recognize.

In the former Soviet Union, problems such as those in the former Yugoslavia are compounded. One is tempted to suggest that the main difference between the former Yugoslavia and the former Soviet Union is that structural adjustment only began in the CIS countries in the 1990s, not the 1980s. Regional economic polarization is overlaid upon a complex pattern of ethnic rivalries. Like the molten magma of an active volcano pushing at fissures in the earth's crust, the question is not whether these economic divisions and cultural rivalries will erupt in violence but where. So far most of the bloodshed has been confined to the southern fringe of the former Soviet empire, which means that it is mainly poor brown people who have suffered and that is the only explanation for the rampant complacency of the Western powers about what has already occurred, particularly in Chechnya. Incredibly, Western politicians have been content to call for 'restraint' from their protégé Boris Yeltsin as his bloodthirsty Boyars exacted retribution on the civil population as revenge for their own military incompetence. President Clinton is on record as comparing the conflict to the American Civil War (presumably with Boris Yeltsin in the role of Abraham Lincoln). The rationale seems to be that as long as the Russian government is committed to the absolutely essential ideology of domestic Market Maoism, then their naked imperialism can be indulgently overlooked (much like that of the original Maoist tyrants in Beijing *vis-à-vis* Tibet). Strangely enough the precedent of plucky little Slovenia has not been mentioned in this context.

One important and overlooked feature of the Chechen conflict is the huge oil deposits under the Caspian Sea, which are on a Middle Eastern scale. Unfortunately, the Caucasus will probably enjoy as much stability as that other unhappy region of the world for this reason if for no other. A bankrupt Russian state cannot afford to miss out on this potential bonanza (although under the current political dispensation it is unlikely that many ordinary Russians will benefit, whatever happens). Chechen diversion of oil revenues gave them a higher standard of living than Russia proper and therefore, like other raw material producing areas of the Russian federation, an incentive to secession. The Baltic republics on the other hand, although poor in raw materials, have become big re-exporters of primary products, particularly metals, illegally exported from the Russian hinterland. This has led some Russian nationalists to compare them with sixteenth-century African trading posts. As we have already noted, the good fortune of others, especially if it is perceived to be at your expense, often excites the predatory instinct.

Other complexities include the internal power struggles within Russia itself in which all these peripheral areas of the so-called 'near abroad' are implicated. The visit of the mayor of Moscow Luzkhov in January 1997 to Sevastopol, capital of the Russian-speaking Crimea but technically still part of the Ukraine, in order to burnish his nationalist credentials is an example of the way in which ethnic tensions and palace power struggles may begin to interact. Ominously, there were units of Ukrainian nationalist volunteers reported to be fighting against the Russian Army in the Chechen war.

A thorough structural adjustment of the Ukraine, probably leading to mass unemployment of Russian speakers in the eastern industrial districts of the country, is current IMF policy. Up to now the government in Kiev has wisely found all sorts of reasons why such a policy cannot be implemented. How long they can hold out against the enormous pressures exerted on them by Western creditors in the middle of a permanent economic crisis is anybody's guess. Non-payment of wages is already a significant source of grievance. The temptation for the Russian-speaking population in the Donbas and the Crimea to avoid structural adjustment implemented by Kiev through irredentist mobilization will be high. It is possible that only when parts of the European heartland such as the Ukraine have been completely destabilized by the Market Maoist dogma that there will be any fundamental rethink of Western policy. By then it will be far too late.

NATO instead of EU?

Various forms of militarism, ethnic and gang violence unleashed in the new era of barbarism have already cost millions of lives among the peoples who previously lived in the two socialist federations, Yugoslavia and the Soviet Union. Among the FSCs sharing borders with these two (that is, nearly all of them), and among the business community operating in the region, the restriction of violence and the maintenance of the rule of law where it has been established have been constantly questioned and debated by analysts. The progressive way to eliminate such a general state of instability would be through economic development, in as much as accelerated integration into the European economic framework could provide useful occupation and an increasing level of incomes for the working population of the region. That would require concerted action on behalf of the major West European governments, now tied down to the project of establishing a single currency within the next five years and depressing their economies for the sake of that.

The only period when West European governments paid more attention to the East was 1993 and 1994 – the early years of the Clinton administration, when the new US foreign policy left the task of dealing with the FSCs to the EU. This was the period when the EU promised future membership for the associated countries, numbering ten. These promises were reinforced for a few, when on 10 July 1997 the European Commission decided that it would launch entry talks with Poland, the Czech Republic, Hungary, Estonia, Slovenia and Cyprus.

Apart from promises, however, the EU has done too little, too late, and in too confused a fashion for the stabilization and development of the FSCs. The Dayton Agreement of late 1995 – a dubious peace treaty for the Balkans – represented an inevitable and robust return of the US to East Central European affairs, although only offering military stabilization without the perspective of economic and social progress. The decision about NATO enlargement is a continuation of this course. The dilemma of 'more jobs or more police' have been answered by US and West European foreign policies to the benefit of the latter at a regional level.

The Poles may be happy to be members of a security alliance with nuclear missiles targeted towards Moscow. However, they should not forget that if Russian tanks really started to move West again, they would have to stand up with conventional weapons and defend Germany before a single missile is launched.

An even greater example of myopia is, however, the expectation that membership in NATO will bring EU membership closer. There are hard economic circumstances that separate the FSCs from the Europe of Maastricht. Real wages are ten times lower than in Germany, the share of agriculture in employment and output is much greater than in most EU countries, and the convergence criteria of EMU are hardly achievable in the next decade, if ever. Recipients of large-scale structural funds like Spain or Portugal may very easily veto the accession of new members if they believe those would take away a part of their external funding, no matter whether the newcomers are inside NATO or not. The case might be that Western governments are giving NATO membership to some FSCs, not as preparation for EU membership but as a substitute for it.

Despite its complexity and controversies, NATO expansion can be made acceptable for a majority of the people in the chosen countries if the terms negotiated and some changes until April 1999 significantly change the character of this exercise. Further negotiations with Russia can eliminate the anti-Russian edge of expansion and prevent the emergence of a new East–West divide. Having suffered so much during the Cold War, peoples in East Central Europe would not like to find themselves in the frontline of another great-power conflict. As a part of the continuing talks, agreements about nuclear non-proliferation can be made to reduce the fear from weapons of mass destruction. Expensive armament projects can be ruled out and thus a need for a rise in military expenditures and foreign borrowing for such purposes can be eliminated. Simultaneously, concrete and practical steps towards EU enlargement can give credibility to the claims that the West would not only allow the military alliance to expand towards the East but economic integration also.

Eastward enlargement is a necessity for the EU if Eastern Europe is to be stabilized without the permanent threat of authorized violence. This would, however, require a more inclusive European integration without the unpopular and insensible drive towards the single currency, but with more conscious development policies, much less room for private interests in resource allocation, and an association with the broadest possible security structure, that is, the Organization for Security and Cooperation in Europe (OSCE). This is not only the interest of the peoples living in the FSCs. What there is to gain for Western Europe is greater security and the benefits of economic cooperation.

Policy makers in both Eastern and Western Europe need to be determined and imaginative to leave behind outdated ideas and develop progressive solutions. In the next chapter we will attempt to outline our own ideas about the concrete steps necessary to take Eastern Europe back from the brink on which it stands as a result of the Great Bourgeois Cultural Revolution. The suggestions are not intended to be exhaustive but rather as a contribution to what we hope will become a wide-ranging debate.

11

Dark Clouds and Spectral Hopes

If one considers all that the transition reforms have achieved and all that they have not achieved, then what has been experienced in Eastern Europe is not just 'some difficulties' with implementation of otherwise well-conceived policies but rather a fundamental failure. Even in the most 'advanced' reform economies, there has had to be an inevitable return to more centralized forms of macroeconomic management. Despite the upbeat marketing patter of Czech, Hungarian, Polish and Slovenian politicians, the underlying weakness of the economic structure remains. In these countries the transitional destruction and chaos of the Great Bourgeois Cultural Revolution have turned out to be far from creative. Elsewhere the results have been little short of catastrophic. The stagflationary effects of stabilization and structural adjustment programmes were entirely predictable; they have been tried and failed elsewhere. Worthwhile industrial restructuring and technological renewal have hardly occurred. As the millennium approaches, pressure for new policies is strengthening (and not only in Eastern Europe). But a coherent alternative paradigm has yet to be consolidated.

There have been Alternatives

We can conclude that the period of the late 1980s and early 1990s has been one of disintegration in Eastern Europe. This has been hidden from view by a masking effect, that is, the reintegration of the region into the international market economy. The naïvety of the first period of reforms is now almost completely dispelled. The true nature of the enormous task facing these societies is becoming more apparent. This gives the hope of more nuanced policies which take into account the peculiarities of individual countries and subregions. It may also lead to lasting stagnation and endemic social misery. Recent Eastern European experience has been a brutal reminder of the long-established thesis of development economics that integration into the international market economy implies disintegration of subsidiary systems. In the peripheries of world

172

capitalism, the market creates islands of development in the sea of underdevelopment. Both development and underdevelopment are simultaneously reproduced by this process; the one is inseparable from the other. As Neil Smith puts it:

> ... capital seeks not an equilibrium built into the landscape but one that is viable precisely in its ability to jump landscapes in a systematic way. Uneven development is social inequality blazoned into the geographical landscape and it is simultaneously the exploitation of that geographical unevenness for certain socially defined ends.[1]

The breakthrough of transnationalization within a period of profound crisis has led inevitably to rapidly increasing social and regional inequalities. In whatever way events now turn, this reality has been the primary result of the early 1990s in Eastern Europe.

Sadly enough neither Liberals nor Social Democrats have had the intellectual self-confidence to present alternatives to the transition juggernaut. Since they do not question the idea that the market economy stands at the end of history, they seem unable to muster any coherent critique even of privatization (despite the absurdly contingent and self-serving justification of its supporters). Moderately progressive politicians are unable to explain to ordinary people how they might conduct business differently apart from some minor changes in personnel. Their fundamental agreement with the present dispensation helps to legitimize the political allocation of public assets to private interests. As a result of this intellectual failure, the loudest and most insistent challenge to these processes of disenfranchisement and exclusion is now represented by the far right, who are throughout Europe in the strongest position they have ever been in since 1945. As we have already noted, this is not necessarily or even primarily an East European phenomenon; this perception is simply a racist stereotype perpetrated by intellectually lazy Western commentators. In fact, the electorates of the East have clearly expressed their preference for 'capitalism with a human face' of the kind they always believed to exist in Western Europe. They have been denied that choice. It is sad that all the struggles of this century to resolve the problems thrown up by capitalist economic development in a civilized fashion have been so easily negated by powerful vested interests. Of course, capitalist economies can in principle be tamed and made to work in the interests of the majority; but not like this.

So what would an alternative paradigm look like? In Hungary, the Keynesian economist Karoly Lorant has suggested that those who want to know how to proceed should invoke Parkinson's Law. First we find out what the Market Maoists are suggesting and then we do the opposite. With due respect to Lorant, the job is obviously a little more complicated than that. As we have seen, the concept of 'transition' is highly problematic, not only intellectually or theoretically, but also from the point of view of political and social stability. The problem in defining an alternative model is that one may easily fall into the fallacy of proposing equally impractical and unworkable blueprints.

The problems experienced today in Eastern Europe are part of a general crisis of liberal social theory. Although there is a longstanding critique of the theoretical underpinnings of the modernization paradigm, it still holds the centre stage as far as policy is concerned. In essence, this paradigm conceives of history as having two stages – first, a long 'traditional age', and then a 'transition' to a modern 'developed' society. Perhaps the most famous of the expositions of this model was that by Walt Rostow, advisor to President Kennedy. Indeed it was the promise of a Rostowian economic 'take-off' which seduced Eastern Europe into the transition project in the first place. But instead of a take-off they have experienced a dreadful crash. The dismissal in Eastern European intellectual circles of what might be called 'post-materialist' values is shallow and misplaced. The general view is that such Western luxuries can only be afforded once society has been 'developed'. The failure of the East European intelligentsia to orient itself in the face of the profound intellectual changes in the West during the last fifty years is ironically a reflection of precisely that underdevelopment which East Europeans are attempting to escape.

As John Howell recounts:

> Alan Greenspan, the chairman of the US Federal Reserve, is alleged to have received a colossal put down from Vaclav Klaus, the Prime Minister of the Czech Republic, when the answer to his question of how GDP was measured in a post-communist economy was greeted by an expression of lack of interest on Klaus's part. However, this question, whether Greenspan knew it or not, was central to the debate of how well Central and Eastern Europe was developing.[2]

A rethinking and subsequent reconstruction of the concept of development requires a profound break with the 'stages' theory of history. We should acknowledge gradualism and evolution in human development and the capacity of political action guided by ethical reasoning to improve economic and social conditions. We have become so intellectually impoverished that the feeble glimmerings of 'growth' in the Eastern economies (after several years of precipitate decline) are regarded as evidence that everything will turn out fine if we just wait for the magic to work. This is quite absurd. In fact, popular tolerance for economic sacrifices is evaporating in these circumstances as it becomes abundantly clear that the crisis has not been a temporary hiatus but rather a harbinger of an economy and society which excludes the majority of its members from meaningful participation and even the hope of elementary social security. As in other parts of the world, there must be much more attention paid to the quality-of-life issues which conventional economic indicators cannot capture. In many ways, gross domestic product is as stilted and meaningless a measure of human welfare as net material product ever was.

The search for alternatives must include open and explicit discussions on an international scale about the future of the nations of Eastern Europe as part of a global reconsideration of the human predicament. The existing institutions of global governance have lost the mandate of heaven. The blame for the failures we have outlined must be shared by both Eastern and Western policy makers. There is no solution to the problems of the East without fundamental rethinking in the West. It is also important to recognize that we cannot rerun the video called 'transition'. What is done is done. Those on the left who think that everything that has happened since 1989 just proves that 'socialism' was right all along are to be seen in the same light as the Market Maoists who insist that all current difficulties are attributable to the failures of 'communism'. It was the failures of communism which allowed the easy triumph of 'savage capitalism' and it was the failures of international capitalism that allowed the triumph of 'savage socialism' in the first place. We must get off this treadmill or face the consequences.

A particularly dangerous fallacy now becoming increasingly popular in some East European societies is the idea that there is some kind of trade-off between democracy and freedom today and prosperity tomorrow. General Lebed's stated admiration for General Pinochet is probably the best-known example of this phenomenon. Democracy does not guarantee prosperity; it is a value in its own right. As George Soros, the currency speculator who destroyed the economic policy of the British Conservative government (taking billions of pounds of British taxpayers' money in the process) has written:

> Open societies tend to be more prosperous, more innovative, more stimulating than closed ones. But there is a danger in proposing

success as the sole basis for holding a belief ... being successful is not identical with being right ... the cult of success can become a source of instability in an open society because it can undermine our sense of right and wrong. That is what is happening in our society today. Our sense of right and wrong is endangered by our preoccupation with success, as measured by money.[3]

Of course, the idea that abandoning democratic values will lead to prosperity is not only morally but also empirically wrong. What is most important is for political leaders to stop promising people what cannot be delivered. A Western standard of living for everyone is simply not on the horizon. Egalitarianism is not therefore an irrational politics of envy. Some reasonable relationship between rewards and sacrifices and a degree of distributive justice are the indispensable components of any stable social order. The fundamental political problem confronting East European societies today is the *fait accompli* of ideologically driven privatization. The winners in this dishonest game have now consolidated their position and they regard their winnings as inviolable. In some respects, this situation mirrors that in post-apartheid South Africa or contemporary post-dictatorship Brazil. Despite democratic formalities the injustices of the past have become etched into the social structure and have become fundamentally unchallengeable. In the social circumstances of Eastern Europe this was never a necessary outcome and one can only bemoan the Market Maoist coup which has allowed it to happen. As the far right in Hungary say: 'The banks have finished the job begun by the tanks.'

For the record, it is important to recognize that alternatives did exist. The very various and contradictory ways in which the neo-liberal paradigm has been implemented – voucher privatizations, foreign buy-outs, shadow capital markets, deregulation, private monopolization and so on – shows that. The only consistency has been the determination to destroy the 'socialist roaders' as a prime political objective. As we have noted the supposedly 'exemplary' Czech voucher privatization has turned out to be the major obstacle to Western-style capital markets in that country. The voucher scheme was a temporarily expedient Market Maoist political tactic, not a coherent economic policy. No other Eastern country has devised a mechanism to create a truly viable capital market either. Without adequate real capital resources how could they? The creation of innovative systems of ownership and accountability were always inevitable in Eastern Europe for that very reason. The pressure to conform to a second-hand approximation of the Anglo-Saxon *rentier* capitalist model is a political mechanism for obscuring this dangerous and inconvenient truth. As Alan Shipman observes: 'Where getting the broad direction right is more important than fine tuning the navigation negotiated or administered dealing often beats market transaction – as the very existence of private corporate structures makes clear.'[4]

Perhaps the best chance for an alternative model was in Poland where a mass trade union movement might have provided the basis for negotiated, inclusive economic change embodying a redefinition of the relationship between the public and the private sectors. Imaginative, innovatory economic policies in Poland might have set a very bad example. As a result, the demobilization and demoralization of the Polish working class became a vital interest of the Market Maoist faction after 1989. Unfortunately the policy has been all too successful. The political price for the Market Maoists has been high however. Leszek Balcerowicz, who lost his parliamentary seat in the election of 1993, has become one of the most unpopular figures in Poland and the former Communist Party of which he was an apostate member has reinvented itself as the 'natural party of government'. From 1993 to 1997 they were able to carry through the marketization policy which they attempted to initiate in 1980 and which was blocked at the time by the appearance of *Solidarność*. Despite the cynical manipulation of popular grievances by Polish right-wing politicians, mass unemployment has rendered organized Polish workers today nearly as powerless as their British counterparts (although most Polish workers would be astonished at the legal restrictions on trade union activity which all mainstream political forces in Britain now regard as unchallengeable). But the anger and frustration created by social exclusion may yet bring forth a bitter harvest. The governing coalition elected in Poland in September 1997, containing as it does both right wing economic populists and convinced neo liberals is inherently unstable.

Alternative policies did exist. The Polish economist Marek Gruchelski rejected that demanding mistress TINA and was a believer in the quest for that hidden treasure TIARA ('There *Is* A Reasonable Alternative'). He was a US-trained specialist then at Warsaw University of Economics and he was highly critical of Balcerowicz and made his own distinctive proposals from 1990 onwards. As Gruchelski put it in 1991:

Even the strongest supporter of the Polish stabilization programme must feel uneasy watching the progressive destruction of our economy. Shock therapy intended to slow down the inflation rate, equalize the market and to stabilize the whole economy has not worked. As a result Poland finds itself in the worst depression since the second world war.

He went on to point out that 'inflation in Poland is mostly caused by drastic growth in costs of production.' For this reason he rejected an expansionary fiscal and monetary policy because 'the Polish economy – being a so-called bottle-neck economy – will not react with increasing production but with price increases and consequently with higher inflation'. (So much for the charge of 'simplistic' Keynesianism with which he was accused.)

From this structural analysis of inflation Gruchelski concluded that 'supply-side' measures were essential to overcoming the crisis. In the conventional lexicon this is simply code for 'privatization'. Not for Gruchelski:

> Privatization is a long-term process requiring huge funds and skilled management. Both are absent in today's Poland and therefore rapid positive changes can't be expected. Rapid privatization, with a non-existent mechanism for the evaluation of national property, simply leads to it being given away.

Poland in 1991 had a surplus of labour and a lack of capital. Gruchelski, recognizing that reality, intended to use existing capital resources to the full. His proposals were geared towards the real economy of work and employment, that is, the labour market. After all, this is the market that matters most to ordinary people. His proposal was that:

> ... simply, industries should operate for the whole year – with only ten days holiday – but workers would work every second day ... unproductive job positions and institutions would be successively eliminated. Workers would be retrained and moved to other jobs or to cover shift work in profitable employment.

Workers would have time on alternate non-working days for such retraining and for participation in the informal economy to boost household incomes. He continued:

> By my estimation this macroeconomic manoeuvre would create a positive climate for overcoming depression and would increase during a five to seven-year period, GNP by up to 50 per cent.
>
> Additionally, the proposed method would improve the effectiveness of investment as a result of the increase in capital turn over and would stimulate business activity. It would:

- Speed up the restructuring of the economy and, at the same time maintain almost full employment
- Increase the potential of industry and the possibility of increased production
- Eliminate or significantly reduce work on night shifts
- Increase wages and salaries according to the growth of production
- Reduce the cost of raw materials and energy
- Decrease the demand for new factory buildings and consequently create possibilities of transferring resources into the construction of new houses thus facilitating increased labour mobility and flexibility.[5]

This is a supply-side policy built around the needs of the Polish working class, which through its self-organization and social struggle had defeated the totalitarian system. It would have implied the continued existence of price controls into the medium term in order to prevent the abuse of residual monopoly power. In many respects it has similarities with the kind of policies adopted in Japan, Korea and Taiwan after World War II. The big difference between those cases and what Gruchelski was proposing for Poland was that in Southeast Asia the 'flexible labour plus full employment' formula was imposed by the state acting in the interests of capital. In Gruchelski's proposal, this flexibility-plus-security formula would have been coordinated by the state in the interests of labour (and in full consultation with their genuine representatives). It is probably only in Poland that such a proposal could have been formulated. It should be noted that such a policy would also have automatically provided a mechanism for the non-monetary control of wage inflation without the necessity for self-defeating deflation of the economy.

In other respects Gruchelski's proposals were consistent with pre-war Polish economic policies. As Taylor noted in 1952, 'If we exclude the USSR, we may say that state capitalism was developed in Poland to a greater extent than in any other European country during this [pre-war] period.'[6]

Most important industries in pre-war Poland were state-owned (including 80 per cent of the chemical industry and 50 per cent of the metallurgical industry). All industries (with the exception of the textile industry) were organized into officially registered cartels which were tightly controlled by the industry ministry to prevent profiteering:

Cartelization kept industrial plant in operation which would have been driven out of existence ... it conserved capital in a country which was dangerously short of capital and it maintained industrial employment in a country where the need for maintaining and increasing industrial employment as against agricultural employment was of primary importance.[7]

The Japanese 'Zaibatsu' and South Korean 'Chaebol' cartels performed similar functions in those two countries at similar stages of their development.

The size of the internal market is crucial for the success of such policies. Poland still represents the single largest unified market in East Central Europe and has attracted considerable inward investment in recent years largely because of this (and continuing tariffs on manufactured imports). In 1936, Polish Industry Minister Kwiatkowski, creator of the port of Gdynia, had initiated the creation of a new Central Industrial District (CID) which was part of a fifteen-year plan for the development of the economy. Taylor writes, 'The ramifications of planning the CID were clearly transforming the whole national economy to a planned economy when that development was ruthlessly cut short by foreign invaders in September 1939.'[8]

Such South-east Asian-style policies were very successful in the Poland of the 1930s in mitigating the effects of the depression. World War I had been particularly destructive in Poland (with both Germans and Russians pursuing scorched-earth policies within the Polish lands) and a totally disjointed infrastructure was inherited from the partition era (without common railway gauges, for example). After struggling out of the post-war slump, Poland was hard hit as a typical peripheralized primary commodity-exporting economy after the global collapse of 1929. Nevertheless, the state-led development policies adopted by Kwiatkowski were widely recognized to have been a notable success by the end of the 1930s – so much so that Poland was probably, to use terminology coined by Peter Evans, a leading 'developmental state' in the world at that time, with a high level of 'embedded autonomy'. As he points out:

> Private capital, especially private capital organised into tight oligopolistic networks, is unlikely to be a political force for competitive markets. Nor can a state which is a passive register of these oligopolistic interests give them what they are unwilling to provide for themselves. Only a state that is capable of acting autonomously can provide this essential collective good.[9]

He also notes: 'Like it or not the state remains central to the process of structural change, even when change is defined as structural adjustment.'[10] In relation to the state he also recognizes that 'even with greater selectivity, strengthening capacity is necessary. Reconstruction, not dismantling, is the order of the day'.[11]

Such a pragmatic approach to the role of the state might also have provided a useful guide to a rational policy of reconstruction in 1990s Poland. It would have been consistent with the reality of the post-communist economy, widespread social expectations and longstanding national traditions although, as Evans cautions, 'constructing the parties and labour movements that form the basis of a broader embedded autonomy is an even more difficult project than constructing a Schumpeterian industrial class'.[12] Difficult – but absolutely essential for any genuine reform of post-communist economies and societies and surely the obvious strategy in unionized Poland.

Gruchelski presented his detailed proposals to trade union leaders, politicians and economists both in Eastern and Western Europe (including John Fleming, then chief economist of the European Bank for Reconstruction and Development, and the then British shadow cabinet). Gruchleski also crossed swords with Leszek Balcerowicz in the specialist press.[13] But the simplistic nostrums of Balcerowicz were much more in tune with the international zeitgeist and his particularly fervent version of the Market Maoist party line was first imported into Poland with the support of Jeffrey Sachs and then re-exported to many other East European societies, notably Russia.

As a result, unemployment in Poland was allowed to soar, reaching an official countrywide peak of around 16 per cent but with individual local labour markets in vulnerable communities totally devastated. Eventually, 'growth' returned, but for the Polish economy as a whole 'over the whole period 1992–95 for every 1 per cent increment in GDP there was a 0.2 per cent decrement in employment' and, in 1996, 'disguised unemployment in the Polish economy remained of the order of 800,000 to 1,000,000 people'. Ominously there was projected to be 'a demographic increase of the supply of labour in 1996–2005'.[14] The drastic effects of Market Maoism on the substantial Polish farming community do not even appear in these baleful figures. As Peter Gowan has pointed out the IMF economists Rollo and Stern have calculated that 'even in the most promising country of the region, Poland, living standards will not return to their 1989 levels until the year 2010 at the earliest' and that

even for a country growing like Poland for the foreseeable future, the population will have to wait for the best part of twenty years simply to return to their living standards under a communist system that had long been in crisis. Even this makes unrealistic assumptions that the West European economies will not enter ... recession, that global casino capitalism will not explode, and that shocks or cycles of other kinds will not hit Poland.[15]

Democracy and Local Initiative

The foregoing analysis has concentrated upon Poland not because conditions there are worse than elsewhere, but because they are the some of the best in Eastern Europe. Poland is touted by the Market Maoists as the 'model' that others are supposed to follow. We think we have shown that this model might have been very different had the destructive delirium of Market Maoism been checked by organized labour armed with appropriate economic policy. Unfortunately this did not occur and unemployment throughout the region has rocketed. As the World Bank admitted in 1996, 'long term unemployment (that persisting for a year or more) increased rapidly in Central and East European countries. So did youth unemployment. Spatial mismatch between jobs and workers produced large and persistent regional differences in unemployment.' They admitted that 'there is little turnover from the pool of unemployed'.[16] All unemployment benefits in Eastern countries are time-limited. Mass poverty is becoming endemic and the comforting belief that people are 'managing somehow' is belied by statistics collected by the Polish government which showed that in 1995 'of the 2,034,000 people in the grey economy only 8.8% reported working more than eleven days per month'.[17] If Poland is in this condition we only need to extrapolate these findings to other, less fortunately placed, societies to recognize the depth of the crisis right across the region.

So what is to be done? It is clear that no sweeping changes of policy are possible in the short run. What surely must be possible are incremental shifts of emphasis from dogmatic to pragmatic approaches. At the very least, fire-sale privatization has to be stopped. Elementary economic theory would suggest that the huge oversupply of assets is forcing down the price to giveaway levels. This is like nationalizing private assets without compensation. This policy is at best an irrelevance and at worst undermines the whole social support for economic reform. Each privatization proposal should be assessed on its merits and should be subordinated to a coherent industrial strategy. (Significantly, the head of the Polish parliamentary commission on privatization, the PSL MP Bogdan Pek, who supported such an approach, was removed from his post by a combination of the votes of the SDRP and Balcerowicz's party, the Freedom Union.) All industries with significant monopoly power, such as public utilities, must remain under social direction and control. The way in which the size of the (supposedly) private sector as opposed to the size of the (supposedly) state sector has been used as a universal measure of the degree of reform should cease. What matters is real economic performance as measured in indicators that matter to ordinary people such as real wages, employment creation and levels of real (not paper) investment. Forcing the increasingly sceptical sheep on Animal Farm to bleat 'private sector good, public sector bad' is not enough.

Investment in people is crucial. Attempts to push the 'marketization' of public services such as health and education should be resisted. It should be remembered that such policies are extremely controversial in the West and have only been implemented at the very end of the Market Maoist revolution. That is because the case for public investment in public goods is intellectually overwhelming. The assertion that societies in economic crisis 'cannot afford' such public services is specious. The fiscal crisis is a symptom of the other failures of the Market Maoist model. For example, the causes of the current economic problems in Germany are not excessive public spending or too generous welfare payments as the Market Maoists contend, it is rather the neo-liberal policy of deflating the economy in order to meet the Maastricht convergence criteria and the hopelessly inadequate policies adopted towards the economic integration of the GDR in the immediate aftermath of 1989. The attempt to use the crisis to erode the rights of German workers is yet another of the manipulations of the Great Bourgeois Cultural Revolution. German trade unions should be prepared to negotiate about labour flexibility; but only on the basis of guaranteed job security and a fundamental change in macroeconomic policy.

The whole Market Maoist model should be rejected and public services should be restructured within a comprehensive strategy for the management of the whole economy. Privatization of these services leads either to private profit at taxpayers expense or acts as a smokescreen for the withdrawal of vital services from the most vulnerable sections of the population. Modern industrial societies should be moving progressively towards the 'demonetarization' of public goods. In the provision of such things as leisure facilities, public transport and preventive health care, 'free is cheaper'.

From a political point of view the Market Maoists may believe that it is possible to create a Latin American-style society in Eastern Europe which will be stable because the poor will accept their lot and are prepared to tolerate huge differences in life chances. They should be reminded that it required two decades of savage repression to inculcate that defeatist psychology in Latin America and that even now it is not clear that the semi-democratic political systems in this region have been stabilized. Redistributive reform was the only mechanism that stabilized Western societies in the earlier part of this century. Why should things be any different today?

Policies which recognize the economic waste of unemployment are essential. Even more so than in Western economies unemployment in the East is simply irrational. Trapped in immobility, the unemployed rapidly become unemployable and a danger to themselves and others. Freed from the pressure to privatize at any price, remaining state-owned enterprises should be given operational incentives which take into account the social costs and benefits of employment. At the very least, enterprises which shed labour must pick up some of the cost of subsequent benefit payments as in the Czech Republic. Such a policy change would imply the setting of sectoral and national targets for wages, productivity and flexibility as suggested by Gruchelski; if politically possible, there should be a negotiated social contracts between capital and labour as in West Germany after 1945.

The nature of the informal economy needs to be rethought. The enthusiasm which has been expressed in some Market Maoist circles for organized crime is a scandal. It should be seen for the evil that it is and well-funded public services (in this case the police service) should be used to combat it. Simultaneously the creation of a viable 'third sector' should be encouraged through legal and fiscal incentives. Wherever possible ordinary people should be encouraged to form associations geared to fulfilling local needs in a sustainable way. The Market Maoist dogma that such structures are 'crypto-socialist' and therefore 'bad' should be treated with the contempt it deserves.

There are many suitable models for such structures from all over the world. The Scottish Community Business movement, for example, was pioneered as a response to mass unemployment in the Strathclyde region in the 1970s and 1980s and now generalized to many depressed regions of Britain. Community businesses are locally owned and controlled and address local needs and they are legally obliged to recycle any profits into the local community. Another obvious example is that of the world-wide credit union movement which is particularly strong in Ireland. The Peruvian cooperative kitchens (the *'comedores'*) which feed millions every day and are 'owned' by their beneficiary members, may be a more appropriate model in those least fortunate societies which are struggling to ensure basic food security. The microcredit structures pioneered by the Grameen Bank in Bangladesh and the South Shore Bank in Chicago at opposite ends of the 'development' spectrum may be also have something to offer. This is not to suggest that any external model can be mechanically applied in entirely different circumstances from that in which it has originally developed.

Even so, the Chinese experience with so-called Township and Village Enterprises (TVEs) is an extraordinary and largely untold story which may have many implications for other post-socialist economies. In the words of the World Bank, 'A TVE is neither state owned in the classic sense nor privately owned in the capitalist sense. They produce mainly consumer goods for domestic and international markets.' Most are owned by local government which acts as a holding company. According to the World Bank the share of TVEs in Chinese GDP rose from 13 per cent in 1985 to 31 per cent in 1994, and output has grown by about 25 per cent per cent a year since the mid-1980s, making TVEs accountable for a third of industrial growth in China. The TVEs have created 95 million jobs in the last fifteen years.[18] These figures show that such 'alternative' structures are not in any way to be seen as 'marginal'. Incredibly, many of the Market Maoist ideologues in central government in Eastern Europe want nothing to do with such 'socialist experiments'. The role of local government in supporting such initiatives has to be recognized and supported. These structures combine the entrepreneurial function with social solidarity.

This is not to suggest that the Dengist Chinese model of social authoritarianism plus the market is in any way admirable in a general sense. In fact it may turn out in the end to be the most unsustainable 'transition' of all, despite the ambivalent admiration showered on it by internally inconsistent Market Maoist ideologues. In Eastern Europe, and in the final analysis in China as well, what is more important than impressive production figures is the mobilization of meaningful social participation and the fulfilment of real human needs both material and non-material. This is a value in itself being based upon a humanistic understanding of what constitutes the good society. As the Latin American scholar and activist John Friedman writes in *Empowerment – The Politics of Alternative Development*:

An alternative development does indeed address the condition of the poor directly. It argues for their involvement in actions that

this truth is acknowledged all the hard questions about economic policy have to be confronted rather than swept under the carpet. We do not rule out the possibility of a complete change of Western policy which might make such an analysis obsolete – but it is very unlikely in the short run. The crisis in Eastern Europe requires solutions now; not after a general crisis has engulfed Western Europe as well.

A transitional solution which attempts to combine the need for adjustment to Western Europe and for immediate rebuilding of Eastern economies would be the development of East European integration at least to the level of a payments union. Such recommendations are not utopian. They have been suggested by George Soros, the Agenda '92 group of economists and in a study entitled *The European Imperative* by the British economist Stuart Holland. According to Holland the main obstacles to an Eastern payments union are political rather than economic:

> The governments of the Central and Eastern European countries are concerned that any such arrangements would act as an obstacle to their membership of the Community. The Community should re-assure them that this will not be the case. The potential gains from establishing a payments union in Central and Eastern Europe are outstanding.[21]

Although deepening regional cooperation could be a step forward, most countries concerned ironically reject this idea as an example of an 'obsolete bloc approach'. One wonders what the founder of the European Community Jean Monnet would have made of such attitudes. Individual governments keep on emphasizing their own achievements and exceptionalities, which is meant to justify their early entry before that of their neighbours. In the case of Hungary, for example, no one seems to have considered the situation which might emerge were such a policy to be successful and perhaps both Hungary and the Czech Republic were admitted (not very likely in any case for the reasons we have given). If that were to happen Hungary would be attached to the European Union only by the short Austrian frontier and it would be surrounded by six non-member states sharing three million ethnic Hungarians between them. Has anybody tried to imagine how Slovakia would behave after the 'Schengenization' of more than 90 per cent of her borders? This is a recipe for destabilization. Regional integration in the East is not an 'obsolete bloc approach' but rather the common sense that dare not speak its name. It is rational and may soon appear inevitable.

Perhaps the single most intractable problem facing the East European economies and societies is that of international debt. In most Eastern countries, interest payments on debt plus uncontrolled capital flight are far greater than any incoming capital resources, pushing them deeper and deeper into a debt trap. Louise Shelley estimated that private capital flight from Russia at anything from $50 to $150 billion dollars from 1991 to 1997 (capital inflow was around $6.5 billion in the same period). These figures put Western 'aid' to Russia and the other CIS states into perspective. These financial processes are in effect testing democratic government and social cohesion to destruction. Whatever other policy measures are adopted, unless the problem of growing indebtedness is solved, then the most terrible consequences can be firmly predicted. As Gavin Williams points out in a challenging paper entitled 'Why Structural Adjustment is Necessary and Why it Doesn't Work':

> No solution ... is compatible with a continued net outflow of foreign exchange to international financial public and commercial banks to service debts. Debt rescheduling does not address this problem. It does not create the conditions for the repayment of debt but defines the conditions under which countries will be permitted not to repay their debts.[22]

Or as Michael Barratt Brown puts it in relation to the former Yugoslavia but with universal implications:

> What we are seeing is not just an explosion of tribal hatred but the panic flight of whole peoples from an economic disaster originating in the mechanisms of the world banking system and its inexorable requirement that the bond be paid at whatever price.[23]

In former Yugoslavia the successor republics are now locked into disputes with each other and the London and Paris Clubs of private and public debtors about who is to inherit the liabilities of the pre-existing state. The devastated society of Bosnia alone owes in the region of $3 billion to international creditors. Any serious attempt to rebuild the shattered infrastructure of these communities will require a complete rethink of existing policies. An encouraging sign was the admittance of Bosnia into the World Bank system despite chronic unpaid arrears; the first time this has happened since Bangladesh seceded from Pakistan in the 1970s. So where the political will exists the rules can be changed (or at least bent). In other parts of Eastern Europe and the Former Soviet Union (and elsewhere) we hope that the necessary political will to defuse the debt bomb is demonstrated before rather than after there are major hostilities. It will be much cheaper in the long run.

So far the powers that be have seen fit to discuss debt relief only in relation to the absolutely desperate countries of sub-Saharan Africa. Even if some lifting of the crushing burden under which these societies labour does eventually take place, the continued infliction of 'conditionality' will render such 'generosity' largely meaningless. Paper write-offs of African debt are reminiscent of the purchase of Indian corn by the British Prime Minister Sir Robert Peel in order to relieve the suffering caused by the Irish Potato Famine:

> The subsequent value to Ireland of Peel's boldness, independence and strength of mind was unfortunately outweighed by his belief in an economic theory which almost every politician of the day, Whig or Tory, held with religious fervour. This theory, usually termed laissez-faire, let people do as they think best, insisted that in the economic sphere individuals should be allowed to pursue their own interests and asserted that the government should interfere as little as possible. Not only were the rights of property sacred; private enterprise was revered and respected and given almost complete liberty...The influence of laissez-faire on the treatment of Ireland during the famine is impossible to exaggerate. Almost without exception the high officials and politicians responsible for Ireland were fervent believers in non interference by government, and the behaviour of the British authorities only becomes explicable when their fanatical belief in private enterprise and their suspicions of any action which might be considered Government intervention are borne in mind.[24]

It is sad and astonishing that these comments about a tragedy of 150 years ago might have been written yesterday.

Faced with the awesome power of modern global finance the only policy can sometimes appear to be appeasement. Certainly individual countries which attempt to buck the system, such as Peru in the 1980s under Alan Garcia which attempted a 'can't pay won't pay' strategy, are doomed. The Peruvians were eventually forced to beg for forgiveness from international financiers on bended knees with tears of repentance in their eyes but only after the internal social crisis in Peru had reached truly horrifying proportions. If there were ever any doubt, this episode proved conclusively that there is no 'nationalist' solution to the problem of international debt. This depressing reality seems to enforce an attitude of defeatist resignation by governments in the face of the ravenous demands of global usury.

Because there was no international support, the Czechs surrendered to the Nazis without a shot fired in 1939. It could be argued that this was the only rational course of action in the circumstances. Ultimately, however, the situation humanity faces will have to be confronted now just as it had to be confronted then. In 1938, the British Prime Minister Neville Chamberlain could argue that Czechoslovakia was 'a far away country of which we know little'. One clear outcome of the globalization of financial markets is that nowhere is 'far away' any more. What happens in Moscow, Mexico and Algiers will affect everybody, everywhere. This much is absolutely clear.

Eastern Europe is actually in a crucial geopolitical position in this crisis. What happens there, matters to the powerful – perhaps not as much as it should – but it does matter. It is in the interests of ordinary people everywhere to overcome this entirely dysfunctional system of political economy. Even the economics profession, which has been the target of many of the criticisms in this book, may have a role in helping to solve the camels and needles problem we have outlined. As the North American Keynesian economist J.K. Galbraith has said, the true vocation of the economist is to 'afflict the comfortable and comfort the afflicted'. Nothing short of an international coalition for change armed with a clear-sighted analysis of the scale of the task which it faces will be sufficient to stop the social breakdown whose signs are all around us. To rebel against this inhuman social order before it is too late is the duty of every right-thinking global citizen. Newly invigorated Eastern European democratic movements might be the pole around which the progressive forces of the world could recompose themselves for an assault upon the citadels of mammon and in opposition to exclusion and intolerance. That surely was the unfulfilled promise of the great moral victory of 1989. But time is running out. It has been said that 'progress is a race between education and chaos'. If this short book has helped to educate the reader about the nature of the problems we all face and stimulated further informed reflection and committed action, then it will have served its purpose.

Notes

Chapter 1 The Long March to the Market

1. Stephen White (ed.), *Political and Economic Encyclopedia of the Soviet Union and Eastern Europe* (London: Longman, 1990) p. 56.
2. David Begg, Stanley Fischer and Rudiger Dornbusch, *Economics* (New York: McGraw Hill, 1987) p. 322.
3. Quoted by Herman Daly in John Cavanaugh, Daphne Wysham and Marcos Arruda (eds), *Beyond Bretton Woods. Alternatives to the Global Economic Order* (London: Pluto Press, 1994) p. 117.
4. World Bank Report, 1988, quoted in Tony Killick (ed.), *The flexible economy – causes and consequences of adaptability of national economies* (London: Overseas Development Institute, 1995) p. 389.
5. *The Wall Street Journal*, 13, 14 and 24 May 1985.
6. Barbara Stallings, 'International influence on economic policy' in Haggard and Kaufman (eds), *The politics of economic adjustment* (Princeton, New Jersey: Princeton University Press, 1995) p. 72.
7. Stallings, 'International influence ...', p. 126.
8. Susan George, 'The Debt Boomerang', *Third World Resurgence*, no. 36.
9. *The Ecologist*, Vol. 22, no. 4, 1992.
10. *The Other Side of the Story: The Real Impact of World Bank IMF Structural Adjustment*, Conference proceedings (New York: Development Group for Alternative Policies, 1993).
11. Haggard and Kaufman, *The politics of economic adjustment*, p. 19.
12. *The Other Side of the Story*.

Chapter 2 The Cold Peace

1. Andras Inotai, 'The West and the transformation of Central and Eastern Europe', *Kozgazdasagi Szemle*, Vol. 40, no. 11, 1993.
2. Daniel Ottolenghi and Alfred Steinherr, 'Yugoslavia: Was it a winner's curse?', *The Economics of Transition*, Vol. 1, no. 2, 1993.
3. Overseas Development Institute, 'Aiding Eastern Europe and the Former Soviet Republics', Briefing paper (London: ODI, November 1992).
4. Youssef Boutros-Ghali, 'Recent International Developments and the North–South Dialogue' in Gianni Vaggi (ed.), *From Debt Crisis to Sustainable Development: Changing Perspectives on North–South Relations* (New York: St Martins Press, 1992).

5. Anne Henderson, 'The International Monetary Fund and the Dilemmas of Adjustment in Eastern Europe: Lessons from the 1980s and prospects for the 1990s', *Journal of International Development*, Vol. 4, no. 3, 1992.
6. World Bank, 'World Economic Outlook' (Washington, DC: World Bank, May 1992), p. 42.
7. Boutros-Ghali, 'Recent International Developments ...', p. 238.

Chapter 3 The Great Bourgeois Cultural Revolution

1. 'Orwell Offered Writers' Blacklist to Anti-Soviet Propaganda Unit', *Guardian*, 11 July 1996.
2. Anders Aslund, *Post Communist Economic Revolutions. How Big a Bang?* (Washington, DC: Center for Strategic and International Studies, 1992) p. 91.
3. Aslund, *Post Communist Economic Revolutions*, p. 37.
4. Quoted in Jonathan Steele, *Eternal Russia* (London: Faber and Faber, 1994) p. 295.
5. Gavril Popov, 'Dangers of Democracy', *New York Review of Books*, 1990.
6. Antonio Gramsci, 'On the Southern Question' in *The modern prince and other writings* (London: International Publishers, 1978) p. 30.
7. Haggard and Kaufman, 'Economic adjustment and the prospects for democracy' in Haggard and Kaufman (eds), *The politics of economic adjustment* (Princeton, New Jersey: Princeton University Press, 1995) p. 321.
8. 'Despair for Sachs as Flames of Chaos Rekindled in Russia', *The European*, 21–27 January 1994.
9. Peter Gowan, 'The dynamics of European enlargement', *Labour Focus on Eastern Europe*, no. 56, Spring 1997, p. 26.

Chapter 4 Price Wars

1. Karl Polanyi, *The Great Transformation* (Boston: Beacon Press, 1957) p. 140.
2. World Bank, *From Plan to Market*, World Development Report (Washington, DC: World Bank, 1996) Figure 1.3.
3. Padma Desai, *The Soviet Economy. Problems and Prospects* (Oxford: Blackwell, 1987) p. xxii.
4. World Bank, *From Plan to Market*, Box 2.7.
5. Robert Harvey, *The Return of the Strong: The Drift to Global Disorder* (London: Macmillan, 1995) p. 176.
6. 'Russian Money Launderers a Threat to the West', *Guardian*, 5 April 1995.
7. World Bank, *From Plan to Market*, Section 2.50.

Chapter 5 The Harder They Come ...

1. Jeffrey Sachs, 'Poland and Eastern Europe: What is to be Done?' in Andras Koves and Paul Marer (eds), *Foreign Economic Liberalization: Transformation in Socialist and Market Economies* (Boulder: Westview Press, 1991).
2. Anders Aslund, *Post Communist Economic Revolutions. How Big a Bang?* (Washington, DC: Center for Strategic and International Studies, 1992) p. 89.
3. Jeffrey Sachs, 'Mexican Precedent for the Ukraine', *Financial Times*, 17 February 1995.
4. Michel Chossudovsky, 'The real causes of Somalia's famine' in *Justice denied – human rights and the international financial institutions* (Geneva: Women's International League for Peace and Freedom, 1994).
5. Will Hutton, *The State We're In* (London: Vintage, 1996) p. 201.
6. International Monetary Fund, 'Republic of Poland. Background paper', 27 December 1995, p. 15.
7. IMF, 'Republic of Poland. Background paper', p. 16.
8. Anthony Robinson, *Financial Times*, 11 December 1996.
9. Norman Davies, *God's Playground. A History of Poland*, Vol. 1 (Oxford: Oxford University Press, 1985) p. 285.
10. Jonathan Spence, *The Search for Modern China* (New York: Norton, 1990) p. 594.
11. 'Russia Harvests the Bitter Fruit of Reform', *Financial Times*, 3 October 1995.
12. 'New Kids on the Block', *Observer*, 21 July 1996.
13. UNICEF, 'Crisis in Mortality, Health and Nutrition-Economies in Transition Studies', UNICEF *Regional Monitoring Report*, No 2, August 1994. Reviewed in *The Independent* 28 January 1994; 'Wave of Misery, Loosed by Fall of the Wall'.
14. quoted in 'Children pay price for democracy', *Guardian Weekly*, 27 April 1997.

Chapter 6 Nouveau *Nomenklatura*

1. Madsen Pirie, *Privatization – A Conceptual Framework* (Hants: Wildwood House, 1988).
2. Leszek Balcerowicz, 'Democracy is No Substitute for Capitalism', *Eastern European Economics*, March/April 1994, p. 44.
3. John Howell, *Understanding Eastern Europe: The Context of Change* (London: Ernst and Young, 1994) p. 72.
4. Howell, *Understanding Eastern Europe*, p. 71.
5. Balcerowicz, 'Democracy is No Substitute ...', p. 39.
6. World Bank, *World Development Report* (Washington, DC: World Bank, 1983) p. 50.
7. Kay and Silberston, 'The New Industrial Policy – Privatization and Regulation, the UK Experience', *Midland Bank Review*, Spring 1984, p. 15.

8. Kay and Silberston, 'The New Industrial Policy', p. 15.
9. Quoted in Kay et al., *Privatization and Deregulation – the UK Experience* (Oxford: The Clarendon Press, 1986) p. 94.
10. Keith Hartley and Attiat F. Ott, 'Privatization – A Conceptual Framework' in Hartley and Parker, *Privatization and Economic Efficiency: A Comparative Analysis of Developed and Developing Countries* (Hants: Edward Elgar, 1991)
11. Pirie, *Privatization*.
12. Hemming and Mansoor, 'Is Privatization the Answer?' *Finance and Development* (1992) p. 33.
13. Hartley and Parker, *Privatization and Economic Efficiency: A Comparative Analysis of Developed and Developing Countries* (Hants: Edward Elgar, 1991).
14. Ramanadham, Venkata Venuri, *Privatization in the UK* (London: Routledge, 1988) p. 271.
15. Balcerowicz, 'Democracy is No Substitute ...', p. 45.
16. Michel Adelbert, *Capitalism against Capitalism* (London: Whurr Publishers, 1993) p. 76.
17. Adelbert, *Capitalism against Capitalism*, p. 75.
18. Jack Wiseman, 'Privatization in Command Economy' in Attiat F. Ott and Keith Hartley (eds), *Privatization and Economic Efficiency ...*, p. 270.
19. Quoted in Martin Brendan, *In the Public Interest? Privatization and Public Sector Reform* (London: Zed Books, 1993) p. 53.
20. Brendan, *In the Public Interest ...*, p. 53.
21. Brendan, *In the Public Interest ...*, p. 54.
22. Brendan, *In the Public Interest ...*, p. 54.
23. 'Russia Set to Spurn Yeltsin and Reform', *Financial Times*, 29 September 1995.
24. 'The Gulag Man Speaks Out', *Guardian*, 29 October 1994.
25. 'Hurd Buries the Serbian Hatchet', *Guardian*, 4 September 1996.
26. Jonathan Steele, *Eternal Russia* (London: Faber and Faber, 1995) p. 229.
27. 'The Good Bad Guys', *Guardian*, 31 July 1995.
28. S. Handelman, *Comrade Criminal: The Theft of the Second Russian Revolution* (London: Michael Joseph, 1994) p. 98.
29. O. Pcheltsinev, 'The results of the three years of reform in the debates of the Russian economists', *Studies on Russian Economic Development*, Vol. 3, no. 3, 1995, p. 168.
30. Christopher Harvie, *Fools Gold: The Story of North Sea Oil* (Harmondsworth: Penguin, 1995) p. 355.
31. 'The Commanding Heights in China Survey', *The Economist*, 28 November 1992.

Chapter 7 The Scissors

1. Vaclav Havel, 'Politics and Conscience' in *Living in Truth* (London: Faber and Faber, 1989) p. 139.

2. Robert Conquest, *The Harvest of Sorrow* (London: Hutchinson, 1986) p. 301.
3. Karl Marx, *Capital*, Vol. 1 (London: Lawrence & Wishart, 1983) p. 681.
4. Conquest, *The Harvest of Sorrow*, p. 171.
5. Feschbach and Friendly, *Ecocide in the USSR* (London: Arum Press, 1992) p. 50.
6. UNICEF, 'Crisis in Mortality, Health and Nutrition – Economies in Transition Studies', *UNICEF Regional Monitoring Report*, No. 2, August 1994.
7. UNICEF, 'Crisis in Mortality ...', p. 77.
8. Don Van Atta (ed.), *The Farmer Threat: The Political Economy of Agrarian Reform in Post Soviet Russia* (Boston: Westview Press, 1993) p. 3.
9. Feschbach and Friendly, *Ecocide in the USSR*, p. 50.
10. World Bank, *World Development Report 1996* (Washington, DC: World Bank, 1996) Section 2.29.
11. Food and Agriculture Organization, *Preliminary Assessment of 1994 Foodcrop Production and the 1994/95 Cereal Import Requirements in the CIS* (Rome: Food and Agriculture Organization, September 1994) p. 5.
12. Alec Nove, *An Economic History of the USSR* (London: Penguin, 1969) p. 95.
13. World Bank, *World Development Report 1996*, Section 2.29.
14. Quoted in *Return to the Good Earth* (Penang, Malaysia: Third World Network, 1990) p. 101.
15. James Goldsmith, *The Trap* (London: Macmillan, 1994) p. 104.
16. 'West Gives Farm Policy Priority Over Security', *Guardian*, 10 October 1994.
17. 'Living Museum on the Land', *Financial Times*, 28 March 1995.
18. Carole Nagengast, *Reluctant Socialists: Rural Entrepreneurs, Class, Culture and the Polish State* (Boston: Westview Press, 1991) p. 215.
19. Clarke (ed.), *Poland: The Economy in the 1980s* (London: Longman, 1989) p. 71.
20. Peter Gibbon, Kjell J. Havnevik and Kenneth H. Hermele, *A Blighted Harvest: The World Bank and African Agriculture in the 1980s* (London: James Currey, 1993) p. 147.
21. 'Living Museum on the Land', *Financial Times*, 28 March 1995.
22. 'Polish Reformers Put EU Cart Before Farmers' Horse', *Guardian*, 16 March 1994.
23. P. Gaspar (ed.), *Changes and Challenges. Economic Transformation in East Central Europe* (Budapest: Akademai Kiado Budapest, 1995) p. 135.
24. Goldsmith, *The Trap*, p. 34.
25. 'West Gives Farm Policy Priority Over Security', *Guardian*, 10 October 1994.
26. 'Rural Poland Faces an Uncertain Future', *Guardian Weekly*, 25 April 1997.
27. *Poland International Economic Report 1995–96* (Warsaw: Warsaw University of Economics, 1996) p. 201.

28. Reid, 'Economic change in the rural US: a search for explanations', quoted in Terry Marsden, Philip Lowe and Sarah Whatmore (eds), *Labour and Locality* (London: David Fulton, 1992) p. 8.
29. Letter from W. Piskorz to *Business Central Europe*, April 1997.
30. Quoted in Harriss (ed.), *Rural Development* (London: Hutchinson, 1982) p. 224.
31. Conquest, *The Harvest of Sorrow*, p. 381.
32. Gavin Williams, 'Taking the Part of Peasants' in Harriss (ed.) *Rural Development*, p. 381.

Chapter 8 Polarities

1. Kramer, 'Eastern Europe Goes to Market', *Foreign Policy*, No. 86, 1992, p. 152.
2. Andrew Glyn, 'Real Wages and Reconstruction Applied Economics', Discussion paper series, no. 147 (Oxford: Institute of Economics and Statistics, 1992); and Standing, Vaughan and Whitehead, 'What Role for Minimum Wages in Central and East Europe?' in *From Protection to Destitution* (Geneva: International Labour Organization, 1995).
3. 'Sad Symbol of Reforms', *Financial Times*, 2 May 1997.
4. Kramer, 'Eastern Europe goes to Market', p. 145.
5. *The Economist*, February 1993.
6. Martin Kovats, 'The good, the bad and the ugly: three faces of "dialogue" – the development of Roma politics in Hungary', *Contemporary Politics*, Vol. 3, no. 1, 1997.
7. Arturo Escobar, *Encountering Development – the making and unmaking of the Third World* (Princeton, New Jersey: Princeton University Press, 1995) p. 78.
8. B. Lomax, 'Impediments to Democratization in Post Communist East Central Europe' in Gordon Wightman (ed.), *Party Formation in East Central Europe* (London: Edward Elgar, 1994).
9. 'Tigers or Tortoises?', *The Economist*, 26 October 1996.
10. Tony Killick (ed.), *The Flexible Economy: causes and consequences of the adaptability of national economies* (London: Overseas Development Institute, 1995) p. 392.

Chapter 9 Left Turn?

1. Joan Nelson, 'Poverty, Equity and the Politics of Adjustment' in Haggard and Kaufman (eds), *The Politics of Economic Adjustment* (Princeton, New Jersey: Princeton University Press, 1992) p. 246 and p. 262.
2. Janos Kornai, 'Transzformacios Visszaeses' in *Kozgazdasagi Szemle* (July–August, 1993).
3. Peter Taylor, *Political Geography: World Economy, Nation State and Locality* (London: Longman, 1996) p. 250.
4. W.B. Yeats, 'The Second Coming'.

5. John Smith, Speech to the Socialist International Committee on Economic Policy, 21 February 1994 (unpublished).
6. H. Compston (ed.), *The New Politics of Unemployment: Radical Policy Initiatives in Western Europe* (London: Routledge, 1996) p. 18.
7. M. Barratt Brown, 'The War in Yugoslavia and the Debt Burden', *Capital and Class*, No. 50, 1993, p. 160.
8. Smith, 'Speech to the Socialist International Committee ...'.

Chapter 10 A Military Solution

1. George Soros, with Byron Wien and Krisztina Koenen, *Soros on Soros: Staying Ahead of the Curve* (New York: John Wiley and Sons, 1995) pp. 158 and 190.
2. 'No a fa, avagy bizalom a jovoben', *Nepszabadsag*, 6 September 1996.
3. Ian Black, 'Nato opens doors to Eastern trio', *The Guardian*, 9 July 1997.
4. Zbigniew Brzezinski and Anthony Lake, 'The Moral and Strategic Imperatives of NATO Enlargement', *International Herald Tribune*, 1 July 1997, p. 10.
5. David Fairhall, 'NATO's chosen recruits prove unfit for service', *The Guardian*, 7 July 1997.
6. 'Eastern promise', *Guardian*, 7 July 1997.
7. *Financial Times*, 21 June 1997, p. 3.
8. 'Eastern promise'.
9. Black, 'Nato opens doors to Eastern trio'.
10. M. Barratt Brown, 'The War in Yugoslavia and the Debt Burden', *Capital and Class*, No. 50, 1993, p. 148.
11. Svetozar Pejovich, 'A property rights analysis of the Yugoslav miracle', *The Annals of the American Academy of Political and Social Sciences*, January 1990, p. 123.
12. Barratt Brown, 'The War in Yugoslavia ...', p. 149.
13. Barratt Brown, 'The War in Yugoslavia ...', p. 156.

Chapter 11 Dark Clouds and Spectral Hopes

1. N. Smith, *Uneven Development: Nature, Capital and the Production of Space* (Oxford: Blackwell, 1984) pp. 149 and 155.
2. Howell, *Understanding Eastern Europe*, p. 159.
3. 'Capital Crimes', *Guardian*, 18 January 1997.
4. Letter from Alan Shipman in *Business Central Europe*, May 1997.
5. M. Gruchelski, 'More Work, More pay', *New Economics Magazine*, Autumn 1991.
6. J. Taylor, *The Economic Development of Poland 1950–1991* (Ithaca: Cornell University Press, 1952) p. 91.
7. Taylor, *The Economic Development of Poland 1950–1991*, p. 93.
8. Taylor, *The Economic Development of Poland 1950–1991*, p. 100.

9. Peter Evans, 'The state as problem and solution: predation, embedded automony and structural change' in Haggard and Kaufman (eds), *The politics of economic adjustment* (Princeton, New Jersey: Princeton University Press, 1995) p. 162.
10. Evans, 'The state as problem ...', p. 140.
11. Evans, 'The state as problem ...', p. 178.
12. Evans, 'The state as problem ...', p. 181.
13. M. Gruchelski, 'Evaluation of the Government Programme', *Eastern European Economics*, March/April 1994.
14. *Poland International Economic Report 1995–96* (Warsaw: Warsaw University of Economics, 1996) p. 66.
15. P. Gowan, 'Neo Liberal Theory and Practice for Eastern Europe' *New Left Review*, no. 213, 1995, p. 56.
16. World Bank, *World Development Report 1996* (Washington, DC: World Bank, 1996) Section 3.3.
17. *Poland International Economic Report 1995–96*, p. 69.
18. World Bank, *World Development Report 196*, Section 3.3.
19. J. Friedman, *Empowerment – The Politics of Alternative Development* (Oxford: Blackwell, 1995) p. 164.
20. Alfred B. Evans Jr, 'The Decline of Rural Living Standards in Russia in the 1990's' *Journal of Communist Studies and Transition Politics*, Vol. 12, no. 3, September 1996.
21. S. Holland, *The European Imperative* (Nottingham: Spokesman, 1993) p. 253.
22. G. Williams, 'Why Structural Adjustment is Necessary and Why it Doesn't Work', Unpublished paper for a seminar of the New Economics Foundation.
23. Barratt Brown, 'The War in Yugoslavia ...', p. 160.
24. Cecil Woodham Smith, *The Great Hunger: Ireland 1845–49* (London: Hamish Hamilton, 1962) p. 54.

Index

Philipines, 5, 10
Pinochet, Augusto, 9, 72, 175
Pirie, Madsen, 83, 89
Piskorz, W, 112
Poland, 2, 4, 20, 24, 26, 28, 33,
  36, 41, 52, 54, 55, 57, 58, 64,
  65, 67, 71, 72, 73, 74, 75, 76,
  81, 93, 102, 108, 109, 110, 112,
  136, 140, 147, 150, 155, 157,
  160, 169, 177, 178, 179, 180,
  181, 182
Polish Democratic Left Alliance
  (SLD), 73, 118, 138
Polish Democratic Union (UD),
  118
Polish Freedom Union (UW), 183
Polish Labour Union (UP), 138
Polish Party 'X', 120
Polish Socialist Party, 138
Polski Stronnictwo Ludowe
  (Polish Peasants Party), 118, 138
Polyani, Karl, 48
'Popiwek', 57, 59
Popov, Gavril, 38
Portugal, 111, 129, 133, 154, 170
Postabank, 80
Preobrazhensky, Evgennii, 37
'Price distortions", 34
Price liberalization, 34, 36, 46,
  51, 52, 53, 59, 61,106, 108, 109
'Price war', 47
'Primitive accumulation", 99, 101
Privatization, 8, 35, 38, 39, 44,
  56, 62, 63, 77, 80, 82, 83, 84,
  85, 86, 87, 88, 89, 90, 91, 93,
  94, 96, 97, 98, 109, 121, 160,
  161, 173, 176, 178, 182, 183

Ramanadham, Venkata Venuri,
  89
'Rational choices', 8, 38, 48, 187
'Rational expectations', 51, 55, 56
Reagan, Ronald, 15, 20, 95, 156
'Recampesinizacion', 186
Redwood, John, 91, 92, 107
Regulation, 48
'Regulatory capture', 151
'Rent seeking', 38
Rifkind, Malcolm, 130

Robinson, Anthony, 74
Rollo, JMC, 181
Rolls Royce, 83
Roma, 122, 123
Romania, 24, 26, 28, 66, 80, 81,
  102, 108, 121, 128, 133, 137,
  139, 148, 156, 160, 161
Rose, Micheal, 155
Rothschild's Bank, 91
Russia, 18, 24, 39, 40, 43, 52, 55,
  58, 62, 64, 70, 78, 81, 94, 95,
  97, 98, 101, 102, 122, 130, 132,
  137, 139, 155, 156, 157, 158,
  168, 181, 186, 189
Russian Liberal Democratic Party,
  40
Russian Social Democratic Party,
  141
Russian Socialist Revolutionary
  Party, 114
Rwanda, 39, 70

Sachs, Jeffrey, 22, 32, 34, 35, 36,
  37, 43, 50, 61, 65, 67, 68, 70,
  73, 94, 134, 146, 161, 165, 181
Saddam Hussein, 5, 166
Sahel, 13
'Samoobrona', 117
Sao Paulo, 13
Sarajevo, 166
Scandinavia, 11, 136
'Scissors crisis', 106
Scumacher, E.F, 116
Schumpeter, Joseph, 47, 60
Schwartzkopf, Norman, 166
Serbia, 95, 139, 166
Serbian Socialist Party, 140
SERPS (State Earnings Related
  Pension), 72
Sevastopol, 168
Shanin, Teodor, 114
Shelley, Louise, 97, 189
Shipman, Allan, 177
'Shock Therapy", 35, 161, 177
Siberia, 43, 187
Silberston, Z.A, 86, 87
Singapore, 144
Skalski, Stanislaw, 117